NEOCONSERVATISM

IRWIN STELZER is a senior fellow and director of the Hudson Institute's regulatory studies program. Prior to joining the Hudson Institute in 1998, Stelzer was resident scholar and director of regulatory policy studies at the American Enterprise Institute. He also is the U.S. economic and political columnist for *The Sunday Times* (London) and *The Courier Mail* (Australia), a contributing editor of *The Weekly Standard* (USA), a member of the Publication Committee of *The Public Interest* and a member of the board of the Regulatory Policy Institute (Oxford).

'Irwin Stelzer is an accomplished economist, businessman and conservative commentator… His outstanding *Neoconservatism* brings together a representative range of neocon thinkers, and is essential reading for anyone seeking to understand this dynamic enterprise, which has joined 'far Right extremism' in the left-wing imagination… Irwin Stelzer's book is the ideal post-Christmas present for anyone eager to face the facts of the world after 9/11.'
Michael Burleigh, *Literary Review*

'This book illustrates just how far Euorpe and America have drifted apart… We may be wary of neocon doctrines, but the least we can do is to take the trouble to acquaint ourselves with our fellow democrats' point of view.'
George Walden, *Sunday Telegraph*

'Who exactly are those mysterious "neocons" who urge hawkish foreign policy on the US?… A new book edited by Irwin Stelzer, a senior fellow of the Hudson Institute think-tank, will not necessarily make many converts but should at least help us to know what we are talking about.'
Samuel Brittan, *Financial Times*

NEOCONSERVATISM

Edited, with an
Introduction by
IRWIN STELZER

Atlantic Books
London

For Cita, who urged me to compile
this volume and, as always,
generously suspended work on her
projects to assist on mine.

CONTENTS

ACKNOWLEDGEMENTS

Irving Kristol and his good wife, historian Gertrude Himmelfarb, were kind enough to review my own introductory essay and in their gentle but firm way to eliminate several errors in the early draft. Charles Murray made certain that I properly described the changes in welfare policy resulting from his work. Toni Allen, a long-time colleague and Hudson Institute adjunct fellow, made her usual contribution to both the substance and accuracy of my own essays, as well as the editing of the others. Leyre Gonzalez, my assistant, used her skills on the internet and her tireless energy to provide valuable research assistance. Herb London made certain that the Hudson Institute provided the resources needed to complete this project. Cita Stelzer deployed her ample editorial and organizational skills to assist me in meeting the publisher's rather tight deadline.

Toby Mundy conceived this project and, along with my wife, Cita, persuaded me to undertake it, an effort on their part that I did not consistently appreciate as I learned that a volume of essays, like a convoy, moves at the speed of the slowest ship. In the end, if closer familiarity with the work of neoconservatives helps to dissipate some of the readers' unreasoning hostility to its doctrines and its advocates, it will have been worth the time and effort.

Most of all, I would like to thank those who allowed us to use their prior works, and those who were good enough to contribute new essays. I have taken the liberty of making a very few minor, non-substantive edits to a few of the previously published essays.

I hope that all of those who helped with this volume will feel amply rewarded if critics of neoconservatism, and the merely puzzled, find these essays a source of a better understanding of what the neoconservative persuasion is all about.

★ ☆ ★

PREFACE TO THE
PAPERBACK EDITION

It was an act of courage for Atlantic Books, my publisher, to produce this volume of essays on neoconservatism when it did. At the time, it seemed that in only a few days America's voters would force George W. Bush to follow in his father's footsteps and become a one-term president; the election had not yet been held in Iraq; the U.S. Secretary of State was doing his best to distance himself from his president's seemingly failed foreign policy; and the American job market was experiencing a painstakingly slow recovery.

It was not unreasonable to guess that the views of neoconservatives soon would be of little interest to anyone, given the looming failure of the policies propounded by many of the contributors to this volume. After all, neocons had produced the foreign policy that created what seemed to be a quagmire in Iraq, and crafted the domestic policy that the president's critics held responsible for soaring budget and trade deficits, and a sluggish labor market. The remainder shelves were likely to be the only places that the few people with a taste for policies that had been consigned to the dustbin of history might find copies of this book.

That was then; this is now. Since this volume of essays first appeared, George W. Bush and Tony Blair, the principal proponents of the war to unseat Saddam Hussein, have been reelected; only Spain's José María Aznar has been turned out, and that for reasons not entirely or even primarily related to the Iraq war. Condoleezza Rice, represented in these pages, has become Secretary of State, and now has both the prestige and institutional resources with which to refine and apply the neoconservative policy she helped to draft — which she is doing with a remarkable combination of doctrinal toughness and captivating style. The United Nations had positioned itself as the world's moral arbiter, and Kofi Annan had declared the Iraq war 'illegal': the UN is now an organization diminished in stature by scandals, mismanagement, and its unworkable structure – just as the neocons predicted it would be.

Meanwhile, Paul Wolfowitz, whose policies were developed and advocated by the Project for the New American Century (PNAC), the organization with which he was closely associated and which was and is chaired by still another contributor to this volume, William ('Bill') Kristol, has now been approved by all shareholders as the new president of the World Bank, where he can be expected to introduce the decidedly neoconservative notion that loans to undemocratic, unaccountable regimes are more likely to end up fattening Swiss bank accounts than feeding starving Africans.

It does not seem excessively triumphalist to say that neoconservatives – more precisely, those of the neoconservative persuasion, as Irving Kristol so accurately describes this non-movement in his essay and Sol Schindler describes in *The Wall Street Journal's* review of this book as 'not a tightly engineered ideology'[1] – are now and will be for the next four years at the center of America's foreign policy establishment. Moreover, they will find continued support from their comrade-in-arms, Tony Blair. Britain's Prime Minister, whose call for pre-emption and the spreading of democracy, reproduced in this volume, pre-dated much of what has come to be America's neoconservative foreign policy, said of that policy: 'Actually, if you put it in different language, it's a progressive agenda.'

Nor would anyone have thought when this book was launched that eight million Iraqis would face down the terrorists and queue at the polls to cast their votes in the first free election of their lifetimes, proudly waving their ink-stained fingers to prove that, yes, they had participated in a process that might – just might – establish a workable democracy in a region of the world where until now only Israel granted its citizens the right to choose their government. Or that Iraq's elected politicians would be able to conclude, with what at this point seems like reasonable success, protracted negotiations to form a government, without, at least so far, fracturing the unity of the Iraqi state.

At the time of writing, the foreign policy laid out in the essays of Condoleezza Rice, Margaret Thatcher, Tony Blair, Robert Kagan, and other contributors seems to have more chance of succeeding in its goal of upsetting the status quo in the Middle East by fostering democracy than could possibly be imagined when this book first landed on bookshop and library shelves.

Neoconservatives called on America's new leaders to abandon their nation's long-standing and continuing collaboration with the corrupt and autocratic regimes of the Middle East that had been the hallmark of American foreign policy at least since World War II. Not merely to do good, but in order to protect the homeland from attack. So Saddam is gone. And with over 100,000 American troops on its border, and the example of Iraq glaring at it 'close-up and personal', as they say in Texas, Syria succumbed to the long-suppressed demand of the

Lebanese people and agreed to withdraw its occupying army and security forces from Lebanon. It is not to diminish the courage of the millions of Lebanese who took to the streets in their 'Cedar Revolution' to note that it occurred only after President Bush made it clear that America would lend all reasonable support to those yearning to replace tyranny with democracy.

There also seems good reason to hope that the fragile democratic openings in other parts of the Middle East will prove durable. Egypt's president Hosni Mubarak has announced that he will for the first time allow contested elections. We do not yet know just how much freedom the regime's opponents will be allowed, but Mubarak's willingness to release dissidents after Secretary Rice cancelled her planned visit to Egypt in order to express America's displeasure at the incarceration of leading anti-regime politicians suggests that he is not immune to pressure from Washington to relax his grip on the political process.

Even Saudi Arabia, as famous for political repression and fostering the doctrines that underlie worldwide terrorism as it is for its God-given abundance of crude oil, is cautiously experimenting with allowing local elections, and promises some day soon that women will be allowed to vote. In part this reform, if such half-measures warrant that term, stems from the rulers' sense that something must be done to placate domestic critics. But in part the ever-so-tiny surrender of power by the regime results from its need to shore up relations with an American president who is no longer satisfied with the 'oil-for-regime-protection' deal struck by Franklin Roosevelt with the royal family six decades ago.

Surely, those who argue that neoconservatism has not played a key role in these and other changes sweeping through the Middle East bear a heavy burden of proof. The neoconservative foreign policy enunciated with such vigor by President Bush in his second inaugural address, his insistence that spreading democracy is important if the West is to win its war on terror, and the ability of America to encourage democratic developments in Afghanistan, Iraq, Egypt, Lebanon, (perhaps) Saudi Arabia, and the Palestinian Authority, at least suggest that many of the contributors to this volume are on the right side of history.

Nor is it implausible that it was the neoconservatives' support for President Bush's steadfast and much-criticized refusal to negotiate with Yasser Arafat that contributed to the possibility – and it is only that – that the death of the terrorist Arafat might create an opening for the peacemakers. Whether Mahmoud Abbas will in the end be able to disarm the terrorists remains to be seen; at this writing, his Fatah faction is in contest with Hamas for political control – a Hamas more interested in ballots than bullets certainly represents progress. And we do not yet know whether President Bush will be able to prevent Israel's Prime Minister, Ariel Sharon, from straying off the path laid out in the roadmap to peace – their meeting at the president's ranch in Crawford, Texas, in April 2005, suggested that Sharon will not easily abandon plans to extend settlements around Jerusalem. But, as with other developments in the Middle East, there is more reason for hope than there has been since Arafat launched his successive Intifadas.

All of these successes for neoconservative-inspired policies are as provisional as they are real. Triumphalism on the part of neoconservatives would be as inappropriate as the continued hand-wringing of their critics, represented by the left-wing press in Britain and the liberal (in the American sense) press in America. So we have Jonathan Steele in the *Guardian*: 'For most Iraqis, with the exception of the Kurds, Washington's "liberation" never was. Wounded national pride was greater than relief at Saddam's departure.' Whether Steele polled the relatives of those whose bodies continue to be uncovered in mass graves is not known.

There is much yet to play for in Iraq. Terrorists still routinely murder Iraqi officials, soldiers and policemen; crime is rife; and public services are spotty at best. It will be some time before we learn whether Iraqis are capable of governing themselves without American troops on the ground to assist indigenous forces to maintain an acceptable approximation of order, and whether the system of government that emerges can credibly be called democratic. Iraq might yet end up a failed state, or fracture under pressures from ethnic groups that have yet to demonstrate they can live in something approaching harmony.

Nor do we yet know whether the Lebanese who united on the single issue of ejecting Syria will find an agenda that converts their one-issue protest into an enduring political movement. Or whether Lebanon will fall under the sway of Hezbollah terrorists.

There are other uncertainties. Mubarak might rig the Egyptian elections. The Palestinian-Israel peace talks might founder on the rocks of renewed terrorism, or intransigence by negotiators on one side or the other. And Saudi Arabia, having offered President Bush a bit of democratization, might revert to type under pressure from followers of Wahabiism, the doctrine that helped spawn al-Qaeda.

But, to borrow from the late British Prime Minister Harold Macmillan, 'the winds of change' are surely blowing through the Middle East, in no small part thanks to a foreign policy that incorporates the wisdom of those whose views are represented in Part II of this volume, and the determination of an American president who believes that Tony Blair had it right when he said, in a talk reproduced here, 'We cannot turn our backs on conflicts and the violation of human rights within other countries if we want still to be secure.'

Thanks in part to the success of the idea that 'the pursuit of freedom and democracy in other people's countries [is] the organizing principle of… foreign policy…, after a certain amount of scoffing and some alarm… the idea is catching on in surprising places…'.[2] This is due not only to the fact that we may be witnessing what might prove to be the end of the beginning – optimists, and most neocons are optimists,[3] would say the beginning of the end – of the war. If so, America, Britain and their allies would have routed a lethal combination of Saddam's remnants; a disgruntled Sunni minority reluctant to surrender its traditional power over the majority Shi'ites; and imported terrorists.

The increasing if at times grudging acceptance of the possibility that the neocons have it right is due, too, to Bush's demonstration that his version of neoconservatism will be applied with sense: the leader of the world's superpower has proven that he knows the difference between Iraq, where military power was the only means for eliminating a terrorist-fostering and abhorrent regime, and Pakistan, an ally so important that it is wise to attempt to change its imperfect system of government by slow persuasion; and Iran, where it is more prudent to give diplomacy a chance before considering the military option, lest pro-American sentiment be squandered by over-hasty intervention.

In short, Bush finds himself in the middle of the spectrum of neoconservative thought, a spectrum that includes on one end Jeane Kirkpatrick's skepticism about attempts to impose democracy everywhere (a view shared by conservative George Will; see his essay), and on the other end the Kristol–Kagan view, expressed in their essay, that the 'purpose of American foreign policy ought to be clear. When it comes to dealing with tyrannical regimes, especially [ed. note: but not only] those with the power to do us or our allies harm, the United States should seek not coexistence but transformation.'

The influential columnist and scholar Charles Krauthammer, a man who styles himself a 'democratic realist', but lives comfortably with many of those of a neoconservative persuasion, distinguishes between an 'open-ended commitment to human freedom, [the] temptation to plant the flag of democracy everywhere', and this axiom: 'We will support democracy everywhere, but we will commit blood and treasure only in places where there is a strategic necessity – meaning, places central to the larger war against the existential enemy, the enemy that poses a global mortal threat to freedom…

We are friends to all, but we come ashore only where it counts.'[4] It is difficult to distinguish that policy from the Bush doctrine *as it is being practiced*. Tony Blair recently described that policy: the Americans know 'that you can't just go round invading every country that you think should be a democracy. What you can, however, do is to say that you are going to encourage people to become more democratic and more open.'[5]

This practical application of neoconservative doctrine allows decidedly non-neo conservatives such as Richard Lowry – he accuses neocons of being possessed of a 'messianic vision', and William Kristol of 'unmitigated... idealistic crusading' – to applaud 'the practical policy of the Bush Administration... The Bush rhetoric is just that – rhetoric, which he has not allowed to trump pragmatic considerations, whether with regard to Russia, China, the Central Asian republics or Saudi Arabia.'[6] But rhetoric matters, most especially to democratic opposition groups that need to know they are not alone in the world. Ronald Reagan understood that – think Solidarity and the Berlin Wall – and so does George W. Bush.

What has become clear since this volume first appeared is that (1) neoconservatism, a broad church, has replaced liberal internationalism – 'the religion of the foreign policy elite... [that has become] an ideology of passivity, acquiescence and almost reflexive anti-interventionism'[7] – as the guiding principle of American foreign policy; (2) neoconservative doctrine is elastic enough to permit the use of both hard and soft power, and to allow distinctions between non-democratic regimes that threaten us, those that support us, and those to which the Western democracies can safely remain indifferent, which pleases both neocons and traditional conservatives; and (3) so far, and subject to reversal by those dreaded 'events, dear boy, events' that so worried Macmillan, neoconservatism seems to be on the right side of history.

In foreign affairs, at least. When it comes to domestic policy, things are not quite so clear. From an extreme position of 'deficits don't matter', the view of some neocons, the American administration has moved to a policy of attempting to contain deficits by reining in, just a little, government spending, and relying on a combination of such cuts in expenses as it can wring from Congress and added revenue from economic growth to meet its goal of sharply reducing the deficit in relation to the nation's income. Even Bruce Bartlett, who reminds us that he 'once argued that the negative effects of deficits are generally exaggerated' now so fears the consequences of 'ever-larger deficits' that he has come out in favor of a value-added tax, which he once opposed.[8]

But at the same time the neoconservative view that government, in the right hands, can be a friend rather than an enemy, remains unchanged. That has allowed the President to preside over the largest expansion of the welfare state since the days of Lyndon B. Johnson's 'Great Society', to the consternation of some but not all neoconservatives, and all traditional conservatives, but to the apparent approval of the voters.[9]

That expansion, however, runs in parallel with an attempt to reduce dependence on government by creating an ownership society. So we have plans for private savings accounts to replace a portion of the government pension system, and private medical accounts to give patients the means with which to shop for health-care services. The underlying goals are pure neoconservative doctrine: greater personal responsibility for one's financial condition, competition to drive the efficiency with which health care is provided, and, in the field of education, insistence on testing so that good teaching and academic achievement can be discovered and rewarded.

Goals are not achievements, however, and it is too early to tell whether a neoconservative administration can convert the former into the latter. The signs are not promising: muddled presentation by the president and his economic team has combined with opposition by those reluctant to support any changes in what liberals see as the jewel in the crown of Franklin Roosevelt's New Deal, to stall the drive to an ownership society.

Efforts to reduce government spending have also run into determined opposition, in this instance from the beneficiaries of that spending: farmers have forced the president to back down on his plan to reduce subsidies, state governors and poverty group lobbyists have forced him to moderate proposed reductions in health-care spending, while Congress continues to demand funding for pet projects – 'pork', in the American political vernacular – that its members feel essential to their reelection prospects in 2006.

Which leaves the much-reported area that has come to be known as 'the culture', an area of neoconservative activity that secular Europe seems to find even more troubling than neocon foreign policy. The Bush administration, out of a combination of conviction and political calculation, continues to pursue policies that appall not only most European elites, but the libertarian wing of the neoconservative persuasion, while appealing to the neocon religious wing:[10] anti-abortion foreign aid restrictions; a constitutional amendment to ban gay marriage; intervention in so called 'right-to-die' cases; the appointment to the chair of the broadcast regulator of a man who certainly agrees with the view reflected in Irving Kristol's essay – that something must be done to curb the output of pornographic and obscene materials that parade across our television screens.

The ability of the administration to maintain the support of both its libertarian and religious wings is a testimonial to the ability of neoconservatism to offer all of its adherents so much that unites them that differences over one or even a few policies have not fractured the rather diverse band that gathers under its banner. Whether that will remain the case if foreign policy recedes into the background and more divisive domestic issues come to dominate American political life is something we will not know until our role in Iraq comes to an end.

Irwin Stelzer, London, May 2005.

1   March 3, 2005.

2   *The Economist*, April 9, 2005.

3   'Neoconservative thought is persuasive precisely because it presents itself not as ideology but as morality – and, moreover, morality charged with optimism,' notes Suzanne Moore in her review of this book. *New Statesman*, November 1, 2004.

4   Charles Krauthammer, 'Democratic Realism: An American Foreign Policy for a Unipolar World', delivered as the Irving Kristol lecture at the American Enterprise Institute in February 2004, subsequently published in Washington, D.C., by AEI Press. See pp.16 and 18–19.

5   Interview with the *Financial Times*, January 26, 2005.

6   *The National Interest*, Spring 2005, pp. 35 and 41.

7   Krauthammer, *op.cit.*, p. 4.

8   Bartlett, a senior fellow at the National Center for Policy Analysis, set forth his revised views in *The New York Times*, April 6, 2005.

9   Domestic nondefense discretionary spending fell 10 percent during President Reagan's first term, and rose by a like percentage in President's Clinton's first term. Under President Bush it has gone up 27 percent. *National Journal*, March 5, 2005, p. 689.

10   'Republicans' Moves to Expand Federal Role Cheer More Than Just Social Conservatives,' announced *The Wall Street Journal* (April 4, 2005). The other members of the cheering section are businessmen who want the federal government to expand its regulatory reach so as to pre-empt the states.

NEOCONSERVATISM
An Introduction

NEOCONSERVATIVES AND THEIR CRITICS
An Introduction

IRWIN STELZER

The war in Iraq is the culmination of a neoconservative takeover of America, if much of the European and some of the American media are to be believed. Thanks to a small cabal of intellectuals – 'conservative ideologues... scornful of... idealistic multilateralism', according to *The Economist*[1] – America has abandoned its traditional foreign policy and become a unilateralist, imperialist hegemon, or hyperpower, given to pre-emptive strikes against any nation that it decides threatens its security. According to critics of neoconservatism, the United States no longer pays what Thomas Jefferson called 'a decent respect to the opinions of mankind'. After years of plotting, this band of neoconservatives, or neocons, led by their most important practitioners, George W. Bush and Dick Cheney, now have control of American foreign and security policy, not to mention domestic policy. But America's difficulties in Iraq have created serious doubts about the ability of the United States to achieve the neoconservative goal of exporting American democracy. 'Now... is the time,' wrote Matthew Parris, almost a year before terrorists became a powerful force on the roads and in the alleys of Iraq, 'to spike the ambitions of the neoconservatives.'[2] Ten months later, *The Economist* picked up the same theme: faced with a mounting toll of death and destruction, 'The neocons themselves are growing queasy.'[3]

Some neocons may indeed be having doubts, but among the steadfast are those – in particular the President of the United States – with the power to decide whether America will continue to pursue the neocon dream.

It is the goal of this collection of essays to replace heat with light, and separate the truths underlying some of the fears of neoconservatism and neocons from the fantasies. A close reading of what prominent neocons have said leads to the conclusion that the foreign policy they advocate, some of which was adopted by the Bush administration in response to the attack on America on September 11, 2001, is less radical, and certainly less novel, than is widely thought. Although neocons are proud to have broken in many ways with the post–Cold War consensus, they can reasonably claim that their ideas have deep roots in early American and British history, and in policies advocated by American presidents such as John Quincy Adams and Theodore Roosevelt, and by British prime ministers Margaret Thatcher and Tony Blair. As such, and because of the quality of the neoconservatives' research and advocacy, their fundamental ideas are likely to survive changes of control of the White House.

So, too, with domestic policy. The programs advocated by neoconservatives in the fields of crime, welfare reform, and what has been called 'the culture war' did not spring fully formed from the minds of those who helped George W. Bush to fashion 'compassionate conservatism'. Instead, these ideas originated with Victorian reformers, were then buried under the mass of legislation that constituted the New Deal of President Franklin D. Roosevelt, and by President Lyndon Johnson's Great Society, to re-emerge in the articles, pamphlets, and proposals of the neocons. In the area of domestic policy the 'neo' prefix may turn out to be as potentially misleading as it can be in the foreign policy field (or at least too all-encompassing to describe what neoconservatism is about).

But we must begin our discussion of the development of neoconservatism with a disclaimer. As David Brooks notes in an essay included in this volume, 'If you ever read a sentence that starts with "Neocons believe", there is a 99.44 per cent chance everything else in that sentence will be untrue.' Brooks is right. There is no such thing as a neoconservative 'movement', in the dictionary sense of 'a body of persons with a common object'. But there is what the acknowledged godfather of neoconservatism, Irving Kristol, calls in one of his essays included here, 'the neoconservative persuasion'; what Joshua Muravchik, in his contribution, calls 'a distinctive neoconservative sensibility'; and what Norman Podhoretz, who used the pages of *Commentary* magazine to develop and win adherents to the foreign policy branch of neoconservatism, calls a 'neoconservative tendency'. Podhoretz prefers the descriptive 'tendency', he says, because neoconservatism 'never had or aspired to the kind of central organization characteristic of a movement'.[4]

In part this disinclination by a group that 'share[s] views on many subjects'[5] to label neoconservatism a 'movement' stems from recognition by those in broad agreement with some of its principles that there are non-trivial differences among them on important points of policy. In part it stems from the fact that many of them have spent their lives railing against a variety of self-styled 'movements' – the peace movement, the communist movement, the environmental movement, and others that view with horror deviations from organizational orthodoxy by their dues-paying members. The intellectuals known as 'neocons', loosely defined, prize their individualism; not for them, grouping with others into an ideological monolith.

All of this suggests that criticism of neoconservatism as a 'cabal' is not well founded. Popular in Europe and in the liberal media in America, the idea goes something like this: a small group of intellectuals, including many future members of the Bush administration, plotted for years, in secret, to replace America's long-standing multinational foreign policy, with its heavy reliance on the United Nations, with a more unilateralist, expansive, and muscular approach to world affairs.

The center of this cabal is said to be the Project for the New American Century (PNAC), an organization founded by William (Bill) Kristol in 1997 in order 'to promote American global leadership'. Its other founders include Dick Cheney, Donald Rumsfeld, Paul Wolfowitz, and Elliott Abrams, all of whom were destined for key positions in the Bush administration – with the exception of Kristol, who uses his editorship of *The Weekly Standard*, an influential Washington-based magazine that at times supports, and at times criticizes, the administration of George W. Bush, to provide a platform for many working neocons.

No one can doubt that PNAC was an important contributor to the Bush administration's foreign policy. To suggest, however, that it is a part of some secret effort to overthrow traditional American foreign policy is simply not true. In a democracy, ideas matter in the crafting of foreign policy, and some of the neocons (but not all) who contributed to the work of PNAC thought hard, quarreled among themselves, wrote with style and wit, spoke at gatherings of important opinion-makers, and circulated memoranda urging America to adopt an approach to the world that is responsive to the new, post-Cold War threats to its security.

This very public battle for the hearts and minds of the foreign policy establishment hardly constitutes the sort of surreptitious scheming favored by cabals. Even Joshua Micah Marshall, who complained in *The New Yorker* that the neocons used the horror of September 11 'to espouse a world view that was unapologetically imperialist', concedes that the neocons' sales technique was no secret. 'You could watch this happening in Washington's think tanks. Over their lunchroom tables, in their seminar rooms, on the covers of their small magazines, the idea of empire got a thorough airing – particularly among ideologues close to the policymakers planning the war on terror.'[6] No plotters, no secret meetings, no cabal. Instead, there was a very public effort to persuade the U.S. government to adopt a view of the world that is radically different from that favored by the post–Cold War foreign-policy establishment, but which nonetheless had roots in earlier American history.

The myth of a secret cabal is not the only one constructed by the neocons' critics. Another is that neoconservative foreign policy is the invention of Jewish intellectuals whose primary interest is the survival and expansion of Israel, rather than the security of the United States. 'Con is short for "conservative" and neo is short for "Jewish",' jokes Brooks in his essay. As John Podhoretz (son of Norman, just as Bill is the son of Irving) describes it in his own book of essays,[7] 'Many Bush opponents have taken to arguing that George W. Bush has come under the control of a collective of Jewish advisers whose true purpose is not the defense of the United States but the furtherance of Israel's security interests.'

Neocon opponents, and some writers who worry less about neoconservatism than about Jewish domination of American policy-making, are convinced this is the case. Steve Bradshaw, the interviewer for the BBC's prestigious *Panorama* television program, informed his audience, 'We picked up a recurrent theme of insider talk in Washington. Some leading neocons, people whisper, are strongly pro-Zionist and want to topple regimes in the Middle East to help Israel as well as the U.S.'

Hardly a mere 'whisper' from these unidentified 'some people' and their like-thinking allies. Robert Fisk, the Middle East correspondent for the *Independent*, told his readers that the Bush administration is being led into a war against Islam by the likes of Ken Adelman (President Ronald Reagan's disarmament director) and Eliot Cohen (Director of the Center for Strategic Studies, a member of the Defense Policy Board and a founding member of PNAC), men 'who have not vouchsafed their own religion'.[8] A long article in *The New Yorker* uses a review of the career of Elliott Abrams, Special Assistant to the President and Senior Director for Near East and North African Affairs, to hint that Abrams gives great weight to Israel's interests when shaping U.S. policy. Also, as Joshua Muravchik points out in his essay, Elizabeth Drew, one of America's more famous journalists, writes, 'Because some… of the neoconservatives are Jewish and virtually all are strong supporters of the Likud party's policies, the accusation has been made that their aim to "democratize" the region is driven by their desire to surround Israel with more sympathetic neighbors. Such a view would explain the otherwise puzzling statements by Wolfowitz and others before the [Iraq] war that "the road to peace in the Middle East goes through Baghdad".' Muravchik's comments on this, and similar charges that neocons are at heart Israeli agents, repay careful reading.

It is one thing to disagree with American policy toward Israel. It is quite another to accuse Jewish neocons of having divided loyalties, and of a plot to tilt America's Middle Eastern policy toward Israel regardless of the interests of the United States. This is the line taken by Michael Lind, who claims, 'For years, American neocons [have been] disseminating the propaganda of the Israeli Right.'9 It is echoed more subtly by Pulitzer Prize-winner Thomas Powers, who first quotes Richard Perle's heated and explicit denial of divided loyalty, and then writes, 'Perle strikes me as a little nervous and defensive on this point. Why not admit openly that of course the fate of Israel is much on his mind?'10 It is not clear why a policy-maker who has 'the fate of Israel' on his or her mind – after all, one hopes that all players in the international power game, including non-Jews, concern themselves with that issue – should be accused of divided loyalty.

It is this myth – Jewish domination of neoconservatism, and neocon subservience to the interests of Israel even when those interests clash with the interests of the United States – that Muravchik lays to rest. He finds the durability of this myth puzzling, since neither Colin Powell nor Condoleezza Rice, the President's principal foreign-policy advisors, are Jewish; nor are Vice President Dick Cheney (thought by some to be the driving force behind the decision to unseat Saddam), Donald Rumsfeld (Secretary of Defense), or George Tenet (until recently director of the Central Intelligence Agency). And Bill Kristol and Richard Perle, both Jewish, were in the forefront of those urging the Clinton administration to intervene in Kosovo to stop the slaughter of tens of thousands of Muslims.

What is more remarkable still about the myth that Jewish neocons dominate administration policy is the close involvement of the Christian right with the Bush government. Leaders of the religious right – evangelicals and Catholics – quite properly style themselves neoconservatives and press for policies on such issues as abortion that the great mass of Jewish voters, 80 per cent of whom voted against George W. Bush in 2000, reject. With the religious right the core of Bush's political support, and Jewish voters second only to blacks in their loyalty to his political opponents, the argument that it is Jews who run the government's foreign policy becomes difficult to maintain. Max Boot's contribution to this volume is a complete consideration of that charge and of many of the others made against neoconservatives.

Another hotly contested question hinges on the foreign-policy goals of the neocons, and their ability to persuade the Bush administration to adopt those goals.

As already noted, neoconservatism is more a tendency than a movement. Indeed, Irving Kristol contends in his essay on the neoconservative persuasion, 'there is no set of neoconservative beliefs concerning foreign policy, only a set of attitudes derived from historical experience.' But these 'attitudes' have definite shape and form in the foreign-policy arena, as shown in the essay by William Kristol and Robert Kagan. The latter, a former State Department official, is the author of *Of Paradise and Power*, perhaps the most influential foreign-policy book in decades.[11] It became essential reading from Britain's Whitehall to America's Foggy Bottom to France's Quai d'Orsay, and in embassies around the world.

The Kristol–Kagan essay in this volume was chosen because it was written before the current invasion of Iraq, so that its policy proposals might be considered for their broad applicability, rather than merely in the specific context of Iraq. In it, the authors argue that it is unrealistic to assume that bad actors will reform, and they call for a policy of 'regime change'. However, they carefully point out that such a policy would not require the United States to 'dispatch troops to topple every regime we found odious'. In the case of Iraq, they regret that in the first Gulf War the coalition did not march to Baghdad 'to remove Saddam Hussein from power, and… [keep] U.S. troops in Iraq long enough to ensure that a friendlier regime took root.' It should be apparent to even the most casual observer of current American policy that the views expressed in this essay became policy, as the contribution to this volume by National Security Advisor Condoleezza Rice makes clear. Explaining President George W. Bush's national security strategy, Dr Rice emphasizes the administration's desire 'to extend the benefits of freedom and prosperity across the globe'.

The doctrine of pre-emption, the perceived need to deal with 'rogue states', and some of the other ingredients of neoconservatism actually have deep roots in American history, and, as Michael Gove points out in his essay, were espoused by British leaders, including Canning, Palmerston, Churchill, and Thatcher, long before they were adopted by George W. Bush (who barely discussed foreign policy during his election campaign). Indeed, Adam Wolfson contends in his essay that the roots of Bush's foreign policy, and in particular its emphasis on pre-emption, can be traced to John Locke's *Second Treatise*, in which he argued that in their defense people must take action before 'it is too late, and the evil is past Cure'.

Although John Lewis Gaddis, of Yale University, believes that President Bush's foreign policy is a disastrous deviation from the more multilateralist policy crafted by Franklin D. Roosevelt, he has pointed out that many of the doctrines underlying the current president's policy have roots in America's history. These policies, most especially pre-emption, originated with President John Quincy Adams in response to circumstances such as Spain's inability to prevent cross-border attacks on America by Indians sheltering in its Florida colony.[12] Early in the twentieth century, Theodore Roosevelt articulated a policy that differs little from that of George W. Bush, with the exception of TR's concentration on the Western Hemisphere: 'Chronic wrongdoing, or an impotence which results in a general loosening of the ties of civilized society, may… ultimately require intervention by some civilized nation, and in the Western Hemisphere… may force the United States, however reluctantly… to the exercise of an international police power.'[13] American neoconservatives have made something of a hero of the president who urged Americans to speak softly and carry a big stick. In their essay, Kristol and Kagan cite with particular approval TR's statement, 'A nation's first duty is within its borders, but it is not thereby absolved from facing its duties in the world as a whole; and if it refuses to do so, it merely forfeits its right to struggle for a place among the people that shape the destiny of mankind.'

A decade after Teddy Roosevelt's statement, another neocon precursor moved into the White House – Woodrow Wilson. Wilson told the world that America had occupied Cuba, 'Not for annexation but to provide the helpless colony with the opportunity for freedom', language similar to that used by George W. Bush and Tony Blair many years later as one of their justifications for unseating Saddam Hussein. Like today's neocons, Wilson sought to remake the world, or substantial portions of it, in America's democratic image. His call for 'self-determination', a concept that he never really defined,[14] is echoed in the Bush–Blair call for free elections that will allow Iraqis to determine their own future.

But neoconservatism is Wilsonianism with a very big difference. Wilson believed that his goal could be achieved by relying on the persuasive powers of multinational institutions such as the League of Nations. Neocons disagree. They would make democracy possible by deposing dictatorial regimes that threaten American security and world order – using military force if all else fails; they would follow regime change with nation-building; and they would rely on varying 'coalitions of the willing', rather than on the United Nations. As Margaret Thatcher points out in her speech at Fulton, Missouri, which is included in this volume, the UN has 'given us neither prosperity nor security'. Neocons such as Jeane Kirkpatrick and Robert Kagan view the UN even more skeptically than does Lady Thatcher – as an organization in which non-democratic regimes are over-represented. They also see it as one in which France seeks to use its veto and influence with its former colonies and its EU colleagues to constrain American freedom of action, by making the UN the sole judge of the moral propriety of American action. In an 'afterword' to the new edition of his *Of Paradise and Power*, Kagan asks, 'Are the UN Security Council, and the structure of international law it sits atop, really the holy grail of international legitimacy, as Europeans today are insisting?' Answer: 'They are not.'[15]

The neocon position might be summed up as diplomacy if possible, force if necessary; the UN if possible, ad hoc coalitions or unilateral action if necessary; pre-emptive strikes if it is reasonable to anticipate hostile action on the part of America's enemies. As Max Boot puts it in his essay, neocons are not 'soft Wilsonians', like former President Jimmy Carter, but are "hard Wilsonians" who place their faith not in pieces of paper but in power, specifically U.S. power'.

Martin Wolf, a perceptive British observer of the world scene, sums up his view of the road from Wilson to Bush by noting 'the neoconservatives… are Wilsonian in their ends but anti-Wilsonian in their means. Unlike Wilson, they believe that the needed transformations can be achieved by U.S. power unbound by international constraint… [Neoconservatives] argue that democracy and freedom are the best way for people to live… Yet… [the U.S.] appears to think, might, not right, makes right.'[16]

Almost, but not quite. Neoconservatives do indeed believe that democracy and freedom are the best way for people to live. But they go beyond mere do-goodism and argue that by spreading democracy the West best ensures the maintenance of a peaceful and prosperous world order. Jeane Kirkpatrick, who served as America's Ambassador to the UN under President Ronald Reagan, long ago pointed out the nexus between democracy and security when she said, 'Democratic nations don't start wars.' Prime Minister Tony Blair shares that view, as he made clear in the speech reproduced here ('The spread of our values makes us safer') and again when he told a joint session of the U.S. Congress on July 17, 2003, 'The spread of freedom is the best security for the free… [T]he liberty we seek is not for some but for all, for that is the only true path to victory in this struggle.'[17]

Besides, neocon advocates of a muscular U.S. foreign policy argue that people everywhere share Western values and desire freedom, as that term is understood in the West. As Blair, a non-neocon raised by neocons to the exalted status that until now was accorded only to Winston Churchill and Margaret Thatcher, put it in his address to Congress, 'Ours are not Western values, they are universal values of the human spirit.' It is this belief in the universality of the desire for Western-style freedom, and its parallel assumption that the U.S. and its allies are capable of transplanting their system of government to often-hostile soils, that George Will so vigorously challenges in his essay here. He is not alone; even James Q. Wilson, a confirmed neocon when it comes to domestic policy, doubts whether America can successfully plant a liberal democracy in the rocky soil of Iraq, citing among other reasons the fact that 'a democratic regime requires a democratic culture, and such a culture grows rather slowly'.[18]

It may be criticism such as this that Condoleezza Rice has in mind when she rejects, in her contribution, 'the condescending view that freedom will not grow in the soil of the Middle East', but she importantly adds, 'We do not seek to impose democracy on others, we seek only to help create conditions in which people can claim a freer future for themselves.'

Neocons are careful to point out that they do not rely solely or even primarily on force to spread democratic values. Blair again: 'In the end, it is not our power alone that will defeat this evil [terrorism]. Our ultimate weapon is not our guns, but our beliefs.'[19] Richard Perle, widely regarded as the hardest of hardliners among the Bush administration's advisors, has pointed out, 'We're not going to make war on the world for democracy... We should be using all instruments of American influence to accomplish that purpose and most of those instruments are not military.'[20]

It might surprise 'soft power' advocates such as Harvard's Joseph Nye[21] to know that they have something of an ally in Perle and other neocons, but they do. Indeed, as the essay by Kristol and Kagan makes clear, Perle is not alone; neocons generally do not rely exclusively on military muscle to defend America's interests. They do want America to devote adequate resources to its military to enable the nation to project overwhelming power wherever and whenever its security requires such deployment, and have loudly criticized the Bush administration for failing to provide sufficient troops to secure Iraq's citizens and infrastructure. But they are sufficiently confident of the sound intellectual basis of their position concerning the universality of the desire for some form of democratic government to be willing also to enter the lists in the war of ideas. More troops, yes; but more seminars as well. Which is why neocons such as Perle and Bill Kristol log tens of thousands of miles every year to engage in debate those who would deny America's need to spread democratic values as part of its program to create a more stable world order.

Nor do neocons call for exclusive reliance on unilateral action. As John Bolton makes clear in this volume, although America views weapons of mass destruction in the hands of terrorists as so grave a threat to its security that it must act alone if it cannot persuade other nations to join it, multilateral non-proliferation agreements are important weapons in 'our non-proliferation arsenal', and multilateral forums have an important role to play in America's security plans. But – and it is this 'but' that raises the hair on the napes of European and North Korean necks – 'While diplomatic efforts and multilateral regimes will remain important to our efforts, we also intend to complement this approach with other measures as we work both in concert with like-minded nations *and on our own* to prevent terrorists and terrorist regimes from acquiring or using WMD [emphasis added].'

According to some neocons, Woodrow Wilson failed, not because America refused to join the League of Nations, but because the League was just as unwilling to enforce its edicts against Mussolini's Ethiopian adventure as the UN Security Council was to insist on Saddam Hussein's compliance with its multiple resolutions demanding that he submit to and cooperate with international weapons inspectors. Hence our willingness to act 'on our own'.

Presidents John Quincy Adams, Theodore Roosevelt, and Woodrow Wilson were not the only progenitors of neocon foreign policy. While many neoconservatives were writing their policy papers and, to use a phrase favored by optimistic politicians in Britain, 'preparing for power', Margaret Thatcher was telling an audience in Fulton, Missouri, that 'rogue states [a phrase she first used in a speech five years earlier] like Syria, Iraq, and Gadaffi's Libya' make the world a dangerous place. Using the occasion of the fiftieth anniversary of Winston Churchill's famous 'Iron Curtain' speech of 1946, Lady Thatcher warned in the talk reproduced in this volume that 'the proliferation of weapons of mass destruction' makes it necessary for 'America and its allies [to]... deal with the problem directly by pre-emptive military means'. As Thatcher biographer John Campbell puts it, 'Her preference was explicitly for pre-emptive military action to remove the threat [posed by rogue states possessing weapons of mass destruction] – a policy that would have to wait for the presidency of the younger George Bush, acting under the provocation of the attack on the World Trade Center in September 2001.'[22] And, by allies, Lady Thatcher meant 'the English-speaking peoples of the West'.[23]

Tony Blair, too, was ahead of George Bush in accepting the view that intervention by Western democracies – in what once were seen as solely the affairs of sovereign states – is sometimes necessary to cope with rogue regimes and terrorists. In a talk that in many ways is a direct descendant of Theodore Roosevelt's statement, quoted above, and which is reprinted in this volume, Blair says that the guide to our actions is the 'moral purpose in defending the values we cherish' – a moral dimension that means that 'When regimes are based on minority rule they lose legitimacy' and that 'Acts of genocide can never be a purely internal matter.'[24] This defense of intervention in what were once viewed as the internal affairs of a nation – intervention justified by the immoral acts of those whom Bush calls 'evildoers' – came well before George W. Bush entered the White House, and the neocons found their American champion.

Since it is not plausible that New Labour's Tony Blair was an early prisoner of the neocon ideologues, we must conclude that the ideas that have come to be associated with neoconservatism are more a product of the circumstances in which the world finds itself, than a result of the success of a cabal of mainly Jewish intellectuals in capturing the hearts and minds of both the Blair and Bush governments.

The attack on the World Trade Center may have been the immediate cause of Bush's adoption of many, although not all, of the doctrines that neocons had been pressing on successive administrations. But it was more than a decade of neocon argument, debate, and policy papers, building on a long history in America and reflecting the views of those such as Lady Thatcher and Prime Minister Blair (who themselves were reflecting their country's own tradition), that gave Bush the intellectual basis for a policy that includes: the use of military force, with the approval of multilateral institutions if possible (the latter a Tony Blair–Colin Powell preference), without such approval if necessary (the path preferred by Dick Cheney and most neocons); the use of pre-emptive strikes rather than conceding to terrorists a first-strike advantage; the inclusion of any nation-states that lend support to or provide havens for terrorists in an 'axis of evil', properly the objects of pre-emptive military strikes; and the pursuit of the 'nation-building' that George W. Bush once derided, and which his Secretary of Defense, Donald Rumsfeld, to this day wishes would be stricken from the agenda of what one observer of the American scene calls the neocon 'democratic imperialists'.[25]

As Robert Cooper – a senior official in the EU – puts it in his *The Breaking of Nations*, a volume that also espouses pre-emption, 'Today we find an administration that arrived in office rejecting "nation-building", engaged in a great nation-building project in Iraq.'[26] This great project is what divides many with a neocon 'sensibility', and convinces conservatives that the neoconservatives do not understand the limits of America's ability to export democracy. Charles Krauthammer points out in a forthcoming book the need to temper the 'universalistic aspirations' of those such as Kristol and Kagan. And George Will, represented in this volume although hardly a neocon, who repeatedly urges the Bush administration to consign the 'neo' to the dustbin of history and retain only the 'con'. His is an even more restricted view of what America is capable of achieving in world affairs. A comparison of Will's views with the doctrines that generally emerge when 'neo' becomes a prefix of 'conservatism' provides a better understanding of the range of views descending on the Bush administration from its influential supporters, and hints at the intensity of the discussions when neocons and sympathetic conservatives gather in the seminar room.

The close similarity between neocon policy proposals and the Bush administration's policy on Iraq – especially its adoption of the goal of replacing Saddam Hussein's homicidal and region-destabilizing dictatorship with a democratic government – may explain why many European and other observers consider neocons to be in control of American foreign policy. But they ignore the extent to which events rather than ideology dictate that policy; events contributed to making Bush a neocon when dealing with Iraq, but left him free to ignore neocon proposals in the very different circumstances surrounding U.S.–China relations.

As Daniel Casse puts it (after paying tribute to neocon efforts 'to redefine the role of American power at a time of retreat and growing isolationism'), 'it is necessary to add that Bush's policy choices have been driven less by ideology than by the clear-cut need to combat terrorism and the states that sponsor it, and to confront rogue regimes whose very existence represents a threat to freedom and security.'[27] To which Max Boot adds in his essay, 'the triumph of neoconservatism was hardly permanent or complete.' We have not seen any attacks on the nuclear facilities of North Korea or Iran. Instead, Bush is relying on the negotiating skills of nations in the region, in the case of North Korea, and on international institutions, in the case of Iran, to cope with the problems created by the spread to these regimes of weapons of mass destruction.

Those who worry about the extent of neocon influence ignore, too, the differences in the policies espoused by those who style themselves neoconservatives. Bill Kristol favored intervention in Kosovo, while Charles Krauthammer opposed it; Kristol and Kagan enthusiastically support American efforts to reform the Middle East by creating a prosperous, democratic state in Iraq, while James Q. Wilson and other neocons view such efforts as doomed to fail. Bush can hardly be said to follow blindly a neocon path when that road contains several forks, leading in opposite directions. Recently, to cite but one example, some neocons have called for more troops and more money to cope with problems in Iraq, while others continue to hunt for an acceptable (and quick) exit strategy. This latter group of neocons has gone from 'triumphalist' to 'depressed', 'angst-ridden', and 'wobbly', according to one observer, who adds, 'Hawks are glumly trying to reconcile the reality in Iraq with the predictions they made before the war. A few have already given up on the idea of a stable democracy in Iraq.'[28]

All of these thinkers support and influence the Bush administration: neocon hawks such as Kristol and Kagan; neocons such as Krauthammer, who emphasized in a recent speech that America's 'unipolar power... must be targeted, focused and limited. We... come ashore only where it really counts';[29] neocons disillusioned that America is seen by many Iraqis as an occupier rather than a liberator; still others whose views have softened as the grisly television images have multiplied; and conservatives who question the entire neocon foreign policy enterprise. Their varied views are represented here to demonstrate that the battle for the hearts and minds of Washington policy-makers goes on, with the neocons' current control of the high ground under continued assault – not only from natural opponents, ranging from isolationists to liberal internationalists who would subsume America in a multilateral global architecture, but also from those with whom they are allied in many battles outside the sphere of foreign policy.

There is another reason for the overestimation of the power of the neocons, one that is due less to a misunderstanding, and more to a desire by congenital America-haters to leave themselves free to scavenge through documents and speeches for inflammatory statements and use them as sticks with which to beat George W. Bush. His critics (especially, but not only, those in Europe) find the President guilty of everything from a low IQ; to a belief in God and the constitutional right of Americans to own guns; to mangled syntax, the latter a crime of which President Dwight D. Eisenhower was also accused and found guilty. Sir Max Hastings, former editor of the conservative *Daily Telegraph* and *Evening Standard*, and a man of the political right, catches the mood of many in Britain and Europe when he writes, 'It is hard not to hate George Bush. His ignorance and conceit, his professed special relationship with God, invite revulsion... He asserted publicly that Saddam Hussein should die... Bush's eagerness to see Saddam swing reflects... an ad hominem desire to complete the liberation of Iraq with a gesture that fits his own brutish view of the world.'[30]

Criticism from the right is not always so intemperate, but when it comes from the mouths of Tory politicians it is more threatening to American policy and to the Anglo-American special relationship than the predictable objections of the left. Tory leader Michael Howard is now suffering a severe case of 'buyer's remorse' because he apparently thinks he missed a political opportunity by supporting the war in Iraq. In softer tones than Hastings but with the unmistakable intention of distancing himself both from the Blair government and from America, Howard is calling on the British government to become more independent of America and its president. In short, both neocon policies and the executor of those policies are under attack from conservative writers and politicians on both sides of the Atlantic.

The left, of course, is not to be outdone. To the list of objections from the right, and those we have already cited from Drew, Lind, and others on the left, add cowardice. To the *Guardian*, Bush is the neocons' 'chicken-hawk president'.[31] And there is more. Michael Gove, whose views on the adaptability of neocon thought to the special circumstances of Britain are represented here, elsewhere notes, 'The Left… particularly hate Bush and his foreign policy mentors because they recognise that the neoconservative belief in a strong and engaged America was responsible for the fall of the Soviet Union and exposes the bankruptcy of their international vision.'[32]

To say that opponents of neoconservative policies overestimate neocon influence is not to say that neocons are mere impotent scribblers and seminar-goers. Indeed, there is no mistaking the influence of neocon thought on American foreign policy. These intellectuals did undoubtedly cause a sea change in American foreign policy – from the post-Cold War consensus back to the Founding Fathers and Teddy Roosevelt, or forward into unexplored territory, depending on your point of view – by laying the basis for President Bush's post-9/11 move from 'soft' to 'hard' Wilsonianism. It is no stretch to say that the views of the U.S. government, laid out here with typical clarity by Condoleezza Rice, are a lineal descendant of a 'Defense Planning Guidance' (DPG) prepared in 1992 by Paul Wolfowitz, then Under Secretary of Defense for Policy in a Pentagon in which Dick Cheney held the job of Secretary of Defense.

Wolfowitz's 1992 memorandum was designed for intra-Defense Department use only. It was one of a series prepared over the years and distributed to key military personnel and civilian policy-makers in the Defense Department to provide a geopolitical framework within which these planners can set force levels and budgets. The Wolfowitz draft was quickly leaked to the press, portrayed as a dangerous deviation from traditional doctrine, and was almost immediately withdrawn and classified by the Department, pending a rewrite by Cheney.

The original document is not available. But we do have rather complete press reports.[33] They reveal that Wolfowitz called for a U.S. military sufficiently powerful to prevent the emergence of any rival in any region of the world; he proposed to encourage the spread of democracy and open economic systems; he argued for the use of military force if necessary to prevent the proliferation of nuclear weapons and 'weapons of mass destruction'; and he suggested reliance on 'ad hoc assemblies' of nations rather than on the United Nations to cope with crises, with 'the United States... positioned to act independently when collective action cannot be orchestrated'. Wolfowitz, whose name has since become synonymous with neocon foreign policy, was expressing a basic view about human nature. Eliot Cohen, who served with Wolfowitz when the latter was a dean at Johns Hopkins University, describes him as possessing 'a basic optimism about the potential of human beings for moderation and self-governance, and a belief in the universal appeal of liberty'.[34] Eight years later PNAC built upon Wolfowitz's DPG, calling for America 'to preserve and extend' its 'preeminent military power... as far into the future as possible'.[35]

But the neocons, although not all-powerful, certainly have reason to claim a policy triumph, even if a limited one. The policy of deferring to the United Nations has been replaced with a policy of ignoring that body if American interests so require; the policy of treating terrorist attacks as criminal acts has been replaced with a policy of treating them as acts of war (the first attack on the World Trade Center in 1993 resulted in a criminal trial; the second and more successful attack in 2001 resulted in a war on terrorists in Afghanistan and Iraq); the policy of responding to attacks with ineffectual isolated missile launches has been replaced with a policy of applying massive force, followed if necessary by occupation and nation-building.

These successes, attributable in part to the scalding impact of September 11, are also in part due to the formidable intellectual firepower behind neoconservative foreign policy. A group with the intelligence and rigor of Wolfowitz, Kagan, Kristol, Rice, Perle, and Cheney has probably not been seen since George Kennan led a team that formulated America's response to the threat of Soviet expansionism. That response – containment – might have been appropriate to its time, but the success of Ronald Reagan in bringing down 'the evil empire' of communism suggests that the policy outlived the era in which it might have been sensible.

In any event, containment bears little relation to the policies of pre-emption and nation-building that move neoconservatism in the direction of a form of imperialism. Indeed, some students prefer to call the more aggressive neoconservatives such as Wolfowitz and Perle 'democratic imperialists'.[36] Neocons believe that a militarily powerful America must play what can reasonably be described as an imperial role if there is to be a new, peaceful world order. Many neocons – the so-called 'democratic imperialist' wing – regret America's unwillingness to adopt an explicitly imperialist role. Imperialists, after all, don't spend a lot of time looking for 'exit strategies', one of the few commonly shared cornerstones of the thinking of both the State Department and Defense Department bureaucracies.

This regret at American reticence is perhaps best expressed by British historian Niall Ferguson. In his latest book and in the numerous articles he has published in America since coming to the U.S. to teach, Ferguson extols the potential advantages to the world of an American imperium, which, to his regret, is rejected by an America unwilling to make 'some profound changes in its economic structure, its social makeup and its political culture',[37] and seeks exit strategies rather than more permanent occupations along the lines of the former British imperialists, who had the grit to stay the civilizing course. If Ferguson is right, then so, too, is Professor Corey Robin of the City University of New York when he writes, 'We thus face a dangerous situation. On the one hand we have neoconservative elites whose vision of American power is recklessly utopian. On the other hand we have a domestic population that shows little interest in any far-flung empire... We may well be entering [a period]... when a republic opts for the frisson of empire, and is forced to confront the fragility and finitude of all political forms, including its own.'[38]

In sum, the neocons have been effective advocates of their foreign-policy views. Although their victory is not a total one, it is fair to say that this loose-knit band of intellectuals and politicians did indeed think, write, and preach its way into the halls of power, in fair and open combat with competing ideas.

And not only in the foreign-policy field. While neocons interested in the role of America in the world were collecting their thoughts in think tanks and publishing their arguments in such journals as Norman Podhoretz's *Commentary*, those whose interests lie in domestic policy were turning to the pages of Irving Kristol's *The Public Interest* and other magazines to argue their case for major changes in domestic policy, especially in regard to the role of the welfare state, attitudes toward crime and civility, and economic policy. The Stream of Op-Ed and magazine articles pouring from scholars infused with a neoconservative sensibility, and the scores of carefully researched papers on *domestic* policy, presented in the ever-available forums provided by think tanks in Washington and at the Manhattan Institute in New York, constitute an output at least equal in quantity and intellectual quality to that produced by neocon *foreign-policy* thinkers, as the essays selected here demonstrate.

Neocons cannot take credit for all of this output. Books such as Charles Murray's *Losing Ground*[39] set the stage for the welfare-to-work reforms that many neocons found appealing, and that were adopted in many states, as well as by Bill Clinton. Murray is no neocon. He styles himself a libertarian, and is skeptical of the ability of the State to manage a welfare program.[40] But he nevertheless was the source of ideas on reforming the welfare state, ideas that were quickly made part of the neocon canon, as Irving Kristol advocates, but eliminating incentives to 'bad' behavior such as out-of-wedlock births, and reserving the resources of the State to ease the plight of what the Victorians called the 'deserving poor'.

This reliance on Victorian ideas is itself part of the neocon intellectual framework: neocons acknowledge a heavy debt in the areas of social and cultural policy to the great student of the Victorian era, Gertrude Himmelfarb (who is married to Irving Kristol). It is no coincidence that George W. Bush chose 'compassionate conservatism' to describe his own brand of conservatism, borrowing from the title of one of Professor Himmelfarb's great works, *Poverty and Compassion: The Moral Imagination of the Late Victorians*.[41] It is not far from Himmelfarb to Murray. Himmelfarb notes, 'The Late Victorians... were agreed that what was important was to do good to others rather than to feel good themselves. Indeed, they were painfully aware that it was sometimes necessary to feel bad in order to do good — to curb their own compassion and restrain their benevolent impulses in the best interests of those they were trying to serve.'[42]

Flash forward to Murray and the welfare reforms he proposed, many of them eventually adopted under the banner of 'tough love' — removing benefits that made the donors feel good, but the recipients behave badly, not only from society's point of view, but from the point of view of their own long-term interests. As Murray put it, 'The barrier to radical reform of social policy is not the pain it would cause the intended beneficiaries of the present system, but the pain it would cause the donors... When reforms do finally occur, they will happen not because stingy people have won, but because generous people have stopped kidding themselves.'[43]

Himmelfarb and Murray provided neoconservatives with the foundation on which to construct their policies toward the welfare state. In defining the proper scope of that state, neoconservatives broke decisively with the conservatives who for a long time had dominated the Republican Party. In what was to set the stage for George Bush's compassionate conservatism, neocons refused to continue the decades-long war waged by their conservative colleagues against the welfare state. As Irving Kristol points out in his essay, 'A Conservative Welfare State', neocons 'assume that the welfare state is with us, for better or worse…'. In a sense, this acceptance of an expanded role for government paralleled the position taken by the foreign policy neocons: government was no longer the enemy of the people, but an instrument that could be a force for good if properly wielded.

Of course, Kristol is not suggesting that the welfare state as we know it today is ideal. Neocons tend to distinguish between Franklin Roosevelt's New Deal and Lyndon Johnson's Great Society. Whereas the New Deal, the first phase of which was introduced in 1932, was based on what Michael Novak calls 'traditional American values', the Great Society programs of 1964 'introduced a new morality' and were 'non-judgmental'. The result is that whereas widows received the bulk of the funds available to aid families and children under New Deal programs, Johnson directed those benefits toward 'divorced, separated, and (no questions asked, no demands made) never-married women'.[44] The neocon bottom line; accept the welfare state, yes; but also return it to its Victorian roots by concentrating resources on the deserving poor.

In short, just as neocons broke with conservatives in the foreign-policy arena when they adopted nation-building as a goal, they also broke with traditional conservatives in the domestic-policy arena by making their peace with the welfare state, on which conservatives had waged war for decades. But they have clung to a portion of their conservative heritage by confining their compassion to the 'deserving poor', and by crafting benefits in a way that rewards, rather than punishes, socially desirable behavior. This is perhaps the most important application of a theory that underlies much neoconservative policy concerning the role of government: get the incentives right – for welfare recipients, polluters, and other private-sector players – and the intrusion of government as a direct regulator of behavior can be minimized.

James Q. Wilson and George L. Kelling addressed another domestic-policy issue, crime, one of the so-called 'quality of life' issues, a category that also includes the increasing coarseness of American culture. Wilson and Kelling laid out what has become a key element in neoconservative policies toward crime in their seminal 'Broken Windows' essay, which is included here. These scholars argue that the best way to fight crime is 'to recognize the importance of maintaining, intact, communities without broken windows'. Public disorder leads to fear, fear to hopelessness, and hopelessness to a loss of control of the streets. Only by recognizing the corrosive effect on public order of what seem like minor offenses, can communities reduce crime. This theory famously underpinned New York Mayor Rudi Giuliani's successful effort to regain control of the city's streets, and led many cities, in America and elsewhere, to adopt similar measures.

Quality of life, argue neocons, includes more than being able to walk the streets in safety. It includes the right to live in a society in which one is not assaulted by obscenity. As Irving Kristol puts it in his typically brilliant blending of principle and pragmatism, a society 'in which obscenity and democracy are regarded as equals... is inherently unstable... [and] will, in the long run, be incompatible with any authentic concern for the quality of life in our democracy'.

It should come as no surprise that the problem of just how to balance freedom of speech (guaranteed to Americans by our Constitution) against the need to preserve a civil society remains unsolved, both in the U.S. and the UK. American politicians and legislators are debating whether the 'F-word' should be viewed as intrinsically obscene, and its use banned from the airwaves, or whether it should be considered by regulators in the context in which it is used. In Britain, the debate over just what may appear on television screens in family viewing hours is ongoing, with Ofcom, the newly established regulator, attempting to create a new set of rules more in keeping with what it perceives to be present-day mores.

Finally, this volume contains a brief look at neoconservative innovations in economic policy. In another sharp break with conservatives, many – indeed, most – neocons have abandoned the adherence to balanced budgets that had long been a cornerstone of conservative policy. To conservatives, the budget must be balanced, and the policies that government pursues are limited by the need to be fiscally responsible, thus defined. Neocons elevated policy over budgets. As Irving Kristol puts it, 'we should figure out what we want before we calculate what we can afford, not the reverse, which is the normal conservative predisposition'. As a corollary of this approach, neoconservatives live quite comfortably with budget deficits, some because they believe that appropriate tax policies will shrink the deficits to manageable proportions, others because they believe deficits to be largely irrelevant to an economy's performance, and still others because they believe deficits prevent the adoption of expensive additions to an already-generous welfare state.

In his essay, Robert L. Bartley, who used the Op-Ed pages of *The Wall Street Journal* to define and defend neoconservative economic policies, discusses the principal contributions of neoconservatives – their suggestions that fear of deficits should not be the driver of economic policy, and that reductions in tax rates, if properly targeted, do not reduce tax receipts proportionately. My own comment on these neocon policies follows Bartley's essay.

The foreign and domestic policy essays thus far discussed leave open two questions. From whence sprang neoconservatism, and what is its future?

The intellectual and political origins are considered in four essays. Kenneth Weinstein begins with a discussion of the importance – or lack of it – of the work of Leo Strauss, a refugee from Nazi Germany and a political philosopher who taught at the University of Chicago and who died in 1973. Critics of neoconservatism see Strauss as the root of neocon vices, a cynic who taught his followers that their intellectual superiority entitled them to tell 'necessary lies to lesser mortals'. Weinstein debunks this view of Strauss, as does Muravchik in his essay. Weinstein argues that Strauss in fact emphasized civic virtue and urged special attention to the threats to democratic republicanism from both 'liberal self-interest run amuck and radical egalitarianism'.

The political roots of neoconservatism may fairly be said to lie on the left of the ideological spectrum or, as Adam Wolfson puts it in his essay, in the 'neo-liberal politics of the 1960s and 1970s'. I am not here referring only to Irving Kristol's famous observation that conservatives are liberals who have been mugged by reality, cited by Jeane Kirkpatrick in her essay, in which she describes her continued 'affinity to traditional liberalism'. Rather, I have in mind the role played by so many who cut their political eye-teeth in the service of Democratic Senator Henry 'Scoop' Jackson. It was Jackson and his young staff, including Richard Perle, who developed many of the neoconservative foreign-policy attitudes reflected in the pages of the 'small magazines' that play such an important role in the making and breaking of policies in America, and who later staffed the Reagan and second Bush administrations.

The senator from the far-west state of Washington has been described as 'a Cold Warrior Democrat and one of neoconservatism's progenitors'.[45] Muravchik lists him, along with Ronald Reagan and Winston Churchill, as one of 'the true neoconservative models in the field of power politics'. The young, Democratic policy wonks who gathered around Jackson insisted that American interests could be protected during the Cold War only by adopting a hardline policy towards the Soviet Union, including predicating normal trade relations on the willingness of the Soviets to allow its persecuted Jews to leave the country in which they were trapped.[46] Détente, which 'realists' Henry Kissinger and Richard Nixon believed would tame the Soviet bear, was no more acceptable to Perle, Douglas Feith (now a key policy-maker at the Pentagon), and others with roots in the Jackson camp than it was to Ronald Reagan. These Jackson Democrats saw little difference between détente with the Soviets and appeasement of Hitler; as neoconservatives they now see little difference between the policies adopted by the UN toward Iraq and terrorists and the European Union towards Palestinian suicide–homicide bombers, and pre-World War II appeasement of Nazism.

So much for the origins of neoconservatism. What about its future? Karlyn Bowman, perhaps America's premier analyst of polling data, notes in her essay that there is reasonably widespread support for the goals of the neoconservatives as articulated by, among others, Irving Kristol, even though most Americans are unfamiliar with the literature of the neocons. It seems that the ideas espoused by these thinkers will probably have an enduring place in American policies.

This brings us to the question of whether basic neocon doctrine is an exportable product. The antipathy of many Europeans to President Bush has already been discussed, and their fear of the consequences of what they see as American unilateralism is too widely known to require discussion here. But the picture is not uniformly bleak. In contrast with the anti-American, anti-neocon views prevailing in Germany and described by Jeffrey Gedmin in his essay, there is the situation in Britain.

As Michael Gove makes clear, the neoconservative doctrines of pre-emption, and the use of power to destroy an enemy's ability to strike with the weapons of the day, have a long history in the UK. To which we might add that the moral dimension of neoconservatism, and the view that its values are universal, are given flesh by Tony Blair, as a reading of his contribution to this volume and his willingness to pay a high political price for his principles attest.

That Britain, with historical and linguistic links to America, should be of a neoconservative persuasion is unsurprising. But if João Carlos Espada is right in his contribution, it is possible that some day the rest of Europe will eventually reject what Espada calls 'a widespread disregard for limited constitutional government [that] has led European politics to be cynically dominated by two illiberal poles: revolutionary "liberals" and counter-revolutionary "conservatives"'.

Unfortunately, Espada may be unduly optimistic – at least, if Germany is a better guide to attitudes than Portugal. Jeffrey Gedmin paints a rather bleak picture of the prospect for neoconservatism in Germany as well as in Europe more generally.

In the end, no one can predict with confidence the future of neoconservatism, whether in the United States, in Great Britain, or in Europe.

Norman Podhoretz, with his usual flourish, pronounced it dead in 1996[47] but his report of the tendency's demise seems to be premature. The policies of pre-emption, unilateral action if necessary, and reduced reliance on multinational institutions have deep roots in both American and British foreign policy, roots that are reflected in current policies in the war on terror. The events of September 11 make it unlikely that any future American president will be prepared to concede a first strike to terrorists, or allow an international body to exercise a veto over the use of American military power. Indeed, the leaders of the Democratic Party have recently made it clear that they are in agreement with President Bush and the neocons on this point. Tony Blair's assertion of the universality of Western ideals, and his willingness to deploy forces in defense of those ideals, in the face of enormous opposition within his own party and increasingly tepid support from the Tories, signal that Britain will stand by America. The same is true of Australia. Perhaps Winston Churchill and Margaret Thatcher were right when they said that it was up to the English-speaking peoples to provide the nucleus of the support for a sensible world order.

Neoconservatives can also claim substantial victories on the domestic front. Charles Murray's emphasis on the unfortunate effects of the incentives provided by a welfare system that was designed with little attention to its effects on the behavior of benefits recipients was adopted by neocons. They developed a program to reform the system, pushing millions off the welfare rolls and into the workplace by reducing what Robert Skidelsky has called the 'conflict between behaving rationally and behaving well'.[48] The Wilson–Kelling approach to policing remains in the forefront of policy debate on techniques for fighting crime, in part due to its advocacy by Rudi Giuliani and the Manhattan Institute, another of those think tanks that joins good ideas with a brilliant 'small magazine'.

Recent public outrage at the tendency of television broadcasters to 'define decency down', to paraphrase Senator Daniel Patrick Moynihan,[49] signals that Irving Kristol's warnings about the dangers of obscenity are receiving renewed attention – he says that the article on obscenity reproduced here is among his most frequently referenced essays – and that there may be a backlash against what Myron Magnet has called 'the thoroughgoing trashing of the culture' that characterized the 1960s.[50]

When it comes to economic policy, neocons can claim some important victories, most notably the subordination of deficits to other policy goals, and the destruction of the assumption that reductions in tax rates will result in equal losses in tax revenues.

It is a testimonial to the quality of neocons' research and their powers of persuasion that they have succeeded despite the fact that the resources available to them are skimpy by comparison with those of their intellectual adversaries. Many of the institutions that provide homes for neocon scholars are dwarfed by those more closely associated with the centrist status quo.

At its peak, PNAC had four employees and an annual budget of about $400,000. Its intellectually congenial American Enterprise Institute has sixty-five scholars and fellows and annual revenues of about $18 million. The even smaller Hudson Institute (with which I am affiliated) operates effectively with a budget of less than $8 million. The more liberal and mainstream Brookings Institution has about 150 scholars, an endowment of some $200 million and an annual budget in the neighborhood of $40 million. Add to that the enormous budgets of the left-leaning universities, including Harvard's John F. Kennedy School – the home of advocates of the 'soft power' alternative to neocon policies – and we have a testimonial to the ability of neocon IQ and imagination to trump the superior financial resources of their political opponents. As two of The Economist's writers put it, '[T]he right has simply been far better at producing agenda-setting ideas. From welfare reform in Wisconsin to policing in New York City, from tax-cutting Proposition 13 in California to regime change in Baghdad, the intellectual impetus has, for better or worse, come from the right... The great liberal universities and foundations have infinitely more resources than the American Enterprise Institute and its allies... But it still seems that liberals are purely reactive.' [51]

The future survival of neoconservative doctrine will depend crucially on the neocons' ability to eliminate the contradiction between their foreign-policy goals and their domestic policies. Muscular foreign policy, and the accompanying expanded military, cost money. Nation-building, reconstructing the Middle East in America's image, and confronting evil wherever it threatens vital U.S. interests, broadly construed, will cost even more. With the current deficit generally considered unsustainable, those neoconservatives who believe that America should 'remain the world's pre-eminent military power, and... remain strong enough to discourage any other power from challenging American pre-eminence', as Robert Kagan summarizes his ideal U.S. policy,[52] will have to rethink their relaxed attitude toward sustained budget deficits.

Neocons' victories in both the domestic and foreign-policy battles have been substantial. Their views on crime, the welfare state, culture and other aspects of domestic-policy, combined with the widespread acceptance of the importance of American power in advancing liberal values[53] – a triumph now being challenged by events in Iraq – provides good reason to ask, 'Who are these people, and precisely what do they think?' I hope that this selection of their thoughts will begin to answer those questions.

Irwin Stelzer, London, May 2004.

1   February 28, 2004, p. 38.

2   *The Times*, July 5, 2003.

3   *The Economist*, May 29, 2004, p. 25.

4   *Commentary*, March 1996, p. 20.

5   *The Economist*, May 29, 2004, p. 25.

6   Joshua Micah Marshall, 'Power Rangers', *The New Yorker*, February 2, 2004, p. 85.

7   John Podhoretz, *Bush Country: How Dubya Became a Great President While Driving Liberals Insane*, New York: St Martin's Press, 2004, p. 59.

8   *Independent*, December 4, 2002.

9   See Michael Lind, 'Churchill for Dummies', *Spectator*, April 24, 2004, p. 25.

10   Thomas Powers, 'Tomorrow the World', *The New York Review of Books*, March 11, 2004, p. 5.

11   Robert Kagan, *Of Paradise and Power: America and Europe in the New World Order*, New York: Alfred A. Knopf, 2003. A later (2004) edition published by Vintage Books contains an important afterword.

12   John Lewis Gaddis, *Surprise, Security, and the American Experience*, Cambridge, Mass. and London: Harvard University Press, 2004, p. 16 and *passim*.

13   Cited by Gaddis in *Surprise, Security, and the American Experience*, p. 21.

14   Margaret Macmillan, *Peacemakers: The Paris Conference of 1919 and Its Attempt to End War*, London: John Murray, 2001, Chapter 1.

15   Robert Kagan, *Of Paradise and Power*, 2004, p. 122.

16   Martin Wolf, *Financial Times*, December 24, 2003.

17   Tony Blair, address to Joint Session of the U.S. Congress, July 17, 2003.

18   James Q. Wilson, 'Why Freedom Can be a Lot More Important than Democracy', *The Sunday Times*, May 2, 2004.

19   Tony Blair, address to Joint Session of the U.S. Congress, July 17, 2003.

20   Richard Perle, interviewed by Walter Pincus in *The Washington Post*, April 8, 2003.

21   See Joseph S. Nye, Jr, *The Paradox of American Power: Why the World's Only Superpower Can't Go it Alone*, New York: Oxford University Press, 2002.

22   John Campbell, *Margaret Thatcher, the Iron Lady*, London: Jonathan Cape, 2003, vol. II, p. 782.

23   Margaret Thatcher, 'New Threats for Old', speech at Westminster College, Fulton, Missouri, March 9, 1996.

24   Tony Blair, speech at the Economic Club, Chicago, April 24, 1999.

25   Gerard Baker, *Financial Times*, December 30, 2003.

26   Robert Cooper, *The Breaking of Nations: Order and Chaos in the Twenty-First Century*, London: Atlantic Books, 2003, p. 50.

27   Daniel Casse, 'Is Bush a Conservative?', *Commentary*, February 2004, p. 22.

28   John Tierney, 'The Hawks Loudly Express their Second Thoughts', *The New York Times*, May 16, 2004.

29   The 2004 Irving Kristol Lecture, delivered by Charles Krauthammer at the annual dinner of the American Enterprise Institute, Washington, D.C., February 12, 2004.

30   Max Hastings relieved himself of these views in the *Guardian*, December 20, 2003.

31   Clark, the *Guardian*, April 7, 2004.

32   Michael Gove, 'The Deadly Mail', *Spectator*, April 17, 2004, p. 15.

33   *The New York Times*, March 8, 1992, and *The Washington Post*, March 11, 1992.

34   Quoted in *The Wall Street Journal Europe*, December 24–8, 2003.

35   'The Project for the New American Century', *Rebuilding America's Defenses: Strategy, Forces and Resources for a New Century*, September 2000, p. i.

36   Ivo H. Daalder and James M. Lindsay, *America Unbound: The Bush Revolution in Foreign Policy*, Washington, D.C.: Brookings Institution Press, 2003, p. 46.

37   Niall Ferguson, *Colossus: The Rise and Fall of the American Empire*, London: Allen Lane/Penguin Books, 2004, p. 301.

38   Corey Robin, 'Grand Designs: How 9/11 Unified Conservatives in Pursuit of Empire', *The Washington Post*, May 2, 2004.

39   Charles Murray, *Losing Ground: American Social Policy, 1950–1980*, New York: Basic Books, 1984.

40   Charles Murray, *What It Means To Be A Libertarian: A Personal Interpretation*, New York: Broadway Books/Bantam-Doubleday-Dell Publishing Group, 1997.

41   Gertrude Himmelfarb, *Poverty and Compassion: The Moral Imagination of the Late Victorians*, New York: Vintage Books, 1991.

42   Himmelfarb, *Poverty and Compassion*, p. 6.

43   Murray, *Losing Ground* p. 236

44   Michael Novak, 'Is There a Third Way?', London: IEA Health and Welfare Unit, 1998, p. 8.

45   Connie Bruck, 'The Diplomatic Round: Back Roads', *The New Yorker*, December 15, 2003, p. 88.

46   The Jackson–Vanick Amendment to U.S. Trade Laws denied most-favored-nation status to all countries that restricted Jewish emigration. The Soviet Union was the obvious target.

47   'Neoconservatism: A Eulogy', *Commentary*, March 1996, pp. 19ff.

48   Robert Skidelsky, *Beyond the Welfare State*, London: The Social Market Foundation, May 1997, p. 83.

49   Moynihan famously worried about society's tendency to to 'define deviancy down'.

50   Myron Magnet, *The Dream and the Nightmare: The Sixties' Legacy to the Underclass*, San Francisco: Encounter Books, 1993, p. 206.

51   John Micklethwait and Adrian Wooldridge, 'For Conservatives, Mission Accomplished' *The New York Times*, May 18, 2004.

52   Kagan, *Of Paradise and Power*, p. 94.

53   Robert Kagan, interviewed by Daniel Finkelstein in *The Times*, April 10, 2004.

PART I

NEOCONSERVATISM
Defined and Demystified

THE
NEOCONSERVATIVE
PERSUASION

Irving Kristol

*The historical task of neoconservatism would seem to be this:
to convert the Republican Party, and American conservatism
in general, against their respective wills, into a new kind of
conservative politics suitable to governing a modern democracy.*

THE NEOCONSERVATIVE PERSUASION

What it was, and what it is

IRVING KRISTOL

[President Bush is] an engaging person, but I think for some reason he's been captured by the neoconservatives around him.

Howard Dean, *U.S. News & World Report*, August 11, 2003

What exactly is neoconservatism? Journalists, and now even presidential candidates, speak with an enviable confidence on who or what is 'neoconservative' and seem to assume the meaning is fully revealed in the name. Those of us who are designated as 'neocons' are amused, flattered, or dismissive, depending on the context. It is reasonable to wonder: is there any 'there' there?

Even I, frequently referred to as the 'godfather' of all those neocons, have had my moments of wonderment. A few years ago I said (and, alas, wrote) that neoconservatism had had its own distinctive qualities in its early years, but by now had been absorbed into the mainstream of American conservatism. I was wrong, and the reason I was wrong is that, ever since its origin among disillusioned liberal intellectuals in the 1970s, what we call neoconservatism has been one of those intellectual undercurrents that surface only intermittently. It is not a 'movement', as the conspiratorial critics would have it. Neoconservatism is what the late historian of Jacksonian America, Marvin Meyers, called a 'persuasion', one that manifests itself over time, but erratically, and one whose meaning we clearly glimpse only in retrospect.

Viewed thus, one can say that the historical task and political purpose of neoconservatism would seem to be this: to convert the Republican Party, and American conservatism in general, against their respective wills, into a new kind of conservative politics suitable to governing a modern democracy. That this new conservative politics is distinctly American is beyond doubt. There is nothing like neoconservatism in Europe, and most European conservatives are highly skeptical of its legitimacy. The fact that conservatism in the United States is so much healthier than in Europe, so much more politically effective, surely has something to do with the existence of neoconservatism. But Europeans, who think it absurd to look to the United States for lessons in political innovation, resolutely refuse to consider this possibility.

Neoconservatism is the first variant of American conservatism in the past century that is in the 'American grain'. It is hopeful, not lugubrious; forward-looking, not nostalgic; and its general tone is cheerful, not grim or dyspeptic. Its twentieth-century heroes tend to be TR [Theodore Roosevelt], FDR [Franklin Delano Roosevelt], and Ronald Reagan. Such Republican and conservative worthies as Calvin Coolidge, Herbert Hoover, Dwight Eisenhower, and Barry Goldwater are politely overlooked. Of course, those worthies are in no way overlooked by a large, probably the largest, segment of the Republican Party, with the result that most Republican politicians know nothing, and could not care less, about neoconservatism. Nevertheless, they cannot be blind to the fact that neoconservative policies, reaching out beyond the traditional political and financial base, have helped make the very idea of political conservatism more acceptable to a majority of American voters. Nor has it passed official notice that it is the neoconservative public policies, not the traditional Republican ones, that result in popular Republican presidencies.

One of these policies, most visible and controversial, is cutting tax rates in order to stimulate steady economic growth. This policy was not invented by neocons, and it was not the particularities of tax cuts that interested them, but rather the steady focus on economic growth. Neocons are familiar with intellectual history and aware that it is only in the last two centuries that democracy has become a respectable option among political thinkers. In earlier times, democracy meant an inherently turbulent political regime, with the 'have-nots' and the 'haves' engaged in a perpetual and utterly destructive class struggle. It was only the prospect of economic growth in which everyone prospered, if not equally or simultaneously, that gave modern democracies their legitimacy and durability.

The cost of this emphasis on economic growth has been an attitude toward public finance that is far less risk averse than is the case among more traditional conservatives. Neocons would prefer not to have large budget deficits, but it is in the nature of democracy – because it seems to be in the nature of human nature – that political demagogy will frequently result in economic recklessness, so that one sometimes must shoulder budgetary deficits as the cost (temporary, one hopes) of pursuing economic growth. It is a basic assumption of neoconservatism that, as a consequence of the spread of affluence among all classes, a property-owning and tax-paying population will, in time, become less vulnerable to egalitarian illusions and demagogic appeals and more sensible about the fundamentals of economic reckoning.

This leads to the issue of the role of the State. Neocons do not like the concentration of services in the welfare state and are happy to study alternative ways of delivering these services. But they are impatient with the Hayekian notion that we are on 'the road to serfdom'. Neocons do not feel that kind of alarm or anxiety about the growth of the State in the past century, seeing it as natural, indeed inevitable. Because they tend to be more interested in history than economics or sociology, they know that the nineteenth-century idea, so neatly propounded by Herbert Spencer in his *The Man Versus the State*, was a historical eccentricity. People have always preferred strong government to weak government, although they certainly have no liking for anything that smacks of overly intrusive government. Neocons feel at home in today's America to a degree that more traditional conservatives do not. Though they find much to be critical about, they tend to seek intellectual guidance in the democratic wisdom of Tocqueville, rather than in the Tory nostalgia of, say, Russell Kirk.

But it is only to a degree that neocons are comfortable in modern America. The steady decline in our democratic culture, sinking to new levels of vulgarity, does unite neocons with traditional conservatives – though not with those libertarian conservatives who are conservative in economics but unmindful of the culture. The upshot is a quite unexpected alliance between neocons, who include a fair proportion of secular intellectuals, and religious traditionalists. They are united on issues concerning the quality of education, the relations of Church and State, the regulation of pornography, and the like, all of which they regard as proper candidates for the government's attention. And since the Republican Party now has a substantial base among the religious, this gives neocons a certain influence and even power. Because religious conservatism is so feeble in Europe, the neoconservative potential there is correspondingly weak.

And then, of course, there is foreign policy, the area of American politics where neoconservatism has recently been the focus of media attention. This is surprising since there is no set of neoconservative beliefs concerning foreign policy, only a set of attitudes derived from historical experience. (The favorite neoconservative text on foreign affairs, thanks to Professors Leo Strauss of

Chicago and Donald Kagan of Yale, is Thucydides on the Peloponnesian War.) These attitudes can be summarized in the following 'theses' (as a Marxist would say): first, patriotism is a natural and healthy sentiment, and should be encouraged by both private and public institutions. Precisely because we are a nation of immigrants, this is a powerful American sentiment. Second, world government is a terrible idea since it can lead to world tyranny. International institutions that point to an ultimate world government should be regarded with the deepest suspicion. Third, statesmen should, above all, have the ability to distinguish friends from enemies. This is not as easy as it sounds, as the history of the Cold War revealed. The number of intelligent men who could not count the Soviet Union as an enemy, even though this was its own self-definition, was absolutely astonishing.

Finally, for a great power, the 'national interest' is not a geographical term, except for fairly prosaic matters like trade and environmental regulation. A smaller nation might appropriately feel that its national interest begins and ends at its borders, so that its foreign policy is almost always in a defensive mode. A larger nation has more extensive interests. And large nations, whose identity is ideological, like the Soviet Union of yesteryear and the United States of today, inevitably have ideological interests in addition to more material concerns. Barring extraordinary events, the United States will always feel obliged to defend, if possible, a democratic nation under attack from non-democratic forces, external or internal. That is why it was in our national interest to come to the defense of France and Britain in World War II. That is why we feel it necessary to defend Israel today, when its survival is threatened. No complicated geopolitical calculations of national interest are necessary.

Behind all this is a fact: the incredible military superiority of the United States vis-à-vis the nations of the rest of the world, in any imaginable combination. This superiority was planned by no one, and even today there are many Americans who are in denial. To a large extent, it all happened as a result of our bad luck. During the fifty years after World War II, while Europe was at peace and the Soviet Union largely relied on surrogates to do its fighting, the United States was involved in a whole series of wars: the Korean War, the Vietnam War, the Gulf War, the Kosovo conflict, the Afghan War, and the Iraq War. The result was that our military spending expanded more or less in line with our economic growth, while Europe's democracies cut back their military spending in favor of social welfare programs. The Soviet Union spent profusely but wastefully, so that its military collapsed along with its economy.

Suddenly, after two decades during which 'imperial decline' and 'imperial overstretch' were the academic and journalistic watchwords, the United States emerged as uniquely powerful. The 'magic' of compound interest over half a century had its effect on our military budget, as did the cumulative scientific and technological research of our armed forces. With power come responsibilities, whether sought or not, whether welcome or not. And it is a fact that if you have the kind of power we now have, either you will find opportunities to use it, or the world will discover them for you.

The older, traditional elements in the Republican Party have difficulty coming to terms with this new reality in foreign affairs, just as they cannot reconcile economic conservatism with social and cultural conservatism. But by one of those accidents that historians ponder, our current President and his administration turn out to be quite at home in this new political environment, although it is clear they did not anticipate this role any more than their party as a whole did. As a result, neoconservatism began enjoying a second life, at a time when its obituaries were still being published.

THE NEOCON CABAL
AND OTHER FANTASIES

David Brooks

*belief in shadowy neocon influence has now hardened
into common knowledge... In truth, the people labeled
neocons... travel in widely different circles and don't
actually have much contact with one another.*

THE NEOCON CABAL
and Other Fantasies

DAVID BROOKS

WASHINGTON

Do you ever get the sense the whole world is becoming unhinged from reality? I started feeling that way awhile ago, when I was still working for *The Weekly Standard* and all these articles began appearing about how Paul Wolfowitz, Richard Perle, Doug Feith, Bill Kristol, and a bunch of 'neoconservatives' at the magazine had taken over U.S. foreign policy.

Theories about the tightly knit neocon cabal came in waves. One day you read that neocons were pushing plans to finish off Iraq and move into Syria. Websites appeared detailing neocon conspiracies; my favorite described a neocon outing organized by Vice President Dick Cheney to hunt for humans. The Asian press had the most lurid stories; the European press the most thorough. Every day, it seemed, *Le Monde* or some deep-thinking German paper would have an exposé on the neocon cabal, complete with charts connecting all the conspirators.

The full-mooners fixated on a think tank called the Project for the New American Century, which has a staff of five and issues memos on foreign policy. To hear these people describe it, PNAC is sort of a Yiddish Trilateral Commission, the nexus of the sprawling neocon tentacles.

We'd sit around the magazine guffawing at the ludicrous stories that kept sprouting, but belief in shadowy neocon influence has now hardened into common knowledge...

In truth, the people labeled neocons (con is short for 'conservative' and neo is short for 'Jewish') travel in widely different circles and don't actually have much contact with one another. The ones outside government have almost no contact with President George W. Bush. There have been hundreds of references, for example, to Richard Perle's insidious power over administration policy, but I've been told by senior administration officials that he has had no significant meetings with Bush or Cheney since they assumed office. If he's shaping their decisions, he must be microwaving his ideas into their fillings.

It's true that both Bush and the people labeled neocons agree that Saddam Hussein represented a unique threat to world peace. But correlation does not mean causation. All evidence suggests that Bush formed his conclusions independently. Besides, if he wanted to follow the neocon line, Bush wouldn't know where to turn because while the neocons agree on Saddam, they disagree vituperatively on just about everything else. (If you ever read a sentence that starts with 'Neocons believe', there is a 99.44 per cent chance everything else in that sentence will be untrue.)

Still, there are apparently millions of people who cling to the notion that the world is controlled by well-organized and malevolent forces. And for a subset of these people, Jews are a handy explanation for everything.

There's something else going on, too. The proliferation of news media outlets and the segmentation of society have meant that it's much easier for people to hive themselves off into like-minded cliques. Some people live in towns where nobody likes President Bush. Others listen to radio networks where nobody likes former President Bill Clinton.

In these communities, half-truths get circulated and exaggerated. Dark accusations are believed because it is delicious to believe them. Vince Foster was murdered. The Saudis warned the Bush administration before 9/11.

You get to choose your own reality. You get to believe what makes you feel good. You can ignore inconvenient facts so rigorously your picture of the world is one big distortion.

And if you can give your foes a collective name – liberals, fundamentalists, or neocons – you can rob them of their individual humanity. All inhibitions are removed. You can say anything about them. You get to feed off their villainy and luxuriate in your own contrasting virtue. You will find books, blowhards, and candidates playing to your delusions, and you can emigrate to your own version of Planet Chomsky. You can live there unburdened by ambiguity.

Improvements in information technology have not made public debate more realistic. On the contrary, anti-Semitism is resurgent. Conspiracy theories are prevalent. Partisanship has left many people unhinged.

Welcome to election year, 2004.

MYTHS ABOUT NEOCONSERVATISM

Max Boot

*By telling... tall tales, critics have twisted the neocons'
identities and thinking on U.S. foreign policy into
an unrecognizable caricature.*

MYTHS ABOUT NEOCONSERVATISM

MAX BOOT

'THE BUSH ADMINISTRATION IS PURSUING A NEOCONSERVATIVE FOREIGN POLICY'

If only it were true! The influence of the neoconservative movement (with which I am often associated) supposedly comes from its agents embedded within the U.S. government. The usual suspects are Paul Wolfowitz, Deputy Secretary of Defense; Douglas Feith, Under Secretary of Defense for Policy; Lewis 'Scooter' Libby, the Vice President's chief of staff; Elliott Abrams, the National Security Council staffer for Near East, South-west Asian, and North African Affairs; and Richard Perle, a member of the Defense Policy Board. Each of these policy-makers has been an outspoken advocate for aggressive and, if necessary, unilateral action by the United States to promote democracy, human rights, and free markets, and to maintain U.S. primacy around the world.

While this list seems impressive, it also reveals that the neocons have no representatives in the administration's top tier. President George W. Bush, Vice President Dick Cheney, Secretary of Defense Donald Rumsfeld, Secretary of State Colin Powell, and National Security Advisor Condoleezza Rice: not a neocon among them. Powell might be best described as a liberal internationalist; the others are traditional national-interest conservatives who, during Bush's 2000 presidential campaign, derided the Clinton administration for its focus on nation-building and human rights. Most of them were highly skeptical of the interventions in the Balkans that neocons championed.

The contention that the neocon faction gained the upper hand in the White House has a superficial plausibility because the Bush administration toppled Saddam Hussein and embraced democracy promotion in the Middle East – both policies long urged by neocons (though not only by neocons) and opposed by self-styled 'realists' who believe in fostering stability above all. But the administration has adopted these policies not because of the impact of the neocons but because of the impact of the four airplanes hijacked on September 11, 2001. Following the worst terrorist attack in U.S. history, Bush realized the United States no longer could afford a 'humble' foreign policy. The ambitious National Security Strategy that the administration issued in September 2002 – with its call for U.S. primacy, the promotion of democracy, and vigorous action, pre-emptive if necessary, to stop terrorism and weapons proliferation – was a quintessentially neoconservative document.

Yet the triumph of neoconservatism was hardly permanent or complete. The administration so far has not adopted neocon arguments to push for regime change in North Korea and Iran. Bush has cooled on the 'axis of evil' talk and has launched negotiations with the regime in North Korea. The President has also established friendlier relations with communist China than many neocons would like, and he launched a high-profile effort to promote a 'road map' for settling the Israeli–Palestinian conflict that most neocons (correctly) predicted would lead nowhere.

'NEOCONS ARE LIBERALS WHO HAVE BEEN MUGGED BY REALITY'

No longer true. Original neoconservatives such as Irving Kristol, who memorably defined neocons as liberals who'd been 'mugged by reality', were (and still are) in favor of welfare benefits, racial equality, and many other liberal tenets. But they were driven rightward by the excesses of the late 1960s and early 1970s, when crime was increasing in the United States, the Soviet Union was gaining ground in the Cold War, and the dominant wing of the Democratic Party was unwilling to get tough on either problem.

A few neocons, like philosopher Sidney Hook or Kristol himself, had once been Marxists or Trotskyites. Most, like former UN Ambassador Jeane Kirkpatrick, simply had been hawkish Democrats who became disenchanted with their party as it drifted further left in the 1970s. Many neocons, such as Richard Perle, originally rallied around Henry 'Scoop' Jackson, a Democratic senator who led the opposition to the Nixon–Ford policy of détente with the Soviet Union. Following the 1980 election, U.S. President Ronald Reagan became the new standard bearer of the neoconservative cause.

A few neocons, like Perle, still identify themselves as Democrats, and a number of 'neoliberals' in the Democratic Party (such as Senator Joseph Lieberman and former UN Ambassador Richard Holbrooke) hold fairly neoconservative views on foreign policy. But most neocons have switched to the Republican Party. On many issues, they are virtually indistinguishable from other conservatives; their main differences are with libertarians who demonize 'big government' and preach an anything-goes morality.

Most younger members of the neoconservative movement, including some descendants of the first generation, such as William Kristol, editor of *The Weekly Standard*, and Robert Kagan, Senior Associate at the Carnegie Endowment for International Peace, have never gone through a leftist phase, which makes the 'neo' prefix no longer technically accurate. Like 'liberal', 'conservative', and other ideological labels, 'neocon' has morphed away from its original definition. It has now become an all-purpose term of abuse for anyone deemed to be hawkish, which is why many of those so described shun the label. Wolfowitz prefers to call himself a 'Scoop Jackson Republican'.

'NEOCONS ARE JEWS WHO SERVE THE INTERESTS OF ISRAEL'

A malicious myth. With varying degrees of delicacy, everyone from fringe U.S. presidential candidates Lyndon LaRouche and Patrick Buchanan to European news outlets such as the BBC and *Le Monde* have used neocon as a synonym for Jew, focusing on Richard Perle, Paul Wolfowitz, Eliot Cohen, and others with obvious Jewish names. Trying to resurrect the old dual-loyalties canard, they cite links between some neocons and the Likud Party to argue that neocons wanted to invade Iraq because they were doing Israel's bidding.

Yes, neocons have links to the Likud Party, but they also have links to the British Tories and other conservative parties around the world, just as some in the Democratic Party have ties to the left-leaning Labour Party in Great Britain and the Labor Party in Israel. These connections reflect ideological, not ethnic, affinity. And while many neocons are Jewish, many are not. Former drug czar Bill Bennett, ex-CIA Director James Woolsey, the Revd Richard John Neuhaus, social scientist James Q. Wilson, theologian Michael Novak, and Jeane Kirkpatrick aren't exactly synagogue-goers. Yet they are as committed to Israel's defense as Jewish neocons are – a commitment based not on shared religion or ethnicity but on shared liberal democratic values. Israel has won the support of most Americans, of all faiths, because it is the only democracy in the Middle East, and because its enemies (Hezbollah, Hamas, Iran, and Syria) also proclaim themselves to be the enemies of the United States.

The charge that neocons are concerned above all with the welfare of Israel is patently false. In the 1980s, they were the leading proponents of democratization in places as disparate as Nicaragua, Poland, and South Korea. In the 1990s, they were the most ardent champions of interventions in Bosnia and Kosovo – missions designed to rescue Muslims, not Jews. Today neocons agitate for democracy in China (even as Israel has sold arms to Beijing!) and against the abuse of Christians in Sudan. Their advocacy of democracy in Iraq and Afghanistan is entirely consistent with this long track record. If neocons were agents of Likud, they would have advocated an invasion not of Iraq or Afghanistan but of Iran, which Israel considers to be the biggest threat to its own security.

'NEOCONS ARE A WELL-FUNDED, WELL-ORGANIZED CABAL'

Hardly. Writers suspicious of neocons have drawn elaborate flow charts to map neoconservative influence, showing the links between journalists (such as Charles Krauthammer and William Kristol), think tanks (the American Enterprise Institute and the Project for the New American Century), and foundations (Bradley, John M. Olin, and Smith Richardson). True, neocons have some support in the media and non-profit worlds. But let's be serious: the Project for the New American Century, the leading neocon foreign-policy think tank, has a staff of five. Its resources pale next to those of the Brookings Institution, Heritage Foundation, and Cato Institute, three of the biggest Washington think tanks, none of them sympathetic to the neoconservative vision of foreign policy. The Bradley, John M. Olin, and Smith Richardson foundations have given some money to neocons (including me), but their combined grants ($68 million per year) are less than a tenth of those doled out by just three liberal foundations – Ford, Rockefeller, and MacArthur ($833 million per year). And funding for neoconservative causes is about to shrink because Olin is going out of business. The leading neoconservative magazines, *The Weekly Standard*, *The Public Interest*, and *Commentary*, have lower circulations than the *National Review*, *The Nation*, or *The New Republic*, to say nothing of *The New Yorker* or *Time*.

Sorry, conspiracy aficionados. Neocons have been relatively influential because of the strength of their arguments, not their connections.

'NEOCONS ARE WILSONIAN IDEALISTS'

True, with an important qualification. The 'Wilsonian' label has been haphazardly affixed to anyone who believes that U.S. foreign policy should be guided by the promotion of American ideals, not just the protection of narrowly defined strategic and economic interests, as realpolitikers believe.

But Wilsonians are not all alike. Liberal 'soft Wilsonians', such as former U.S. President Jimmy Carter and, previously, U.S. President Woodrow Wilson himself, share a faith that multilateral organizations such as the League of Nations or the United Nations should be the main venues through which the United States promotes its ideals, and that international law should be the United States' main policy tool. They are willing to use force, but preferably only when (as in Haiti or Kosovo) the intervention is untainted by any hint of national interest.

The neocons have scant regard for Wilson himself, whom they regard as hopelessly naive. Instead, they are 'hard Wilsonians', who place their faith not in pieces of paper but in power, specifically U.S. power. Their heroes are Theodore Roosevelt, Franklin Roosevelt, Harry Truman, and Ronald Reagan – all U.S. presidents who successfully wielded power in the service of a higher purpose. Neocons believe the United States should use force when necessary to champion its ideals as well as its interests, not only out of sheer humanitarianism but also because the spread of liberal democracy improves U.S. security, while crimes against humanity inevitably make the world a more dangerous place.

'NEOCONS ARE TARGETING NORTH KOREA AND IRAN NEXT'

True. The greatest danger to the United States today is the possibility that some rogue state will develop nuclear weapons and then share them with terrorist groups. Iran and North Korea are the two likeliest culprits. Neither would be willing to negotiate away its nuclear arsenal; no treaty would be any trustworthier than the 1994 Agreed Framework that North Korea violated. Neocons think the only way to ensure U.S. security is to topple the tyrannical regimes in Pyongyang and Tehran.

This objective does not mean, however, that neocons are agitating for pre-emptive war. They do not rule out force if necessary. But their preferred solution is to use political, diplomatic, economic, and military pressure, short of actual war, to bring down these dictators – the same strategy the United States followed with the Soviet Union during the Cold War. The Iranian and North Korean peoples want to be free; the United States should help them by every means possible, while doing nothing to provide support for their oppressors. Regime change may seem like a radical policy but it is actually the best way to prevent a nuclear crisis that could lead to war. Endless negotiating with these governments – the preferred strategy of self-described pragmatists and moderates – is likely to bring about the very crisis it is meant to avert.

'NEOCONS OPPOSE MULTILATERALISM'

False. Neocons don't have a problem with alliances. They are wary of granting multilateral institutions (such as the United Nations) a veto over U.S. action, or joining deeply flawed international agreements (such as the landmine convention) simply for the sake of multilateral harmony. But that's a long way from unilateralism, which, if it means anything, implies a preference for going it alone.

To be sure, a faction within the Republican Party might properly be described as unilateralist. These traditional conservatives believe that the guiding principles of U.S. foreign policy should be, in columnist George Will's formulation, to: 'Preserve U.S. sovereignty and freedom of action by marginalizing the United Nations. Reserve military interventions for reasons of U.S. national security, not altruism. Avoid peacekeeping operations that compromise the military's war-fighting proficiencies. Beware of the political hubris inherent in the intensely unconservative project of "nation-building".'

Neocons, by contrast, are committed above all to U.S. global leadership, and they know that the costs of such leadership (including peacekeeping and nation-building) are so high that the United States needs allies to share the burden. For this reason, neocons have been vocal advocates of expanding NATO and sending its forces into Afghanistan and Iraq. Like most conservatives, neocons are deeply suspicious of the United Nations, which they fear is animated by anti-Americanism. But, unlike some on the right, they are happy to make common cause with the United Nations when doing so will serve U.S. interests. Some neocons (myself included) are even willing to cede the United Nations some authority in Iraq in order to bring more countries into the coalition.

'NEOCONS ARE POLITICAL FUNDAMENTALISTS'

Give me a break. According to some of their more heated critics, neocons view the world in Manichean terms. Guided by the spirits of philosopher Leo Strauss and Russian revolutionary Leon Trotsky, the neocons allegedly have contempt for the democratic masses and believe in spreading 'noble lies' to mislead the public. The 'exaggerated' threat posed by Saddam Hussein is cited as their latest deception.

This portrayal is a crude caricature of a group that believes American values are worth defending at home and abroad. That conviction was, in fact, the view of Strauss himself. A largely apolitical Professor of Classics at the University of Chicago who died in 1973, Strauss was a refugee from Nazi Germany who saw the evils of totalitarianism at first hand. He did not propose – as neocon-bashers charge – that a privileged few should run society while deceiving everyone else about their intentions. He was a firm believer in U.S. democracy, which, he thought, needed to be defended by a well-educated elite, lest it go the way of the Weimar Republic. Strauss's views inspired some early neocons; few read him today, contrary to all the articles asserting that (as the French weekly magazine *Le Nouvel Observateur* put it) Strauss is the neocons' 'mentor'.

Even more absurd is the charge that the neocons are secret adherents to Trotsky's theory of the permanent revolution. The former Red Army commander may have opened a few leftists' eyes to the evils of Stalinism in the 1930s, but he was no proto-neocon. He was a communist, who, even after his expulsion from Russia, remained committed to establishing a 'dictatorship of the proletariat'. The only kind of revolution he favored was one that would bring him and his comrades to power. As neocon author Joshua Muravchik has pointed out, Trotsky would not have supported a democratic war of liberation in Iraq; his sympathies would have been with Saddam.

'FAILURE IN IRAQ HAS DISCREDITED THE NEOCONS'

Too early to say. The emerging media consensus that the U.S. occupation has fizzled is ludicrously premature. Sure, there have been a lot of well-publicized problems, such as terrorism, crime, and electricity shortages. But a lot of less-publicized progress is also evident – the creation of a Governing Council, the election of city councils and mayors, the emergence of the freest political parties and media in the Arab world, the reconstruction of looted schools and government buildings, and the establishment of a legal framework for a free-enterprise system. The continuing U.S. casualties are lamentable but the losses so far are low by the standards of guerrilla wars... There is no reason, other than 1960s nostalgia, to expect a Vietnam redux. But if the occupation does turn into a fiasco, as numerous critics expect, the neocons will be a convenient scapegoat.

To a large extent, this blame is unfair. Many of the early problems of the occupation were due to the administration's failure to commit sufficient resources to Iraq. This oversight was largely the fault of policy-makers, such as Rumsfeld, who remain skeptical of nation-building. Neocons have been pushing for a more vigorous nation-building effort in both Afghanistan and Iraq and for a concomitant expansion of the active-duty military to provide the necessary troops. Unfortunately, this advice was largely unheeded by the administration. And when the White House finally realized it needed to spend more on rebuilding Iraq and Afghanistan, Republican isolationists and fiscal conservatives in Congress raised obstacles. If neocons had been in control, they would have done far more, far earlier, in both Afghanistan and Iraq, possibly averting some of the post-war problems. But fairly or not, neocons will doubtless be held responsible for the outcome in both countries; their numerous enemies, on both the left and the right, will see to that.

PART II

NEOCONSERVATIVES AND FOREIGN POLICY

with some comments
by friendly dissenters

NATIONAL INTEREST AND GLOBAL RESPONSIBILITY

William Kristol and Robert Kagan

Our present danger is one of declining military strength,
flagging will and confusion about our role in the world…
It is likely to yield very real external dangers. The task
for America… [is] preserving and reinforcing America's
benevolent global hegemony.

NATIONAL INTEREST AND GLOBAL RESPONSIBILITY

WILLIAM KRISTOL AND ROBERT KAGAN

The 1990s, for all their peace and prosperity, were a squandered decade. The decade began with America's triumph in the Cold War and its smashing victory over Iraq in Desert Storm. In the wake of those twin triumphs, the United States had assumed an unprecedented position of power and influence in the world. By the traditional measures of national power, the United States held a position unmatched since Rome dominated the Mediterranean world. American military power dwarfed that of any other nation, both in its war-fighting capabilities and in its ability to intervene in conflicts anywhere in the world on short notice. There was a common acceptance, even by potential adversaries, that America's position as the sole global superpower might not be challenged for decades to come. Meanwhile, the American economic precepts of liberal capitalism and free trade had become almost universally accepted as the best model for creating wealth, and the United States itself stood at the center of that international economic order. The American political precepts of liberal democracy had spread across continents and cultures as other peoples cast off or modified autocratic methods of governance and adopted, or at least paid lip-service to, the American credo of individual rights and freedoms. American culture, for better or for worse, had become the dominant global culture. To a degree scarcely imaginable at mid-century, or even as late as the 1970s, the world had indeed been transformed in America's image.

Our country, in other words, was – or could have been – present at another creation similar to the one Dean Acheson saw emerge after World War II. For the first time in its history, the United States had the chance to shape the international system in ways that would enhance its security and advance its principles without opposition from a powerful, determined adversary. A prostrate and democratizing Russia had neither the ability nor the inclination to challenge the American-led international democratic order. Though it turned toward harsh repression at home in 1989, China had barely begun to increase its military capabilities, and rather than thinking about launching a challenge to American dominance in East Asia, China's military leaders stood in awe of the military prowess and technological superiority America had exhibited in the Gulf War...

The task for America at the start of the 1990s ought to have been obvious. It was to prolong this extraordinary moment and to guard the international system from any threats that might challenge it. This meant, above all, preserving and reinforcing America's benevolent global hegemony, which undergirded what President George H. W. Bush rightly called a 'new world order'. The goal of American foreign policy should have been to turn what Charles Krauthammer called a 'unipolar moment' into a unipolar era.

The great promise of the post-Cold War era, however, began to dim almost immediately – and even before Bill Clinton was elected. The United States, which had mustered the world's most awesome military force to expel Saddam Hussein from Kuwait, failed to see that mission through to its proper conclusion: the removal of Saddam from power in Baghdad. Instead, vastly superior U.S. forces stood by in March 1991 as Shi'ite and Kurdish uprisings against Saddam were brutally crushed and the Iraqi tyrant, so recently in fear of his life, began to re-establish his control over the country. Three months later, Yugoslav President Slobodan Milošević launched an offensive against the breakaway province of Slovenia, following up with a much larger attack on Croatia. In the spring of 1992, Serb forces began their bloody siege of Sarajevo and a war of ethnic cleansing that would cost the lives of 200,000 Bosnian Muslims over the next three years. In the second half of 1992, meanwhile, American intelligence learned that North Korea had begun surreptitiously producing materials for nuclear weapons.

Saddam Hussein, Slobodan Milošević, and the totalitarian regime of North Korea, each in their own way, would be the source of one crisis after another throughout the remainder of the decade. Each of these dangerous dictatorships appears certain to survive the end of the twentieth century and go on to present continuing risks to the United States and its allies in the new millennium. And their very survival throughout the 1990s has established a disturbing principle in the post-Cold War world: that dictators can challenge the peace, slaughter innocents in their own or in neighboring states, threaten their neighbors with missile attacks – and still hang on to power. This constitutes a great failure in American foreign policy, one that will surely come back to haunt us.

But these were not the only failures that made the 1990s a decade of squandered opportunity for American foreign policy. The past decade also saw the rise of an increasingly hostile and belligerent China, which had drawn its own conclusions about U.S. behavior after the Gulf War. While every other great power in the world cut its defense budget throughout the 1990s, China alone embarked on a huge military build-up, augmenting both its conventional and its nuclear arsenal in an effort to project power beyond its shores and deter the United States from defending its friends and allies. China used this power to seize contested islands in the South China Sea, to intimidate its neighbors in East Asia, and, in the most alarming display of military might, to frighten the people of Taiwan by launching ballistic missiles off their shores. Throughout the 1990s, moreover, the Chinese government continued and intensified the repression of domestic dissent, both political and religious, that began with the massacre in Tiananmen Square. The American response to China's aggressive behavior at home and abroad has, with but a few exceptions, been one of appeasement.

In the face of the moral and strategic challenges confronting it, the United States engaged in a gradual but steady moral and strategic disarmament. Rather than seeking to unseat the dangerous dictatorships in Baghdad and Belgrade, the Clinton administration combined empty threats and ineffectual military operations with diplomatic accommodation. Rather than press hard for changes of regime in Pyongyang and Beijing, the Clinton administration – and in the case of China, the Bush administration before it – tried to purchase better behavior through 'engagement'. Rather than confronting the moral and strategic challenge presented by these evil regimes, the United States tried to do business with them in pursuit of the illusion of 'stability'. Rather than squarely facing our world responsibilities, American political leaders chose drift and evasion.

In the meantime, the United States allowed its military strength to deteriorate to the point where its ability to defend its interests and deter future challenges is now in doubt. From 1989 to 1999, the defense budget and the size of the armed forces were cut by a third; the share of America's GNP devoted to defense spending was halved, from nearly six to around three per cent; and the amount of money spent on weapons procurement and research and development declined about fifty per cent. There was indeed a 'peace dividend', and as a result, by the end of the decade the U.S. military was inadequately equipped and stretched to the point of exhaustion. And while defense experts spent the 1990s debating whether it was more important to maintain current readiness or to sacrifice present capabilities in order to prepare for future challenges, the United States, under the strain of excessive budget cuts, did neither.

Yet ten years from now, and perhaps a good deal sooner, we likely will be living in a world in which Iraq, Iran, North Korea, and China all possess the ability to strike the continental United States with nuclear weapons. Within the next decade we may have to decide whether to defend Taiwan against a Chinese attack. We could face another attempt by a rearmed Saddam Hussein to seize Kuwait's oil fields. An authoritarian regime in Russia could move to reclaim some of what it lost in 1991.

Other, still greater challenges can be glimpsed on the horizon, involving a host of unanswerable questions. What will China be in ten years: a modernizing economy peacefully integrating itself into the international system, an economic basket case ruled by a desperate dictatorship and a hypernationalistic military, or something in between? What will Russia be: a struggling democracy shedding its old imperial skin, or a corrupt autocracy striving to take back some of what it lost in 1989 and 1991? And there are other imponderables that derive from these. If Japan feels increasingly threatened by North Korean missiles and growing Chinese power, will it decide to rearm and perhaps build its own nuclear arsenal? What would Germany do if faced by an increasingly disaffected, revanchist, and bellicose Russia?

These threats and challenges do not exhaust the possibilities, for if history is any guide we are likely to face dangers, even within the next decade, that we cannot even imagine today. Much can happen in ten years. In 1788 for instance, while Louis XVI sat comfortably on his French throne, French philosophers preached the dawning of a new age of peace based on commerce, and no one had ever heard of Napoleon Bonaparte. Ten years later, a French king had lost his head and Napoleon was rampaging across Europe. In 1910, Norman Angell won international acclaim for a book, *The Great Illusion*, in which he declared that the growth of trade between capitalist countries had made war between the great powers obsolete. By 1920, the world had suffered through the costliest war in human history, fought among the world's great capitalist trading powers, and had seen a communist takeover in Russia, a development that was literally unimaginable a decade earlier. In 1928, the American economy was soaring, Weimar Germany was ruled by a moderate democrat, and Europe was at peace. Ten years later, the United States was struggling to emerge from the Great Depression, and Neville Chamberlain was handing Czechoslovakia over to Adolf Hitler.

While none of this argues that the world *must* become a vastly more dangerous place, the point is that the world *can* grow perilous with astonishing speed. Should this happen once more, it would be terrible to have to look back on the current era as a great though fleeting opportunity that was recklessly wasted. Everything depends on what we do now.

NO 'RETURN TO NORMALCY'

Contrary to prevailing wisdom, the missed opportunities of the 1990s cannot be made up for merely by tinkering around the edges of America's current foreign and defense policies. The middle path many of our political leaders would prefer, with token increases in the defense budget and a more 'humble' view of America's role in the world, will not suffice. What is needed today is not better management of the status quo, but a fundamental change in the way our leaders and the public think about America's role in the world.

Serious thinking about that role should begin by recalling those tenets that guided American policy through the more successful phases of the Cold War. Many writers treat America's Cold War strategy as an aberration in the history of American foreign policy. Jeane Kirkpatrick expressed the common view of both liberal and conservative foreign-policy thinkers when she wrote at the decade's start that, while the United States had 'performed heroically in a time when heroism was required', the day had passed when Americans ought to bear such 'unusual burdens'. With a return to 'normal' times, the United States could 'again become a normal nation'. In the absence of a rival on the scale of the Soviet Union, the United States should conduct itself like any other great power on the international scene, looking to secure only its immediate, tangible interests, and abjuring the broader responsibilities it had once assumed as leader of the Free World.

What is striking about this point of view is how at odds it is with the assumptions embraced by the leaders who established the guiding principles of American foreign policy at the end of World War II. We often forget that the plans for world order devised by American policy-makers in the early 1940s were not aimed at containing the Soviet Union, which many of them still viewed as a potential partner. Rather, those policy-makers were looking backward to the circumstances that had led to the catastrophe of global war. Their purpose was to construct a more stable international order than the one that had imploded in 1939; an economic system that furthered the aim of international stability by promoting growth and free trade; and a framework for international security that, although it placed too much faith in the ability of the great powers to work together, rested ultimately on the fact that American power had become the keystone in the arch of world order.

American leaders in the early to mid-1940s believed, in fact, that the 'return to normalcy' that President Harding had endorsed in 1920 was the fatal error that led to the irresponsible isolationism of the 1930s. Franklin Roosevelt said in 1941 that 'We will not accept a world, like the postwar world of the 1920s, in which the seeds of Hitlerism can again be planted and allowed to grow.' Men like James Forrestal and Dean Acheson believed the United States had supplanted Great Britain as the world's leader and that, as Forrestal put it in 1941, 'America must be the dominant power of the twentieth century.'

Henry Luce spoke for most influential Americans inside and outside the Roosevelt administration when he insisted that it had fallen to the United States not only to win the war against Germany and Japan, but to create both 'a vital international economy' and 'an international moral order' that would together spread American political and economic principles — and in the process avoid the catastrophe of a third world war. Such thinking was reflected in Roosevelt's Atlantic Charter and, more concretely, in the creation of the international financial system at Bretton Woods in 1944 and of the United Nations a year later.

Thus, before the Soviet Union had emerged as the great challenge to American security and American principles, American leaders had arrived at the conclusion that it would be necessary for the United States (together, they hoped, with the other great powers) to deter aggression globally, whoever the aggressor might be. In fact, during the war years they were at least as worried about the possible re-emergence of Germany and Japan as about the Soviets. John Lewis Gaddis has summarized American thinking in the years between 1941 and 1946 thus: 'The American President and his key advisers were determined to secure the United States against whatever dangers might confront it after victory, but they lacked a clear sense of what those might be or where they might arise. Their thinking about postwar security was, as a consequence, more general than specific.'

Few influential government officials, moreover, were under the illusion that 'collective security' and the United Nations could be counted on to keep the peace. In 1945 Harry Truman declared that the United States had become 'one of the most powerful forces for good on earth', and the task now was to 'keep it so' and to 'lead the world to peace and prosperity'. The United States had 'achieved a world leadership which does not depend solely upon our military and naval might', Truman asserted. But it was his intention, despite demobilization, to ensure that the United States would remain 'the greatest naval power on earth' and would maintain 'one of the most powerful air forces in the world'. Americans, Truman declared, would use 'our military strength solely to preserve the peace of the world. For we now know that this is the only sure way to make our own freedom secure.'

The unwillingness to sustain the level of military spending and preparedness required to fulfill this expansive vision was a failure of American foreign policy in the immediate aftermath of the war. It took the Iron Curtain and the outbreak of war in Korea to fully awaken Americans to the need for an assertive and forward-leaning foreign policy. But while the United States promptly rose to meet these challenges, a certain intellectual clarity was lost in the transition from the immediate post-war years to the beginning of the Cold War era. The original post-war goal of promoting and defending a decent world order became conflated with the goal of meeting the challenge of Soviet power. The policies that the United States should have pursued even in the absence of a Soviet challenge – seeking a stable and prosperous international economic order; playing a large role in Europe, Asia, and the Middle East; upholding rules of international behavior that benefited Americans; promoting democratic reform where possible and advancing American principles abroad – all these became associated with the strategy of containing the Soviet Union. In fact, America was pursuing two goals at once during the Cold War: first, the promotion of a world order conducive to American interests and principles; and second, a defense against the most immediate and menacing obstacle to achieving that order. The stakes surrounding the outcome of that latter effort became so high, in fact, that when the Cold War ended, many Americans had forgotten about the former.

LEADERSHIP

But the collapse of the Soviet empire has not altered the fundamental purposes of American foreign policy. Just as sensible Americans after World War II did not imagine that the United States should retreat from global involvement and await the rise of the next equivalent to Nazi Germany, so American statesmen today ought to recognize that their charge is not to await the arrival of the next great threat, but rather to shape the international environment to prevent such a threat from arising in the first place. To put it another way: the overarching goal of American foreign policy – to preserve and extend an international order that is in accord with both our interests and our principles – endures.

Certainly, the dramatic shift in international strategic circumstances occasioned by the Soviet collapse requires a shift in the manner in which this goal is pursued. But it is not a shift to 'normalcy'. In the post-Cold War era, the maintenance of a decent and hospitable international order requires continued American leadership in resisting, and where possible undermining, rising dictators and hostile ideologies; in supporting American interests and liberal democratic principles; and in providing assistance to those struggling against the more extreme manifestations of human evil. If America refrains from shaping this order, we can be sure that others will shape it in ways that reflect neither our interests nor our values.

This does not mean that the United States must root out evil wherever and whenever it rears its head. Nor does it suggest that the United States must embark on a crusade against every dictatorship. No doctrine of foreign policy can do away with the need for judgment and prudence, for weighing competing moral considerations. No foreign policy doctrine can provide precise and unvarying answers to the question of where, when, and how the United States ought to intervene abroad. It is easy to say that the United States must have criteria for choosing when to intervene. But it is a good deal harder to formulate those criteria than simply to say they must exist. Henry Kissinger writes in *Diplomacy* that what is most needed in American foreign policy are 'criteria for selectivity'. But he does not venture to suggest exactly what those criteria might be. Yet if one admits that closely linked matters of prestige, principle, and morality play a role in shaping foreign policy, then rigid criteria for intervention quickly prove illusory. As Kissinger well knows, the complicated workings of foreign policy and the exceptional position of the United States should guard us against believing that the national interest can be measured in a quasi-scientific fashion, or that areas of 'vital' national interest can be located, and other areas excluded, by purely geopolitical determinations. Determining what is in America's national interest is an art, not a science. It requires not only the measurement of power but also an appreciation of beliefs, principles, and perceptions, which cannot be quantified. That is why we choose statesmen, not mathematicians, to conduct foreign policy. That is why we will occasionally have to intervene abroad even when we cannot prove that a narrowly construed 'vital interest' of the United States is at stake.

It is worth pointing out, though, that a foreign policy premised on American hegemony, and on the blending of principle with material interest, may in fact mean fewer, not more, overseas interventions than under the 'vital interest' standard. Had the [first] Bush administration, for example, realized early on that there was no clear distinction between American moral concerns in Bosnia and America's national interest there, the United States, with the enormous credibility earned in the Gulf War, might have been able to put a stop to Milošević's ambitions with a well-timed threat of punishing military action. But because the Bush team placed Bosnia outside the sphere of 'vital' American interests, the resulting crisis eventually required the deployment of thousands of troops on the ground.

The same could be said of American interventions in Panama and the Gulf. A passive world-view encouraged American leaders to ignore troubling developments which eventually metastasized into full-blown threats to American security. Manuel Noriega and Saddam Hussein were given reason to believe that the United States did not consider its interests threatened by their behavior, only to discover that they had been misled. In each case, a broader and more forward-leaning conception of the national interest might have made the later, large, and potentially costly interventions unnecessary.

The question, then, is not whether the United States should intervene everywhere or nowhere. The decision Americans need to make is whether the United States should generally lean forward, as it were, or sit back. A strategy aimed at preserving American hegemony should embrace the former stance, being more rather than less inclined to weigh in when crises erupt, and preferably before they erupt. This is the standard of a global superpower that intends to shape the international environment to its own advantage. By contrast, the vital interest standard is that of a 'normal' power that awaits a dramatic challenge before it rouses itself into action.

TOOLS AND TACTICS

Is the task of maintaining American primacy and making a consistent effort to shape the international environment beyond the capacity of Americans? Not if American leaders have the understanding and the political will to do what is necessary. Moreover, what is required is not particularly forbidding. For much of the task ahead consists of building on already existing real strengths.

Despite its degradation in the last decade, for example, the United States still wields the strongest military force in the world. It has demonstrated its prowess in war on several occasions since the end of the Cold War – in Panama in 1989, in the Persian Gulf in 1991, and most recently [before the second Gulf War, Ed.] in the air war over Kosovo. Those victories owed their success to a force built in the Reagan years. This is a legacy the United States has lived off for over a decade, an account it has drawn too far down. Today the United States spends too little on its military capabilities, in terms of both present readiness and investment in future weapons technologies. The gap between America's strategic ends and the means available to accomplish those ends is growing, a fact that becomes more evident each time the United States deploys forces abroad.

To repair these deficiencies and to create a force that can shape the international environment today, tomorrow, and twenty years from now will probably require spending... about three and a half per cent of GDP on defense, still low by the standards of the past fifty years, and far lower than most great powers have spent on their militaries throughout history. Is the aim of maintaining American primacy not worth a hike in defense spending from 3 to 3.5 per cent of GDP?

The United States also inherited from the Cold War a legacy of strong alliances in Europe and Asia, and with Israel in the Middle East. Those alliances are a bulwark of American power and, more important still, they constitute the heart of the liberal democratic civilization that the United States seeks to preserve and extend. Critics of a strategy of American pre-eminence sometimes claim that it is a call for unilateralism. It is not. The notion that the United States could somehow 'go it alone' and maintain its pre-eminence without its allies is strategically misguided. It is also morally bankrupt. What would 'American leadership' mean in the absence of its democratic allies? What kind of nation would the United States be if it allowed Great Britain, Germany, Japan, Israel, Poland, and other democratic nations to fend for themselves against the myriad challenges they will face?

In fact, a strategy aimed at preserving American pre-eminence would require an even greater U.S. commitment to its allies. The United States would not be merely an 'offshore balancer', a savior of last resort, as many recommend. It would not be a 'reluctant sheriff', rousing itself to action only when the threatened townsfolk turn to it in desperation. American pre-eminence cannot be maintained from a distance, by means of some post-Cold War version of the Nixon doctrine, whereby the United States hangs back and keeps its powder dry. The United States would instead conceive of itself as at once a European power, an Asian power, a Middle Eastern power, and, of course, a Western Hemispheric power. It would act as if threats to the interests of our allies are threats to us, which indeed they are. It would act as if instability in important regions of the world, and the flouting of civilized rules of conduct in those regions, are threats that affect us with almost the same immediacy as if they were occurring on our doorstep. To act otherwise would make the United States appear a most unreliable partner in world affairs, which would erode both American pre-eminence and the international order, and gradually undermine the very alliances on which U.S. security depends. Eventually, the crises *would* appear at our doorstep.

This is what it means to be a global superpower with global responsibilities. The costs of assuming these responsibilities are more than made up by the benefits to American long-term interests. It is short-sighted to imagine that a policy of 'keeping our powder dry' is either safer or less expensive than a policy that aims to preclude and deter the emergence of new threats, that has the United States arriving quickly at the scene of potential trouble before it has fully erupted, that addresses threats to the national interest before they have developed into full-blown crises. Senator Kay Bailey Hutchison expressed a common but mistaken view last year when she wrote that 'a superpower is more credible and effective when it maintains a measured distance from all regional conflicts'. In fact, this is precisely the way for a superpower to cease being a superpower.

A strong America capable of projecting force quickly and with devastating effect to important regions of the world would make it less likely that challengers to regional stability would attempt to alter the status quo in their favor. It might even deter such challengers from undertaking expensive efforts to arm themselves in the first place. An America whose willingness to project force is in doubt, on the other hand, can only encourage such challenges. In Europe, in Asia, and in the Middle East, the message we should be sending to potential foes is: 'Don't even think about it.' That kind of deterrence offers the best recipe for lasting peace; it is much cheaper than fighting the wars that would follow should we fail to build such a deterrent capacity.

This ability to project force overseas, however, will increasingly be jeopardized over the coming years as smaller powers acquire weapons of mass destruction and the missiles to launch them at American forces, at our allies, and at the American homeland. The sine qua non for a strategy of American global pre-eminence, therefore, is a missile defense system that can protect all three of these targets. Only a well-protected America will be capable of deterring – and when necessary moving against – 'rogue' regimes when they rise to challenge regional stability. Only a United States reasonably well shielded from the blackmail of nuclear, biological, or chemical weapons will be able to shape the international environment to suit its interests and principles.

With the necessary military strength, strong and well-led alliances, and adequate missile defense, the United States can set about making trouble for hostile and potentially hostile nations, rather than waiting for them to make trouble for us. Just as the most successful strategy in the Cold War combined containment of the Soviet Union with an effort to undermine the moral legitimacy of the Moscow regime, so in the post-Cold War era a principal aim of American foreign policy should be to bring about a change of regime in hostile nations – in Baghdad and Belgrade, in Pyongyang and Beijing, and wherever tyrannical governments acquire the military power to threaten their neighbors, our allies, and the United States itself.

REGIME CHANGE

The idea, common to many foreign-policy minimalists and commerce-oriented liberals alike, that the United States can 'do business' with any regime, no matter how odious and hostile to our basic principles, is both strategically unsound and unhistorical. The United States has in the past worked with right-wing dictatorships as a bulwark against communist aggression or against radical Muslim fundamentalism. It has at times formed tactical alliances with the most brutal regimes – with Stalin's Soviet Union against Nazi Germany, and with Mao's China against the Soviet Union. But these should properly be viewed as tactical deviations from a broad strategy of promoting liberal democratic governance throughout the world, the result of circumstances in which our security was immediately threatened or where there was no viable democratic alternative.

Relationships with tyrannical regimes, moreover, are inherently difficult to sustain. The problem is not merely that such relationships become distasteful to Americans. More important, in today's environment American interests and those of tyrannical regimes inevitably clash. For the force of American ideals and the influence of the international economic system, both of which are upheld by American power and influence, tend to corrode the pillars on which authoritarian and totalitarian regimes rest. To bolster their legitimacy, such regimes therefore resort frequently to provocation, either with arms build-ups designed to intimidate both the United States and its allies, as in the case of China and North Korea, or by regional conquest, as in the case of Iraq and

Serbia. With no means of acquiring legitimacy for their domestic policies, they, like the Soviet rulers described by George Kennan, seek the nationalist legitimacy that comes from 'standing up' to an external enemy. Hence, the Chinese government knows there can be no real 'strategic partnership' with the United States. The North Korean government knows there can be no true 'normalization' with South Korea and the West. Saddam Hussein knows he cannot simply give up the struggle and try to live peaceably with his neighbors and with his own people. Slobodan Milošević knows that he cannot truly integrate himself into the European community. The price of such accommodations would be loss of power.

When it comes to dealing with such regimes, then, the United States will not succeed in persuading them to play by the existing – which is to say American – rules of the game. We cannot expect to limit their acquisition or sale of dangerous weapons by relying on their voluntary adherence to international non-proliferation agreements. We cannot hope to stem their aggression by appealing to their consciences and asking them to accept the 'norms' of the civilized world. For those 'norms' serve as obstacles to their ambitions and even threats to their existence. They have, and will continue to have, a clear and immutable interest in flouting them.

Here we would do well to cast another glance backward, for this is hardly the first time we have confronted the question of how to manage relations with dictatorial adversaries. During the 1970s, the view of U.S.–Soviet relations promulgated by much of the American foreign-policy establishment was that the key to peace and stability lay in an effort to reach mutual understanding with Moscow. The way to deal with the threat of apocalypse posed by the Soviet and American nuclear arsenals was through mutual arms control. The way to cope with Soviet adventurism abroad was to bind Moscow's leaders into a 'web of interdependence' and thereby compel them to recognize the advantages of responsible international behavior. But these measures proved futile, as Soviet leaders would not and probably could not fulfill their side of the proposed bargain without undermining their rule at home. The source of confrontation between the two sides was not mutual misunderstanding, a lack of interdependence, or the military arsenals amassed by both sides. It was the nature of the Soviet regime. When that regime came to an end, so did the arms race, so did Russian aggression beyond its borders, and so did the Cold War. This lesson can be applied to the post-Cold War era. The most effective form of non-proliferation when it comes to regimes such as those in North Korea and Iraq is not a continuing effort to bribe them into adhering to international arms control agreements, but an effort to bring about the demise of the regimes themselves.

To be sure, the United States cannot simply wish hostile regimes out of existence. The United States would not dispatch troops to topple every regime we found odious. An American strategy that included regime change as a central component would neither promise nor expect rapid transformations in every rogue state or threatening power. But such a strategy would depart from recent American policy in fundamental ways. Instead of ending the Gulf War in 1991 after the liberation of Kuwait, an American strategy built around the principle of regime change would have sent U.S. forces on to Baghdad to remove Saddam Hussein from power, and it would have kept U.S. troops in Iraq long enough to ensure that a friendlier regime took root. Such a strategy would not only have employed ground forces in Kosovo last year [1999] but would have sent sufficient NATO forces to Serbia to topple the Milošević regime. Those who believe such efforts would have been impossible to implement, or who caution against the difficulties of occupying and reforming such countries, or who insist that the removal of one man provides no solution to a problem, may wish to reflect on the American experiences in Germany and Japan – or even the Dominican Republic and Panama. In any case, if the United States is prepared to summon the forces necessary to carry out a Desert Storm, and to take the risks associated with expelling the world's fourth-largest army from Kuwait, it is absurd, and in the event self-defeating, not to complete the job.

Tactics for pursuing a strategy of regime change would vary according to circumstances. In some cases, the best policy might be support for rebel groups, along the lines of the Reagan Doctrine as it was applied in Nicaragua and elsewhere. In other cases, it might mean support for dissidents by either overt or covert means, and/or economic sanctions and diplomatic isolation. These tactics may or may not succeed immediately and would constantly have to be adjusted as circumstances in these regimes changed. But the purpose of American foreign policy ought to be clear. When it comes to dealing with tyrannical regimes, especially those with the power to do us or our allies harm, the United States should seek not coexistence but transformation.

To many the idea of America using its power to promote changes of regime in nations ruled by dictators rings of utopianism. But in fact, it is eminently realistic. There is something perverse in declaring the impossibility of promoting democratic change abroad in light of the record of the past three decades. After we have already seen dictatorships toppled by democratic forces in such unlikely places as the Philippines, Indonesia, Chile, Nicaragua,

Paraguay, Taiwan, and South Korea, how utopian is it to imagine a change of regime in a place like Iraq? How utopian is it to work for the fall of the Communist Party oligarchy in China after a far more powerful and, arguably, more stable such oligarchy fell in the Soviet Union? With democratic change sweeping the world at an unprecedented rate over these past thirty years, is it 'realistic' to insist that no further victories can be won?

If anything, we ought to be fairly optimistic that such change can be hastened by the right blend of American policies. The Chinese regime, for example, shows many signs of instability. The inherent contradiction between its dictatorial rule and its desire for economic growth so preoccupies the Beijing government that it feels compelled to crack down even on non-political, semi-religious sects like the Falun Gong. The United States and the West can either make it easier or more difficult for the People's Republic of China to resolve these contradictions. Our policy in this instance ought to be the latter, so that we can hasten the day when the conflicting currents of Chinese society prove beyond the capacity of its dictatorial government to manage.

But as disturbing as recent developments in China are, a strategy aimed at preserving American pre-eminence cannot and should not be based on the threat posed by any single nation. We need not go searching for an enemy to justify the requirement for a strong military and a strong moral component in our foreign policy. Even if the threat from China were to disappear tomorrow, that would not relieve us of the need for a strong and active role in the world. Nor would it absolve us of the responsibilities that fate has placed on our shoulders. Given the dangers we know currently exist, and given the certainty that unknown perils await us over the horizon, there can be no respite from this burden.

It is fair to ask how the rest of the world will respond to a prolonged period of American dominance. Those regimes that find an American-led world order inhospitable to their existence will seek to cut away at American power, will form tactical alliances with other dictatorships and 'rogue' states for the common purpose of unsettling the international order, and will look for ways to divide the United States from its allies. China's proliferation of weapons and selling of weapons technologies to Iran, its provision of financial support to Milošević, its attempt to find common ground with Russia against American 'hegemonism' – all represent opportunistic attempts to undercut American dominance. Russia can similarly be expected to search for opportunities to weaken U.S. political, diplomatic, and military preponderance in the world. Even an ally such as France may be prepared to lend itself to these efforts,

viewing a unified Europe as a check on American power and using the UN
Security Council as an arena for forging diplomatic roadblocks, along with
China and Russia, against effective U.S.-led international action, whether in
the Balkans or in the Persian Gulf.

All this is to be expected as part of the price for American global pre-
eminence. It does not, however, add up to a convincing argument against
preserving that pre-eminence. The main issue is not American 'arrogance'. It
is the inescapable reality of American power in all its many forms. Those who
suggest that these international resentments could somehow be eliminated by
a more restrained American foreign policy are deluding themselves. Even a
United States that never again intervened in a place like Kosovo or expressed
disapproval of China's human rights practices would still find itself the target
of jealousy, resentment, and in some cases even fear. A more polite but still pre-
eminently powerful United States would continue to stand in the way of
Chinese ambitions in East Asia, would still exist as a daily reminder of Russia's
vastly diminished standing in the world, and would still grate on French
insecurities. Unless the United States is prepared to shed its real power and
influence, allowing other nations genuinely to achieve a position of relative
parity on the world stage, would-be challengers of the international order – as
well as those merely resentful at the disparity of power – will still have much
to resent.

But neither should Americans fear that any effective grouping of nations is
likely to emerge to challenge American power. Much of the current
international attack on American 'hegemonism' is posturing. Allies such as the
French may cavil about the American 'hyperpower', but they recognize their
dependence on the United States as the guarantor of an international order
that greatly benefits France. (Indeed, it is precisely this recognition that breeds
French resentment.) As for Russia and China, the prospect of effective joint
action between those two nations against the United States is slight. Their long
history of mutual mistrust is compounded by the fact that they do not share
common strategic goals – even with regard to the United States. While
Chinese leaders consider the United States an enemy, a sporadically
democratizing Russia has a more ambivalent view. Post-Soviet Russia seeks
inclusion in an American-led West, both for economic and ideological reasons.

As a practical matter, as William C. Wohlforth has argued, it will be very
difficult for other nations to gang up on the United States precisely because it
is so powerful. But the unwillingness of other powers to gang up on the United
States also has something to do with the fact that it does not pursue a narrow,

selfish definition of its national interest, but generally finds its interests in a benevolent international order. In other words, it is precisely because American foreign policy is infused with an unusually high degree of morality that other nations find they have less to fear from its otherwise daunting power.

OUR INHERITANCE

At the beginning of this century, Theodore Roosevelt worried that Americans had become so 'isolated from the struggles of the rest of the world, and so immersed in our material prosperity', that they were becoming 'effete'. Roosevelt implored Americans to look beyond the immediate needs of their daily lives and embrace as a nation a higher purpose in the world. He aspired to greatness for America, and he believed that a nation could only be great if it accepted its responsibilities to advance civilization and improve the world's condition. 'A nation's first duty is within its borders,' Roosevelt declared, 'but it is not thereby absolved from facing its duties in the world as a whole; and if it refuses to do so, it merely forfeits its right to struggle for a place among the people that shape the destiny of mankind.'

In appealing to Americans to support a robust brand of internationalism, Roosevelt possessed the insight to appeal to their sense of nationalism. It was a nationalism, however, of a uniquely American variety: not an insular, blood-and-soil nationalism, but one that derived its meaning and coherence from being rooted in universal principles first enunciated in the Declaration of Independence. Roosevelt was no utopian; he had contempt for those who believed the international environment could be so transformed as to rid the world of war, put an end to international conflict, and, indeed, put an end to the notion of nationhood itself. Roosevelt was an idealist of a different sort. He did not attempt to wish away the realities of power, but insisted that the defenders of civilization must exercise their power against civilization's opponents. 'Warlike intervention by the civilized powers,' he insisted, 'would contribute directly to the peace of the world.'

Americans should once again embrace a broad understanding of the 'national interest', one in keeping with Roosevelt's vision. In recent years, many American foreign policy thinkers, and some politicians, have come to define the 'national interest' as consisting of a grid of ground, sea lanes, industrial centers, strategic choke-points, and the like. This was a definition of interests foisted upon our foreign policy establishment by 'realists' in the middle of the century. It is not a definition that would have been welcomed by previous generations of Americans. If someone had asked Alexander Hamilton what the 'national interest' was, he would have cited prosperity and security, but he would also have invoked the need to lift his young country into a place of honor among the world's great powers. Past American presidents and statesmen would never have imagined that the national interest, a term that can encompass a people's noblest aspirations, would come to possess such a narrow and limited meaning as many American thinkers give it today.

Honor and greatness in the service of liberal principles used to be understood as worthy goals of American foreign policy. In insisting that the 'national interest' extended beyond material security and prosperity, and in summoning Americans to seek honor as a nation, Theodore Roosevelt echoed the views of the American founders. And almost fifty years after Roosevelt, Reinhold Niebuhr insisted that America's 'sense of responsibility to a world community beyond our own borders is a virtue', and this virtue was in no way diminished by the fact that this sense of responsibility also 'derived from the prudent understanding of our own interests'. Common wisdom holds that Americans do not care about their nation's role in the world. But it has been a long time since any of their leaders asked them to care, or made an appeal to the elevated patriotism that joins interest and justice, which has characterized the American republic from its beginning.

The American-led world that emerged after the Cold War is a more just world than any imaginable alternative. A multipolar world, in which power is shared more equally among great powers – including China and Russia – would be far more dangerous, and it would also be far less congenial to democracy and to individual liberties. Americans should understand that their support for American pre-eminence is as much a strike for international justice as any people is capable of making. It is also a strike for American interests, and for what might be called the American spirit. George Kennan wrote more than fifty years ago that the American people should feel a 'certain gratitude to a Providence, which by providing [them] with this implacable challenge, has made their entire security as a nation dependent on pulling themselves together and accepting the responsibilities of moral and political leadership that history plainly intended them to bear'.

The 'implacable challenge' facing Americans has, of course, changed. Our fundamental responsibilities have not.

POSTSCRIPT – JUNE 2004
Neoconservatism Remains the Bedrock of U.S. Foreign Policy

WILLIAM KRISTOL

The essay you've just read appeared as the introduction to a book, *Present Dangers: Crisis and Opportunity in American Foreign and Defense Policy*, in the fall of 2000. The 'neoconservative' (as we would now say – the term was not much in use then) authors of the essays in *Present Dangers* had mostly been associated with the magazine *The Weekly Standard* (founded in September 1995), and with the think tank the Project for the New American Century (begun in 1997) – and before that, in the 1980s, with the Reagan administration. Among the more prominent recent products of this loose-knit group had been a July 1996 Kagan–Kristol article in *Foreign Affairs*, 'Towards a Neo-Reaganite Foreign Policy', and a September 2000 report by the Project for the New American Century, 'Rebuilding America's Defenses'.

None of this work had much immediate impact in the late 1990s. What was accomplished, in a relatively short period of time, was to bring back to life a certain strain of foreign-policy inspired by Harry Truman, Henry 'Scoop' Jackson, and Ronald Reagan. The strain of thought – it wouldn't yet be called a school of thought – was taken seriously in late 1990s foreign policy circles in Washington. But it was a minority strain even among Republicans and conservatives, as exemplified by neoconservative support for U.S. intervention in the Balkans.

Then George W. Bush was elected. Still nothing much happened. Then came 9/11. Suddenly there was a lot more receptivity to the argument that the world was more dangerous than it seemed in the 1990s. Suddenly political leaders were open to the claim that American leadership, American strength, and American principles were needed to deal adequately with these dangers. Suddenly an emphasis on containment and 'realism' seemed less compelling, and the case for regime change and democracy promotion as goals of American foreign policy seemed more convincing. Suddenly it didn't seem outlandish to suggest that moral clarity could be an important quality of a successful American foreign policy. And so this new school of thought seemed to influence, maybe even to guide, the Bush administration, as it removed the Taliban in late 2001, articulated a new national security strategy in September 2002, and moved to go to war against Saddam in March 2003.

How does this (neoconservative) strain of thinking stand today? It has probably been weakened by the Bush administration's poor performance in implementing what could be characterized as its recommended foreign policy. Yet, in another sense, neoconservatism is today stronger than ever, for it continues to provide the most plausible basic guidance for America's role in today's world.

The difficulties and troubles in Iraq have damaged neoconservative advocates of the war. On the other hand, for all the bitter criticism of its performance by opponents (and friends) of the Bush administration, no one seriously thinks we can go back to the nineties. No one seriously thinks we don't have to act decisively in the face of the threats of terror, weapons of mass destruction, radical Islam, and dictatorship and extremism in the Middle East. No one seriously thinks it's possible to deal with these problems without American leadership, American strength – and, yes, at the end of the day, American military power. And very few thoughtful people seriously believe that the old 'realist' prescription of working with local dictators will work – which means we have to be serious, in a 'neo-Reaganite' or neoconservative way, about regime change and the promotion of liberal democracy, especially in the Middle East.

So, in an important way, the neoconservative analysis is, I think, broadly vindicated. Of course, the Bush administration made the big mistake of trying to will the ends without the means. There was no big increase in the size of the military, no overhaul of our political, diplomatic, and intelligence institutions, no suitable commitment of resources, no radical adjustments of government bureaucracy and mindset needed to adjust to the post-9/11 world.

This failure in execution has been a big one. It has put the neoconservative 'project' at risk. Much more important, it has put American foreign policy at risk, and has endangered our safety and the safety and well-being of the world. But the errors have not been fatal, and there is time to correct the mistakes. It is, I suppose, not unusual for democracies to be resistant to change, and not unusual for democratic political leaders to be slow to make the big changes needed to cope with the new challenges they face. I remain confident we will now make the necessary changes, and I remain convinced that, in fact, the only successful American foreign policy on offer is a neoconservative one. Indeed, I suspect the only successful European foreign policy would be a neoconservative one, and believe that eventually the Europeans, too – at least some of them – will face up to reality.

THE PRESIDENT'S NATIONAL SECURITY STRATEGY

Condoleezza Rice

*As the world's most powerful nation, the United States has
a special responsibility to help make the world more secure...
There has never been a moral or legal requirement that a country
wait to be attacked before it can address existential threats.*

THE PRESIDENT'S NATIONAL SECURITY STRATEGY

CONDOLEEZZA RICE

The fall of the Berlin Wall and the fall of the World Trade Center were the bookends of a long transition period. During that period those of us who think about foreign policy for a living searched for an overarching, explanatory theory or framework that would describe the new threats and the proper response to them. Some said that nations and their militaries were no longer relevant, only global markets knitted together by new technologies. Others foresaw a future dominated by ethnic conflict. And some even thought that in the future the primary energies of America's armed forces would be devoted to managing civil conflict and humanitarian assistance.

It will take years to understand the long-term effects of September 11. But there are certain verities that the tragedy brought home to us in the most vivid way.

Perhaps most fundamentally, 9/11 crystallized our vulnerability. It also threw into sharp relief the nature of the threats we face today. Today's threats come less from massing armies than from small, shadowy bands of terrorists – less from strong states than from weak or failed states. And after 9/11, there is no longer any doubt that today America faces an existential threat to our security – a threat as great as any we faced during the Civil War, the so-called 'Good War', or the Cold War.

President Bush's new National Security Strategy offers a bold vision for protecting our nation that captures today's new realities and new opportunities.

It calls on America to use our position of unparalleled strength and influence to create a balance of power that favors freedom. As the President says in the cover letter: we seek to create the 'conditions in which all nations and all societies can choose for themselves the rewards and challenges of political and economic liberty'.

This strategy has three pillars:

- We will **defend the peace** by opposing and preventing violence by terrorists and outlaw regimes.
- We will **preserve the peace** by fostering an era of good relations among the world's great powers.
- And we will **extend the peace** by seeking to extend the benefits of freedom and prosperity across the globe.

Defending our nation from its enemies is the first and fundamental commitment of the federal government. And as the world's most powerful nation, the United States has a special responsibility to help make the world more secure.

In fighting global terror, we will work with coalition partners on every continent, using every tool in our arsenal – from diplomacy and better defenses to law enforcement, intelligence, cutting off terrorist financing, and, if needed, military power.

We will break up terror networks, hold to account nations that harbor terrorists, and confront aggressive tyrants holding or seeking nuclear, chemical, and biological weapons that might be passed to terrorist allies. These are different faces of the same evil. Terrorists need a place to plot, train, and organize. Tyrants allied with terrorists can greatly extend the reach of their deadly mischief. Terrorists allied with tyrants can acquire technologies allowing them to murder on an ever more massive scale. Each threat magnifies the danger of the other. And the only path to safety is to effectively confront both terrorists and tyrants...

The National Security Strategy does not overturn five decades of doctrine and jettison either containment or deterrence. These strategic concepts can and will continue to be employed where appropriate. But some threats are so potentially catastrophic – and can arrive with so little warning, by means that are untraceable – that they cannot be contained. Extremists who seem to view suicide as a sacrament are unlikely to ever be deterred. And new technology requires new thinking about when a threat actually becomes 'imminent'. So as a matter of common sense, the United States must be prepared to take action, when necessary, before threats have fully materialized.

Pre-emption is not a new concept. There has never been a moral or legal requirement that a country wait to be attacked before it can address existential threats. As George Shultz recently wrote, 'If there is a rattlesnake in the yard, you don't wait for it to strike before you take action in self-defense.' The United States has long affirmed the right to anticipatory self-defense – from the Cuban Missile Crisis in 1962 to the crisis on the Korean peninsula in 1994.

But this approach must be treated with great caution. The number of cases in which it might be justified will always be small. It does not give a green light – to the United States or any other nation – to act first without exhausting other means, including diplomacy. Pre-emptive action does not come at the beginning of a long chain of effort. The threat must be very grave. And the risks of waiting must far outweigh the risks of action.

To support all these means of defending the peace, the United States will build and maintain twenty-first-century military forces that are beyond challenge.

We will seek to dissuade any potential adversary from pursuing a military build-up in the hope of surpassing, or equaling, the power of the United States and our allies.

Some have criticized this frankness as impolitic. But surely clarity is a virtue here. Dissuading military competition can prevent potential conflict and costly global arms races. And the United States invites – indeed, we exhort – our freedom-loving allies, such as those in Europe, to increase their military capabilities.

The burden of maintaining a balance of power that favors freedom should be shouldered by all nations that favor freedom. What none of us should want is the emergence of a militarily powerful adversary who does not share our common values.

Thankfully, this possibility seems more remote today than at any point in our lifetimes. We have an historic opportunity to break the destructive pattern of great power rivalry that has bedeviled the world since the rise of the nation-state in the seventeenth century. Today, the world's great centers of power are united by common interests, common dangers, and – increasingly – common values. The United States will make this a key strategy for preserving the peace for many decades to come.

There is an old argument between the so-called 'realistic' school of foreign affairs and the 'idealistic' school. To oversimplify, realists downplay the importance of values and the internal structures of states, emphasizing instead the balance of power as the key to stability and peace. Idealists emphasize the primacy of values such as freedom and democracy and human rights in ensuring that just political order is obtained. As a professor, I recognize that this debate has won tenure for and sustained the careers of many generations of scholars. As a policy-maker, I can tell you that these categories obscure reality.

In real life, power and values are married completely. Power matters in the conduct of world affairs. Great powers matter a great deal – they have the ability to influence the lives of millions and change history. And the values of great powers matter as well. If the Soviet Union had won the Cold War, the world would look very different today – Germany today might look like the old German Democratic Republic, or Latin America like Cuba.

Today, there is an increasing awareness – on every continent – of a paradigm of progress, founded on political and economic liberty. The United States, our NATO allies, our neighbors in the Western Hemisphere, Japan, and our other friends and allies in Asia and Africa all share a broad commitment to democracy, the rule of law, a market-based economy, and open trade.

In addition, since September 11 all the world's great powers see themselves as falling on the same side of a profound divide between the forces of chaos and order, and they are acting accordingly.

America and Europe have long shared a commitment to liberty. We also now understand that being the target of trained killers is a powerful tonic that makes disputes over other important issues look like the policy differences they are, instead of fundamental clashes of values.

The United States is also cooperating with India across a range of issues – even as we work closely with Pakistan.

Russia is an important partner in the war on terror and is reaching towards a future of greater democracy and economic freedom. As it does so, our relationship will continue to broaden and deepen. The passing of the ABM Treaty and the signing of the Moscow Treaty reducing strategic arms by two-thirds make clear that the days of Russian military confrontation with the West are over.

China and the United States are cooperating on issues ranging from the fight against terror to maintaining stability on the Korean peninsula. And China's transition continues. Admittedly, in some areas, its leaders still follow practices that are abhorrent. Yet China's leaders have said that their main goal is to raise living standards for the Chinese people. They will find that reaching that goal in today's world will depend more on developing China's human capital than it will on China's natural resources or territorial possessions.

And as China's populace become more educated, more free to think, and more entrepreneurial, we believe this will inevitably lead to greater political freedom. You cannot expect people to think on the job, but not at home.

This confluence of common interests and increasingly common values creates a moment of enormous opportunities. Instead of repeating the historic pattern where great power rivalry exacerbates local conflicts, we can use great power cooperation to solve conflicts, from the Middle East to Kashmir, Congo, and beyond. Great power cooperation also creates an opportunity for multilateral institutions – such as the UN, NATO, and the WTO – to prove their worth. That's the challenge set forth by the President three weeks ago [September 2002] to the UN concerning Iraq. And great power cooperation can be the basis for moving forward on problems that require multilateral solutions – from terror to the environment.

To build a balance of power that favors freedom, we must also extend the peace by extending the benefits of liberty and prosperity as broadly as possible. As the President has said, we have a responsibility to build a world that is not only safer, but better.

The United States will fight poverty, disease, and oppression because it is the right thing to do – and the smart thing to do. We have seen how poor states can become weak or even failed states, vulnerable to hijacking by terrorist networks – with potentially catastrophic consequences. And in societies where legal avenues for political dissent are stifled, the temptation to speak through violence grows.

We will lead efforts to build a global trading system that is growing and more free. Here in our own hemisphere, for example, we are committed to completing a Free Trade Area of the Americas by 2005. We are also starting negotiations on a free trade agreement with the Southern African Customs Union. Expanding trade is essential to the development efforts of poor nations and to the economic health of all nations.

We will continue to lead the world in efforts to combat HIV/Aids – a pandemic which challenges our humanity and threatens whole societies.

We will seek to bring every nation into an expanding circle of development. Earlier this year the President proposed a 50 per cent increase in U.S. development assistance. But he also made clear that new money means new terms. The new resources will only be available to countries that work to govern justly, invest in the health and education of their people, and encourage economic liberty.

We know from experience that corruption, bad policies, and bad practices can make aid money worse than useless. In such environments, aid props up bad policy, chasing out investment and perpetuating misery. Good policy, on the other hand, attracts private capital and expands trade. In a sound policy environment, development aid is a catalyst, not a crutch.

At the core of America's foreign policy is our resolve to stand on the side of men and women in every nation who stand for what the President has called the 'non-negotiable demands of human dignity' – free speech, equal justice, respect for women, religious tolerance, and limits on the power of the State.

These principles are universal – and President Bush has made them part of the debate in regions where many thought that merely to raise them was imprudent or impossible.

From Cairo and Ramallah to Tehran and Tashkent, the President has made clear that values must be a vital part of our relationships with other countries. In our development aid, our diplomacy, our international broadcasting, and in our educational assistance, the United States will promote moderation, tolerance, and human rights. And we look forward to one day standing for these aspirations in a free and unified Iraq.

We reject the condescending view that freedom will not grow in the soil of the Middle East – or that Muslims somehow do not share in the desire to be free. The celebrations we saw on the streets of Kabul... proved otherwise. And in a recent UN report, a panel of thirty Arab intellectuals recognized that for their nations to fully join in the progress of our times will require greater political and economic freedom, the empowerment of women, and better, more modern education.

We do not seek to impose democracy on others, we seek only to help create conditions in which people can claim a freer future for themselves. We recognize as well that there is no 'one size fits all' answer. Our vision of the future is not one where every person eats Big Macs and drinks Coke – or where every nation has a bicameral legislature with 535 members and a judiciary that follows the principles of Marbury vs. Madison.

Germany, Indonesia, Japan, the Philippines, South Africa, South Korea, Taiwan, and Turkey show that freedom manifests itself differently around the globe – and that new liberties can find an honored place amid ancient traditions. In countries such as Bahrain, Jordan, Morocco, and Qatar, reform is under way, taking shape according to different local circumstances. And in Afghanistan this year, a traditional Loya Jirga assembly was the vehicle for creating the most broadly representative government in Afghan history.

Because of our own history, the United States knows we must be patient – and humble. Change – even if it is for the better – is often difficult. And progress is sometimes slow. America has not always lived up to our own high standards. When the Founding Fathers said, 'We, the people,' they didn't mean Me. Democracy is hard work. And 226 years later, we are still practicing each day to get it right.

We have the ability to forge a twenty-first century that lives up to our hopes and not down to our fears. But only if we go about our work with purpose and clarity. Only if we are unwavering in our refusal to live in a world governed by terror and chaos. Only if we are unwilling to ignore growing dangers from aggressive tyrants and deadly technologies. And only if we are persistent and patient in exercising our influence in the service of our ideals, and not just ourselves.

NEW THREATS FOR OLD

Margaret Thatcher

*The rise of Islamic militancy... point[s] to instability and conflict...
The international bodies... have given us neither prosperity
nor security... The single most awesome threat of modern times
[is] the proliferation of weapons of mass destruction
[in the hands of] rogue states.*

NEW THREATS FOR OLD

MARGARET THATCHER

When my distinguished predecessor delivered his Fulton speech, exactly fifty years ago, he journeyed hither by train in the company of the President of the United States. On the way, they played poker to pass the time. And the President won $75 dollars – quite a sum in those non-inflationary times for an unemployed former prime minister. But in view of the historic impact of his speech on American opinion and subsequently on U.S. foreign policy, Sir Winston Churchill later recorded that his loss was one of the best investments he had ever made.

I did not travel here by train; nor in the company of the President of the United States; nor did I play poker. I don't have the right kind of face for it. But there is some similarity in the circumstances of fifty years ago and today.

Mr. Churchill spoke not long after World War II. Toward the end of that great conflict, the wartime allies had forged new international institutions for post-war cooperation. There was in those days great optimism, not least in the United States, about a world without conflict presided over benevolently by bodies like the United Nations, the IMF, the World Bank, and the GATT. But the high hopes reposed in them were increasingly disappointed as Stalin lowered the Iron Curtain over Eastern Europe, made no secret of his global ambitions, and became antagonist rather than ally. Churchill's speech here was the first serious warning of what was afoot, and it helped to wake up the entire West.

In due course, that speech bore rich fruit in the new institutions forged to strengthen the West against Stalin's assault.

The Marshall Plan laid the foundations for Europe's post-war economic recovery.

The Truman Doctrine made plain that America would resist communist subversion of democracy.

The North Atlantic Treaty Organization mobilized America's allies for mutual defense against the Soviet steamroller.

And the European Coal and Steel Community, devised to help reconcile former European enemies, evolved over time into the European Community.

Stalin had overplayed his hand. By attempting to destroy international cooperation, he succeeded in stimulating it along more realistic lines – and not just through Western 'Cold War' institutions like NATO. As the West recovered and united, growing in prosperity and confidence, so it also breathed new life into some of the first set of post-war institutions like the GATT and the IMF. Without the Russians to obstruct them, these bodies helped to usher in what the Marxist historian, Eric Hobsbawm, has ruefully christened the 'Golden Age of Capitalism'. The standard of living of ordinary people rose to levels that would have astonished our grandparents; there were regional wars, but no direct clash between the superpowers; and the economic, technological, and military superiority of the West eventually reached such a peak that the communist system was forced into, first reform, then surrender, and finally liquidation.

None of this, however, was preordained. It happened in large part because of what Churchill said here fifty years ago. He spoke at a watershed: one set of international institutions had shown themselves to be wanting; another had yet to be born. And it was his speech, not the 'force' celebrated by Marx, which turned out to be the midwife of history.

Today we are at what could be a similar watershed. The long twilight struggle of the Cold War ended five years ago [1991] with complete victory for the West and for the subject peoples of the communist empire – and I very much include the Russian people in that description. It ended amid high hopes of a New World Order. But those hopes have been grievously disappointed. Somalia, Bosnia, and the rise of Islamic militancy all point to instability and conflict rather than cooperation and harmony.

The international bodies, in which our hopes were reposed anew after 1989 and 1991, have given us neither prosperity nor security. There is a pervasive anxiety about the drift of events. It remains to be seen whether this generation will respond to these threats with the imagination and courage of Sir Winston, President Truman, and the wise men of those years.

THE POST-COLD WAR WORLD

But, first, how did we get to our present straits?

Like the break-up of all empires, the break-up of the Soviet empire wrought enormous changes way beyond its borders.

Many of these were indisputably for the good:

- a more cooperative superpower relationship between the U.S. and Russia;
- the spread of democracy and civil society in Eastern Europe and the Baltics;
- better prospects for resolving regional conflicts like those in South Africa and the Middle East, once Soviet mischief-making had been removed;
- the discrediting of socialist economic planning by the exposure of its disastrous consequences in Russia and Eastern Europe;
- and the removal of Soviet obstruction from the United Nations and its agencies.

These were – and still are – real benefits for which we should be grateful.

But in the euphoria which accompanied the Cold War's end – just as in what Churchill's private secretary called 'the fatal hiatus' of 1944 to 1946 – we failed to notice other, less appealing, consequences of the peace.

Like a giant refrigerator that had finally broken down after years of poor maintenance, the Soviet empire in its collapse released all the ills of ethnic, social, and political backwardness which it had frozen in suspended animation for so long.

— Suddenly, border disputes between the successor states erupted into small wars in, for instance, Armenia and Georgia.

— Within these new countries the ethnic divisions aggravated by Soviet policies of Russification and forced population transfer produced violence, instability, and quarrels over citizenship.

— The absence of the legal and customary foundations of a free economy led to a distorted 'robber capitalism', one dominated by the combined forces of the mafia and the old communist *nomenklatura*, with little appeal to ordinary people.

— The moral vacuum created by communism in everyday life was filled for some by a revived Orthodox Church, but for others by the rise in crime, corruption, gambling, and drug addiction – all contributing to a spreading ethic of luck, a belief that economic life is a zero-sum game, and an irrational nostalgia for a totalitarian order without totalitarian methods.

— And, in these Hobbesian conditions, primitive political ideologies which have been extinct in Western Europe and America for two generations surfaced and flourished, all peddling fantasies of imperial glory to compensate for domestic squalor.

No one can forecast with confidence where this will lead. I believe that it will take long years of civic experience and patient institution-building for Russia to become a normal society. Neo-communists may well return to power in the immediate future, postponing normality; but whoever wins the forthcoming Russian elections will almost certainly institute a more assertive foreign policy, one less friendly to the U.S.

NEW THREATS FOR OLD

A revival of Russian power will create new problems – just when the world is struggling to cope with problems which the Soviet collapse has itself created outside the old borders of the USSR.

When Soviet power broke down, so did the control it exercised, however fitfully and irresponsibly, over rogue states like Syria, Iraq, and Gadaffi's Libya. They have in effect been released to commit whatever mischief they wish without bothering to check with their arms supplier and bank manager. Note that Saddam Hussein's invasion of Kuwait took place after the USSR was gravely weakened and had ceased to be Iraq's protector.

The Soviet collapse has also aggravated the single most awesome threat of modern times: the proliferation of weapons of mass destruction. These weapons – and the ability to develop and deliver them – are today acquired by middle-income countries with modest populations such as Iraq, Iran, Libya, and Syria – acquired sometimes from other powers like China and North Korea, but most ominously from former Soviet arsenals, or unemployed scientists, or from organized criminal rings, all via a growing international black market.

According to Stephen J. Hadley, formerly President Bush's assistant secretary for international security policy:'By the end of the decade, we could see over twenty countries with ballistic missiles, nine with nuclear weapons, ten with biological weapons, and up to thirty with chemical weapons.'

According to other official U.S. sources, all of north-east Asia, south-east Asia, much of the Pacific, and most of Russia could soon be threatened by the latest North Korean missiles. Once they are available in the Middle East and North Africa, all the capitals of Europe will be within target range; and on present trends a direct threat to American shores is likely to mature early in the next century.

Add weapons of mass destruction to rogue states and you have a highly toxic compound. As the CIA has pointed out: 'Of the nations that have or are acquiring weapons of mass destruction, many are led by megalomaniacs and strongmen of proven inhumanity or by weak, unstable, or illegitimate governments.' In some instances, the potential capabilities at the command of these unpredictable figures is either equal to – or even more destructive than – the Soviet threat to the West in the 1960s. It is that serious.

Indeed, it is even more serious than that. We in the West may have to deal with a number of possible adversaries, each with different characteristics. In some cases their mentalities differ from ours even more than did those of our old Cold War enemy. So the potential for misunderstanding is great and we must therefore be very clear in our own minds about our strategic intentions, and just as clear in signalling these to potential aggressors.

And that is only the gravest threat. There are others.

Within the Islamic world the Soviet collapse undermined the legitimacy of radical secular regimes and gave an impetus to the rise of radical Islam. Radical Islamist movements now constitute a major revolutionary threat not only to the Saddams and Assads but also to conservative Arab regimes, who are allies of the West. Indeed, they challenge the very idea of a Western economic presence. Hence, the random acts of violence designed to drive American companies and tourists out of the Islamic world.

In short, the world remains a very dangerous place, menaced by more unstable and complex threats than a decade ago. But because the risk of total nuclear annihilation has been removed, we in the West have lapsed into an alarming complacency about the risks that remain. We have run down our defenses and relaxed our guard. And to comfort ourselves that we were doing the right thing, we have increasingly placed our trust in international institutions to safeguard our future. But international bodies have not generally performed well. Indeed, we have learned that they cannot perform well unless we refrain from utopian aims, give them practical tasks, and provide them with the means and backing to carry them out.

INSTITUTIONAL FAILURE

The United Nations
Perhaps the best example of utopian aims is multilateralism; this is the doctrine that international actions are most justified when they are untainted by the national interests of the countries which are called upon to carry them out. Multilateralism briefly became the doctrine of several Western powers in the early nineties, when the United Nations Security Council was no longer hamstrung by the Soviet veto. It seemed to promise a new age in which the UN would act as world policeman to settle regional conflicts.

Of course, there was always a fair amount of hypocrisy embedded in multilateralist doctrine. The Haiti intervention by U.S. forces acting under a United Nations mandate, for instance, was defended as an exercise in restoring a Haitian democracy that had never existed; but it might be better described in the language of Clausewitz as the continuation of American immigration control by other means. But honest multilateralism without the spur of national interest has led to intervention without clear aims.

No one could criticize the humane impulse to step in and relieve the suffering created by the civil war in Somalia. But it soon became clear that the humanitarian effort could not enjoy long-term success without a return to civil order. And no internal force was available to supply this.

Hence, the intervention created a painful choice: either the UN would make Somalia into a colony and spend decades engaged in 'nation-building', or the UN forces would eventually withdraw and Somalia revert to its prior anarchy. Since America and the UN were unwilling to govern Somalia for thirty years, it followed that the job of feeding the hungry and helping the sick must be left to civilian aid agencies and private charities.

Conclusion: military intervention without an attainable purpose creates as many problems as it solves.

This was further demonstrated in the former Yugoslavia, where early action to arm the victims of aggression so that they could defend themselves would have been far more effective than the UN's half-hearted, multilateral intervention. A neutral peacekeeping operation, lightly armed, in an area where there was no peace to keep, served mainly to consolidate the gains from aggression. Eventually, the UN peacekeepers became hostages, used by the aggressor to deter more effective action against him. All in all, a sorry episode, ended by the Croatian army, NATO air power, and American diplomacy.

The combined effect of interventions in Bosnia, Somalia, and, indeed, Rwanda has been to shake the self-confidence of key Western powers and to tarnish the reputation of the UN. And now a dangerous trend is evident: as the Haiti case shows, the Security Council seems increasingly prepared to widen the legal basis for intervention. We are seeing, in fact, that classically dangerous combination – a growing disproportion between theoretical claims and practical means.

Ballistic missile defense

Compare this hubris with the failure to act effectively against the proliferation of nuclear, chemical, and biological weapons, and the means to deliver them.

As I have already argued, these are falling into dangerous hands.

Given the intellectual climate in the West today, it is probably unrealistic to expect military intervention to remove the source of the threat, as for example against North Korea – except perhaps when the offender invites us to do so by invading a small neighboring country. Even then, as we now know, our success in destroying Saddam's nuclear and chemical weapons capability was limited.

And we cannot be sure that the efforts by inspectors of the International Atomic Energy Authority to prevent Saddam putting civil nuclear power to military uses have been any more successful; indeed, we may reasonably suspect that they have not.

What then can we do? There is no mysterious diplomatic means to disarm a state which is not willing to be disarmed. As Frederick the Great mordantly observed: 'Diplomacy without arms is like music without instruments.' Arms control and non-proliferation measures have a role in restraining rogue states, but only when combined with other measures.

If America and its allies cannot deal with the problem directly by pre-emptive military means, they must at least diminish the incentive for the Saddams, the Gaddafis, and others to acquire new weapons in the first place. That means the West must install effective ballistic missile defense which would protect us and our armed forces, reduce or even nullify the rogue state's arsenal, and enable us to retaliate.

So the potential contribution of ballistic missile defense to peace and stability seems to me to be very great.

First and most obviously it promises the possibility of protection if deterrence fails; or if there is a limited and unauthorized use of nuclear missiles.

Second, it would also preserve the capability of the West to project its power overseas.

Third, it would diminish the dangers of one country overturning the regional balance of power by acquiring these weapons.

Fourth, it would strengthen our existing deterrent against a hostile nuclear superpower by preserving the West's powers of retaliation.

And fifth, it would enhance diplomacy's power to restrain proliferation by diminishing the utility of offensive systems.

Acquiring an effective global defense against ballistic missiles is therefore a matter of the greatest importance and urgency. But the risk is that thousands of people may be killed by an attack which forethought and wise preparation might have prevented.

It is, of course, often the case in foreign affairs that statesmen are dealing with problems for which there is no ready solution. They must manage them as best they can.

The European Union and Central Europe

That might be true of nuclear proliferation, but no such excuses can be made for the European Union's activities at the end of the Cold War. It faced a task so obvious and achievable as to count as an almost explicit duty laid down by History: namely, the speedy incorporation of the new Central European democracies – Poland, Hungary, and what was then Czechoslovakia – within the EU's economic and political structures.

Early entry into Europe was the wish of the new democracies; it would help to stabilize them politically and smooth their transition to market economies; and it would ratify the post–Cold War settlement in Europe. Given the stormy past of that region – the inhabitants are said to produce more history than they can consume locally – everyone should have wished to see it settled economically and politically inside a stable European structure.

Why was this not done? Why was every obstacle put in the way of the new market democracies? Why were their exports subject to the kind of absurd quotas that have until now been reserved for Japan? And why is there still no room at the inn?

The answer is that the European Union was too busy contemplating its own navel. Both the Commission and a majority of member governments were committed to an early 'deepening' of the EU (that is, centralizing more power in the EU's supranational institutions), and they felt that a 'widening' of it (that is, admitting new members) would complicate, obstruct, or even prevent this process.

So, while the 'deepening' went ahead, they arranged to keep the Central Europeans out by the diplomats' favorite tactic: negotiations to admit them. In making this decision, the European Union put extravagant and abstract schemes ahead of practical necessities in the manner of doctrinaire 'projectors' from Jonathan Swift down to the present.

And with the usual disastrous results. The 'visionary' schemes of 'deepening' either have failed or are failing.

The 'fixed' exchange rates of the European Exchange Rate Mechanism have made the yo-yo seem like a symbol of rigidity; they crashed in and out of it in September 1992 and have shown no signs of obeying the diktats of Brussels since then.

The next stage of monetary union agreed at Maastricht – the single currency – is due in 1999 when member states will have to achieve strict budgetary criteria. With three years to go, only Luxembourg fully meets these tests; the attempts by other countries to meet them on time have pushed up unemployment, hiked interest rates, depressed economic activity, and created civil unrest.

And for what? Across the continent businessmen and bankers increasingly question the economic need for a single currency at all. It is essentially a political symbol – the currency of a European state and people which don't actually exist, except perhaps in the mind of a Brussels bureaucrat...

NATO

Which brings me to my last example of institutional failure, mercifully a partial one counterbalanced by some successes, namely NATO. NATO is a very fine military instrument; it won the Cold War when it had a clear military doctrine. But an instrument cannot define its own purposes, and since the dissolution of the Warsaw Pact, Western statesmen have found it difficult to give NATO a clear one.

Indeed, they have shilly-shallied on the four major questions facing the Alliance:

1. Should Russia be regarded as a potential threat or a partner? (Russia may be about to answer that in a clearer fashion than we would like.)
2. Should NATO turn its attention to 'out of area' where most of the post-Cold War threats, such as nuclear proliferation, now lie?
3. Should NATO admit the new democracies of Central Europe as full members with full responsibilities as quickly as prudently possible?
4. Should Europe develop its own 'defense identity' in NATO, even though this is a concept driven entirely by politics and has damaging military implications?

Such questions tend to be decided not in the abstract, not at intergovernmental conferences convened to look into the crystal ball, but on the anvil of necessity in the heat of crisis. And that is exactly what happened in the long-running crisis over Bosnia.

At first, the supporters of a European foreign policy and a European defense identity declared the former Yugoslavia 'Europe's crisis' and asked the

U.S. to keep out. The U.S. was glad to do so. But the European Union's farcical involvement only made matters worse and, after a while, was effectively abandoned.

Then the United Nations became involved, and asked NATO to be its military agent in its peacekeeping operations.

Finally, when the UN–NATO personnel were taken hostage, the U.S. intervened, employed NATO air-power with real effect, forced the combatants to the conference table, for better or worse imposed an agreement on them, and now heads a large NATO contingent that is enforcing it.

In the course of stamping its authority on events, the U.S. also stamped its authority on the European members of NATO. And since the logistical supply chain goes through Hungary, it drew the Central Europeans into NATO operations in a small way. Whether NATO will apply the logic of this crisis in future strategic planning remains to be seen; but for the armchair theorists of a closed, passive, and divided NATO, Bosnia has been no end of a lesson.

These various institutional failures are worrying enough in their own terms and in our own times. If we look ahead still further to the end of the twenty-first century, however, an alarming and unstable future is on the cards.

The West and the rest

Consider the number of medium-to-large states in the world that have now embarked on a free-market revolution: India, China, Brazil, possibly Russia. Add to these the present economic great powers: the USA and Japan, and, if the federalists get their way, a European superstate with its own independent foreign and defense policy separate from, and perhaps inimical to, the United States. What we see here in 2096 is an unstable world in which there are more than half a dozen 'great powers', all with their own clients, all vulnerable if they stand alone, all capable of increasing their power and influence if they form the right kind of alliance, and all engaged willy-nilly in perpetual diplomatic maneuvers to ensure that their relative positions improve rather than deteriorate. In other words, 2096 might look like 1914 played on a somewhat larger stage.

That need not come to pass if the Atlantic Alliance remains as it is today: in essence, America as the dominant power surrounded by allies which generally follow its lead. Such are the realities of population, resources, technology, and capital that if America remains the dominant partner in a united West, and militarily engaged in Europe, then the West can continue to be the dominant power in the world as a whole.

WHAT IS TO BE DONE?

I believe that what is now required is a new and imaginative Atlantic initiative. Its purpose must be to redefine Atlanticism in the light of the challenges I have been describing. There are rare moments when history is open and its course changed by means such as these. We may be at just such a moment now.

Reviving the Alliance

First, security. As my discussion of the Bosnian crisis demonstrated, the key lies in two reforms: opening NATO membership to Poland, Hungary, and the Czech Republic, and extending NATO's role so that it is able to operate out of area.

Both reforms will require a change in NATO's existing procedures. An attack on the territory of one member must, of course, continue to be regarded unambiguously as an attack on that of all; but that principle of universality need not apply to out-of-area activities. Indeed, it needs to be recognized that a wider role for NATO cannot be achieved if every member state has to participate in an out-of-area operation before it can go ahead. What is required are flexible arrangements which, to use a fashionable phrase, permit the creation of 'coalitions of the willing'.

Would NATO expansion mark a new division of Europe and give Russia the right to intervene in states outside the fold? Not in the least. Among other reasons, we could hold out the possibility of admitting those countries which subsequently demonstrate a commitment to democratic values and which have trained military forces up to an acceptable standard. That would be a powerful incentive for such states to pursue the path of democratic reform and defense preparedness.

NATO also provides the best available mechanism for coordinating the contribution of America's allies to a global system of ballistic missile defense: that is, one providing protection against missile attack from whatever source it comes.

If, however, the United States is to build this global ballistic defense system with its allies, it needs the assurance that the Alliance is a permanent one resting on the solid foundations of American leadership. That raises, in my view, very serious doubts about the currently fashionable idea of a separate European 'defense identity' within the Alliance.

Essentially, this is another piece of political symbolism, associated among European federalists with long-term aspirations for a European state with its own foreign and defense policy. It would create the armed forces of a country which does not exist. But, like the single currency, it would have damaging practical consequences in the here and now.

In the first place, it contains the germs of a major future transatlantic rift. And in the second, it has no military rationale or benefits. Indeed, it has potentially severe military drawbacks. Even a French general admitted that during the Gulf War the U.S. forces were 'the eyes and ears' of the French troops. Without America, NATO is a political talking shop, not a military force.

Nor is that likely to be changed in any reasonably foreseeable circumstances. Defense expenditure has been falling sharply in almost all European states in recent years. Even if this process were now halted and reversed, it would take many years before Europe could hope to replace what America presently makes available to the Alliance by way of command and control facilities, airlift capacity, surveillance, and sheer firepower. Defense policy cannot be built upon political symbolism and utopian projects of nation-building which ignore or even defy military logic and fiscal prudence.

Transatlantic free trade

But even a vigorous and successful NATO would not survive indefinitely in a West divided along the lines of trade and economics. One of the great threats to Atlantic unity in recent years has been the succession of trade wars, ranging from steel to pasta, which have strained relations across the Atlantic. So the second element of a New Atlantic Initiative must take the form of a concerted program to liberalize trade, thereby stimulating growth and creating badly needed new jobs. More specifically, we need to move towards a Transatlantic Free Trade Area, uniting the North American Free Trade Area with a European Union enlarged to incorporate the Central European countries.

I realize that this may not seem the most propitious moment in American politics to advocate a new trade agreement. But the arguments against free trade between advanced industrial countries and poor Third World ones – even if I accepted them, which I do not – certainly do not apply to a Transatlantic Free Trade deal.

Such a trade bloc would unite countries with similar incomes and levels of regulation. It would therefore involve much less disruption and temporary job loss – while still bringing significant gains in efficiency and prosperity. This has been recognized by American labor unions, notably by Mr. Lane Kirkland in a series of important speeches. And it would create a trade bloc of unparalleled wealth (and therefore influence) in world trade negotiations.

Of course, economic gains are only half of the argument for a TAFTA. It would also provide a solid economic underpinning to America's continued military commitment to Europe, while strengthening the still fragile economies and political structures of Central Europe. It would be, in effect, the economic equivalent of NATO and, as such, the second pillar of Atlantic unity under American leadership.

Political foundations

Yet, let us never forget that there is a third pillar – the political one.

The West is not just some Cold War construct, devoid of significance in today's freer, more fluid world. It rests upon distinctive values and virtues, ideas and ideals, and above all upon a common experience of liberty.

True, the Asia–Pacific may be fast becoming the new center of global economic power. Quite rightly, both the United States and Britain take an ever closer interest in developments there.

But it is the West – above all perhaps, the English-speaking peoples of the West – that has formed that system of liberal democracy which is politically dominant and which we all know offers the best hope of global peace and prosperity. In order to uphold these things, the Atlantic political relationship must be constantly nurtured and renewed.

So we must breathe new life into the consultative political institutions of the West such as the Atlantic Council and the North Atlantic Assembly. All too often, they lack influence and presence in public debate. Above all, however – loath as I am to suggest another gathering of international leaders – I would propose an annual summit of the heads of government of all the North Atlantic countries, under the chairmanship of the President of the United States.

What all this adds up to is not another supranational entity. That would be unwieldy and unworkable. It is something more subtle, but I hope more durable: a form of Atlantic partnership which attempts to solve common problems while respecting the sovereignty of the member states. In the course of identifying those problems and cooperating to solve them, governments would gradually discover that they were shaping an Atlantic public opinion and political consciousness.

FIFTY YEARS ON

The reaction, fifty years ago, to that earlier Fulton speech was swift, dramatic and, at first, highly critical. Indeed, to judge from the critics you would have imagined that it was not Stalin but Churchill who had drawn down the Iron Curtain.

But for all the immediate disharmony, it soon became evident that Fulton had struck a deeper chord. It resulted in a decisive shift in opinion: by May, the opinion polls recorded that 83 per cent of Americans now favored the idea of a permanent alliance between the United States and Britain, which was subsequently broadened into NATO.

By speaking as and when he did, Churchill guarded against a repetition of the withdrawal of America from Europe which, after 1919, allowed the instability to emerge that plunged the whole world – including America – into a second war.

Like my uniquely distinguished predecessor, I too may be accused of alarmism in pointing to new dangers to which present institutions – and attitudes – are proving unequal. But, also like him, I have every confidence in the resources and the values of the Western civilization we are defending.

In particular, I believe (to use Churchill's words) that: 'If all British moral and material forces and convictions are joined with your own in fraternal association, the highroads of the future will be clear, not only for us but for all, not only for our time, but for a century to come.'

That at least has not changed in fifty years.

DOCTRINE OF THE INTERNATIONAL COMMUNITY

Tony Blair

*Appeasement does not work. If we let an evil dictator range
unchallenged, we have to spill infinitely more blood and
treasure to stop him later... We cannot turn our backs on...
the violation of human rights within other countries if
we want still to be secure.*

DOCTRINE OF THE INTERNATIONAL COMMUNITY
Kosovo

TONY BLAIR

GLOBAL INTERDEPENDENCE

Twenty years ago we would not have been fighting in Kosovo. We would have turned our backs on it. The fact that we are engaged is the result of a wide range of changes – the end of the Cold War; changing technology; the spread of democracy. But it is bigger than that.

I believe the world has changed in a more fundamental way. Globalization has transformed our economies and our working practices. But globalization is not just economic. It is also a political and security phenomenon.

We live in a world where isolationism has ceased to have a reason to exist. By necessity we have to cooperate with each other across nations.

Many of our domestic problems are caused on the other side of the world. Financial instability in Asia destroys jobs in Chicago and in my own constituency in County Durham. Poverty in the Caribbean means more drugs on the streets in Washington and London. Conflict in the Balkans causes more refugees in Germany and here in the U.S. These problems can only be addressed by international cooperation.

We are all internationalists now, whether we like it or not. We cannot refuse to participate in global markets if we want to prosper. We cannot ignore new political ideas in other countries if we want to innovate. We cannot turn our backs on conflicts and the violation of human rights within other countries if we want still to be secure.

On the eve of a new millennium we are now in a new world. We need new rules for international cooperation and new ways of organizing our international institutions.

After World War II, we developed a series of international institutions to cope with the strains of rebuilding a devastated world: Bretton Woods, the United Nations, NATO, the EU. Even then, it was clear that the world was becoming increasingly interdependent. The doctrine of isolationism had been a casualty of a world war, where the United States and others finally realized standing aside was not an option.

Today the impulse towards interdependence is immeasurably greater. We are witnessing the beginnings of a new doctrine of international community. By this I mean the explicit recognition that today more than ever before we are mutually dependent, that national interest is to a significant extent governed by international collaboration, and that we need a clear and coherent debate as to the direction this doctrine takes us in each field of international endeavor. Just as within domestic politics, the notion of community – the belief that partnership and cooperation are essential to advance self-interest – is coming into its own; so it needs to find its own international echo. Global financial markets, the global environment, global security and disarmament issues: none of these can be solved without intense international cooperation.

As yet, however, our approach tends toward being ad hoc. There is a global financial crisis: we react, it fades; our reaction becomes less urgent. Kyoto can stimulate our conscience about environmental degradation but we need constant reminders to refocus on it. We are continually fending off the danger of letting wherever CNN roves be the cattle prod to take a global conflict seriously.

We need to focus in a serious and sustained way on the principles of the doctrine of international community and on the institutions that deliver them. This means:

1. In global finance, a thorough, far-reaching overhaul and reform of the system of international financial regulation. We should begin it at the G7 at Cologne.
2. A new push on free trade in the WTO with the new round beginning in Seattle this autumn[1999].
3. A reconsideration of the role, workings, and decision-making process of the UN, and in particular the UN Security Council.
4. For NATO, once Kosovo is successfully concluded, a critical examination of the lessons to be learned, and the changes we need to make in organization and structure.
5. In respect of Kyoto and the environment, far closer working between the

main industrial nations and the developing world as to how the Kyoto targets can be met and the practical measures necessary to slow down and stop global warming, and;

6. A serious examination of the issue of Third World debt, again beginning at Cologne.

In addition, the EU and U.S. should prepare to make real step-change in working more closely together. Recent trade disputes have been a bad omen in this regard. We really are failing to see the bigger picture with disputes over the banana regime... or whatever else. There are huge issues at stake in our cooperation. The EU and the U.S. need each other and need to put that relationship above arguments that are ultimately not fundamental.

Now is the time to begin work in earnest on these issues. I know President Clinton will stand ready to give a lead on many of them. In Kosovo but on many other occasions, I have had occasion to be truly thankful that the United States has a president with his vision and steadfastness.

GLOBALIZATION

Globalization is most obvious in the economic sphere. We live in a completely new world. Every day about $1 trillion moves across the foreign exchanges, most of it in London. Here in Chicago the Mercantile Exchange and the Chicago Board of Trade contracts [are] worth more than $1.2 billion per day.

Any government that thinks it can go it alone is wrong. If the markets don't like your policies they will punish you.

The same is true of trade. Protectionism is the swiftest road to poverty. Only by competing internationally can our companies and our economics grow and succeed. But it has to be an international system based on rules. That means accepting the judgments of international organizations even when you do not like them. And it means using the new trade round to be launched at Seattle to extend free trade.

The international financial system is not working as it should. The Asian financial crisis of last year, and the knock-on impact on Brazil, demonstrate that.

The fact is that the Bretton Woods machinery was set up for the post-war world. The world has moved on. And we need to modernize the international financial architecture to make it appropriate for the new world.

The lesson of the Asian crisis is above all that it is better to invest in countries where you have openness, independent central banks, properly functioning financial systems, and independent courts, where you do not have to bribe or rely on favors from those in power.

We have therefore proposed that we should make greater transparency the keystone of reform. Transparency about individual countries' economic policies through adherence to new codes of conduct on monetary and fiscal policy; about individual companies' financial positions through new internationally agreed accounting standards and a new code of corporate governance; and greater openness too about IMF and World Bank discussions and policies.

We also need improved financial supervision both in individual countries through stronger and more effective peer group reviews, and internationally through the foundation of a new Financial Stability Forum. And we need more effective ways of resolving crises, like that in Brazil. The new contingent credit line at the IMF will assist countries pursuing sensible economic reforms and prevent damaging contagion. But we should also think creatively about how the private sector can help to resolve short-term financial crises...

I want to see a wider dialogue between Russia and the G7 focusing on all of the structural and legal reforms that are needed to improve the economic prospects for ordinary Russians. Russia is a unique economy with its own special problems and its own unique potential. We all need to build on the lessons of the last few years and develop a long-term strategy for reform that respects Russia's history, her culture, and her aspirations. If Russia is prepared, with our understanding and cooperation, to take the difficult economic action it needs to reform its economy – to build a sound and well-regulated financial system, to restructure and close down bankrupt enterprises, to develop and enforce a clear and fair legal system, and to reduce the damage caused by nuclear waste – the G7 must be prepared to think imaginatively about how it can best support these efforts.

We will be putting forward concrete ideas on how to do this at the Cologne Summit – by opening up our markets to Russian products by providing technical advice and sharing our expertise with the Russians, by providing support both bilaterally and through the IMF, the World Bank, and the other international economic instituitions, and the Paris Club for the Russian reform efforts.

I believe passionately that we will all benefit hugely from a thriving Russia making use of its immense natural resources, its huge internal market, and its talented and well-educated people. Russia's past has been as a world power that we felt confronted by. We must work with her to make her future as a world power with whom we cooperate in trust and to mutual benefit.

INTERNATIONAL SECURITY

The principles of international community apply also to international security.

We now have a decade of experience since the end of the Cold War. It has certainly been a less easy time than many hoped in the euphoria that followed the collapse of the Berlin Wall. Our armed forces have been busier than ever – delivering humanitarian aid, deterring attacks on defenseless people, backing up UN resolutions, and occasionally engaging in major wars as we did in the Gulf in 1991 and are currently doing in the Balkans.

Have the difficulties of the past decade simply been the aftershocks of the end of the Cold War? Will things soon settle down, or does it represent a pattern that will extend into the future?

Many of our problems have been caused by two dangerous and ruthless men – Saddam Hussein and Slobodan Milošević. Both have been prepared to wage vicious campaigns against sections of their own community. As a result of these destructive policies both have brought calamity on their own peoples. Instead of enjoying its oil wealth Iraq has been reduced to poverty, with political life stultified through fear. Milošević took over a substantial, ethnically diverse state, well placed to take advantage of new economic opportunities. His drive for ethnic concentration has left him with something much smaller, a ruined economy, and soon a totally ruined military machine.

One of the reasons why it is now so important to win the conflict is to ensure that others do not make the same mistake in the future. That in itself will be a major step to ensuring that the next decade and the next century will not be as difficult as the past. If NATO fails in Kosovo, the next dictator to be threatened with military force may well not believe our resolve to carry the threat through.

At the end of this century the U.S. has emerged as by far the strongest state. It has no dreams of world conquest and is not seeking colonies. If anything Americans are too ready to see no need to get involved in [the] affairs of the rest of the world. America's allies are always both relieved and gratified by its continuing readiness to shoulder burdens and responsibilities that come with its sole superpower status. We understand that this is something that we have no right to take for granted, and must match with our own efforts. That is the basis for the recent initiative I took with President Chirac of France to improve Europe's own defense capabilities.

As we address these problems at this weekend's [1999] NATO Summit we may be tempted to think back to the clarity and simplicity of the Cold War. But now we have to establish a new framework. No longer is our existence as states under threat. Now our actions are guided by a more subtle blend of mutual self-interest and moral purpose in defending the values we cherish. In the end values and interests merge. If we can establish and spread the values of liberty, the rule of law, human rights, and an open society then that is in our national interests too. The spread of our values makes us safer. As John F. Kennedy put it, 'Freedom is indivisible and when one man is enslaved who is free?'

The most pressing foreign-policy problem we face is to identify the circumstances in which we should get actively involved in other people's conflicts. Non-interference has long been considered an important principle of international order. And it is not one we would want to jettison too readily. One state should not feel it has the right to change the political system of another or foment subversion or seize pieces of territory to which it feels it should have some claim. But the principle of non-interference must be qualified in important respects. Acts of genocide can never be a purely internal matter. When oppression produces massive flows of refugees which unsettle neighboring countries then they can properly be described as 'threats to international peace and security'. When regimes are based on minority rule they lose legitimacy – look at South Africa.

There are many regimes that are undemocratic and engaged in barbarous acts. If we wanted to right every wrong that we see in the modern world then we would do little else than intervene in the affairs of other countries. We would not be able to cope.

So how do we decide when and whether to intervene? I think we need to bear in mind five major considerations.

First, are we sure of our case? War is an imperfect instrument for righting humanitarian distress; but armed force is sometimes the only means of dealing with dictators. Second, have we exhausted all diplomatic options? We should always give peace every chance, as we have in the case of Kosovo. Third, on the basis of a practical assessment of the situation, are there military operations we can sensibly and prudently undertake? Fourth, are we prepared for the long term? In the past we talked too much of exit strategies. But having made a commitment we cannot simply walk away once the fight is over; better to stay with moderate numbers of troops than return for repeat performances with large numbers. And finally, do we have national interests involved? The mass expulsion of ethnic Albanians from Kosovo demanded the notice of the rest of the world. But it does make a difference that this is taking place in such a combustible part of Europe.

I am not suggesting that these are absolute tests. But they are the kind of issues we need to think about in deciding in the future when and whether we will intervene.

Any new rules, however, will only work if we have reformed international institutions with which to apply them.

If we want a world ruled by law and by international cooperation then we have to support the UN as its central pillar. But we need to find a new way to make the UN and its Security Council work if we are not to return to the deadlock that undermined the effectiveness of the Security Council during the Cold War. This should be a task for members of the Permanent Five to consider once the Kosovo conflict is complete.

POLITICS

This speech has been dedicated to the cause of internationalism and against isolationism. On Sunday [April 25, 1999], along with other nations' leaders, including President Clinton, I shall take part in a discussion of political ideas. It is loosely based around the notion of the Third Way, an attempt by center and center-left governments to redefine a political program that is neither old left nor 1980s right. In the field of politics, too, ideas are becoming globalized. As problems become global – competitiveness, changes in technology, crime, drugs, family breakdown – so the search for solutions becomes global too. What amazes me, when I talk to other countries' leaders, is not the differences but the points in common. We are all coping with the same issues: achieving prosperity in a world of rapid economic and technological change; social stability in the face of changing family and community mores; a role for government in an era where we have learned big government doesn't work, but no government works even less.

Certain key ideas and principles are emerging. Britain is following them. It is one of the things that often makes it difficult for commentators to define the New Labour government. We are parodied as either being Mrs. Thatcher with a smile instead of a handbag; or as really old-style socialists in drag, desperate to conceal our true identity. In reality, we are neither. The political debates of the twentieth century – the massive ideological battleground between left and right – are over. Echoes remain, but they mislead as much as they illuminate.

Let me summarize the new political agenda we stand for:

1. Financial prudence as the foundation of economic success. In Britain, we have eliminated the massive budget deficit we inherited; put in new fiscal rules; granted Bank of England independence – and we're proud of it.

2. On top of that foundation, there is a new economic role for government. We don't believe in laissez-faire. But the role is not picking winners, heavy-handed intervention, old-style corporatism, but: education, skills, technology, small-business entrepreneurship. Of these, education is recognized now as much for its economic as its social necessity. It is our top priority as a government.

3. We are reforming welfare systems and public services. In Britain, we are introducing measures to tackle failing schools and reform the teaching profession that would have been unthinkable by any government even a few years ago. Plus big changes to the NHS. For the first two years of this government, welfare bills have fallen for the first time in two decades.

4. We are all tough on crime, tough on the causes of crime. The debate between 'liberals' and 'hardliners' is over. No one disputes the causes of crime. In particular social exclusion – a hardcore of society outside its mainstream – needs a special focus. We won't solve it just by general economic success. But we don't excuse crime either. Criminals get punished. That's justice. Fairness.

5. We are reinventing or reforming government itself. The government machine is being overhauled. Here, Al Gore has led the way. But the whole basis of how we deliver government services is being altered.

For Britain, there is a special dimension to this.

We are modernizing our Constitution. We have devolved power to a new Parliament in Scotland and a new Assembly in Wales. We are handing power back to local government, because we believe that power should be exercised as close as possible to the people it affects. We have introduced the concept of elected mayors which, strange as it may seem to you here in Chicago, has not existed in the past in Britain. The first election for a Mayor of London will take place next year. And we are removing the constitutional anomalies from the past, like hereditary peers voting on legislation, that have proved too difficult to tackle previously.

We also want to change the way in which Northern Ireland is governed, and let me say something on this.

We have made great progress in bringing peace to Northern Ireland. The Good Friday Agreement last year was a breakthrough. We have to make one last heave to get over the one remaining obstacle, so that we can establish the executive and the North/South bodies and hand over power to the elected Assembly. The stand-off on decommissioning cannot be allowed to derail the process when we have come so far. Bertie Ahern, the Irish Taoiseach, and I are determined to find a way through. The people will never forgive the politicians unless we resolve it.

And I would like to thank President Clinton and the Irish-American community in the U.S. for the great contribution they have made to coming this far. I know you will assist us again in the final straight.

And the final thing we all have in common, the new center, center-left governments, is we are internationalists and that returns me to my original theme.

For Britain, the biggest decision we face in the next couple of decades is our relationship with Europe. For far too long British ambivalence to Europe has made us irrelevant in Europe, and consequently of less importance to the United States. We have finally done away with the false proposition that we must choose between two diverging paths – the transatlantic relationship or Europe. For the first time in the last three decades we have a government that is both pro-Europe and pro-American. I firmly believe that it is in Britain's interest, but it is also in the interests of the U.S. and of Europe.

Being pro-Europe does not mean that we are content with the way it is. We believe it needs radical reform. And I believe we are winning the battle for economic reform within the EU. Two weeks ago the Conservative Spanish Prime Minister and I issued a joint declaration on economic reform. Shortly, the German Social Democratic Chancellor Schröeder and I will be issuing a declaration on the same subject. We all understand the need to ensure flexible labor markets, to remove regulatory burdens, and to untie the hands of business if we are going to succeed. The tide of Euro-sclerosis has begun to turn: the Third Way in Europe as much as in Britain.

As to Britain and the euro, we will make our decision not on political grounds but on the basis of our national economic interests. We must, however, ensure that we are ready to enter if we make the decision to do so. And the government has put a national changeover plan in place to convert sterling that will make that possible if we decide to do so.

I also pledge that we will prevent the European Union becoming a closed fortress. Europe must be a force for openness and free trade. Indeed, it is

fundamental to my whole thesis tonight that we can only survive in a global
world if we remove barriers and improve cooperation.

CONCLUSION

This has been a very broad-ranging speech, but maybe the time is right for
that. One final word on the USA itself. You are the most powerful country in
the world, and the richest. You are a great nation. You have so much to give
and to teach the world; and I know you would say, in all modesty, a little to
learn from it too. It must be difficult and occasionally irritating to find
yourselves the recipient of every demand, to be called upon in every crisis, to
be expected always and everywhere to do what needs to be done. The cry
'What's it got to do with us' must be regularly heard on the lips of your people
and be the staple of many a politician running for office.

Yet just as with the parable of the individuals and the talents, so those
nations which have the power, have the responsibility. We need you engaged.
We need the dialogue with you. Europe over time will become stronger and
stronger; but its time is some way off.

I say to you: never fall again for the doctrine of isolationism. The world
cannot afford it. Stay a country, outward looking, with the vision and
imagination that is in your nature. And realize that in Britain you have a friend
and an ally that will stand with you, work with you, fashion with you the
design of a future built on peace and prosperity for all, which is the only dream
that makes humanity worth preserving.

BEYOND THE
AXIS OF EVIL

Additional Threats from
Weapons of Mass Destruction

John R. Bolton

*The spread of weapons of mass destruction... is... the gravest
security threat we now face... States that sponsor terror and
pursue WMD must stop... those that do not can expect
to become our targets.*

BEYOND THE AXIS OF EVIL
Additional Threats from Weapons of Mass Destruction

JOHN R. BOLTON

The spread of weapons of mass destruction to state sponsors of terrorism and terrorist groups is, in my estimation, the gravest security threat we now face. States engaging in this behavior – some of them parties to international treaties prohibiting such activities – must be held accountable and must know that only by renouncing terrorism and verifiably forsaking WMD can they rejoin the community of nations...

THE NEW SECURITY ENVIRONMENT

The attacks of September 11 reinforced with blinding clarity the need to be steadfast in the face of emerging threats to our security. The international security environment has changed, and our greatest threat comes not from the specter of nuclear war between two superpowers, as it did during the Cold War, but from transnational terrorist cells that will strike without warning using weapons of mass destruction. Every nation – not just the United States – has had to reassess its security situation and to decide where it stands on the war on terrorism.

In the context of this new international security situation, we are working hard to create a comprehensive security strategy with Russia, a plan President Bush calls the New Strategic Framework. The New Strategic Framework involves reducing offensive nuclear weapons, creating limited defensive systems that deter the threat of missile attacks, strengthening non-proliferation and counter-proliferation measures, and cooperating with Russia to combat terrorism. It is based on the premise that the more cooperative post-Cold War relationship between Russia and the United States makes new approaches to these issues possible.

Accordingly, President Bush has announced that the United States will reduce its strategic nuclear force to a total of between 1,700 and 2,200 operationally deployed strategic nuclear warheads over the next ten years. President Putin has made a similarly bold and historic decision with respect to Russian strategic nuclear forces.

Strengthening the U.S.–Russian relationship has been a priority of the Bush administration, even prior to the September 11 attacks. In the current security climate, cooperation with Russia becomes even more important so that we can work together to combat terrorism and the spread of weapons of mass destruction, which threaten both our countries.

PREVENTING TERRORISM'S NEXT WAVE

President Bush believes it is critical not to underestimate the threat from terrorist groups and rogue states intent on obtaining weapons of mass destruction. As he said on the six-month anniversary of the attacks, 'Every nation in our coalition must take seriously the growing threat of terror on a catastrophic scale – terror armed with biological, chemical, or nuclear weapons.' We must not doubt for a moment the possible catastrophic consequences of terrorists or their rogue state sponsors who are willing to use disease as a weapon to spread chemical agents to inflict pain and death, or to send suicide-bound adherents armed with radiological weapons on missions of mass murder.

Every nation must commit itself to preventing the acquisition of such weapons by state sponsors of terrorism or terrorist groups. As President Bush said: 'Our lives, our way of life, and our every hope for the world depend on a single commitment: the authors of mass murder must be defeated, and never allowed to gain or use the weapons of mass destruction.' To this end, we use a variety of methods to combat the spread of weapons of mass destruction, including export controls, missile defense, arms control, non-proliferation, and counter-proliferation measures.

In the past, the United States relied principally on passive measures to stem proliferation. Arms control and non-proliferation regimes, export controls, and diplomatic overtures were the primary tools used in this fight. But September 11, the subsequent anthrax attacks, and our discoveries regarding al-Qaeda and its WMD aspirations have required the U.S. to complement these more traditional strategies with a new approach. The Bush administration is committed to combating the spread of nuclear, chemical, and biological weapons, missiles, and related equipment, and is determined to prevent the use of these deadly weapons against our citizens, troops, allies, and friends. While diplomatic efforts and multilateral regimes will remain important to our efforts, we also intend to complement this approach with other measures as we work both in concert with like-minded nations and on our own to prevent terrorists and terrorist regimes from acquiring or using WMD. In the past, we looked at proliferation and terrorism as entirely separate issues. As Secretary Powell said in his Senate testimony on April 24, 'There are terrorists in the world who would like nothing better than to get their hands on and use nuclear, chemical, or biological weapons. So there is a definite link between terrorism and WMD. Not to recognize that link would be foolhardy to the extreme.'

America is determined to prevent the next wave of terror. States that sponsor terror and pursue WMD must stop. States that renounce terror and abandon WMD can become part of our effort. But those that do not can expect to become our targets. This means directing firm international condemnation toward states that shelter – and in some cases directly sponsor – terrorists within their borders. It means uncovering their activities that may be in violation of international treaties. It means having a direct dialogue with the rest of the world about what is at stake. It means taking action against proliferators, middlemen, and weapons brokers by exposing them, sanctioning their behavior, and working with other countries to prosecute them or otherwise bring a halt to their activities. It means taking law-enforcement action against suspect shipments, front companies, and financial institutions that launder proliferators' funds. And it requires, above all, effective use, improvement, and enforcement of the multilateral tools at our disposal – both arms-control and non-proliferation treaties and export-control regimes.

THE PROBLEM OF NON-COMPLIANCE

Multilateral agreements are important to our non-proliferation arsenal. This administration strongly supports treaties such as the Treaty on the Non-Proliferation of Nuclear Weapons (NPT), the Chemical Weapons Convention, and the Biological Weapons Convention. But in order to be effective and provide the assurances they are designed to bring, they must be carefully and universally adhered to by *all* signatories. Therefore, strict compliance with existing treaties remains a major goal of our arms control policy.

This has been our aim in particular with the Biological Weapons Convention (BWC). In 1969, President Nixon announced that the United States would unilaterally renounce biological weapons. The U.S. example was soon followed by other countries, and by 1972 the BWC was opened for signature. This international treaty, to which more than 140 countries are parties, prohibits the development, production, stockpiling, acquisition, or retention of biological and toxin weapons.

While the vast majority of the BWC's parties have conscientiously met their commitments, the United States is extremely concerned that several states are conducting offensive biological weapons programs while publicly avowing compliance with the agreement. To expose some of these violators to the international community, last November [2001], I named publicly several states the U.S. government knows to be producing biological warfare agents in violation of the BWC.

Foremost is Iraq. Although it became a signatory to the BWC in 1972 and became a state party in 1991, Iraq has developed, produced, and stockpiled biological warfare agents and weapons. The United States strongly suspects that Iraq has taken advantage of more than three years of no UN inspections to improve all phases of its offensive BW program. Iraq also has developed, produced, and stockpiled chemical weapons, and has shown a continuing interest in developing nuclear weapons and longer-range missiles.

Next is North Korea. North Korea has a dedicated, national-level effort to achieve a BW capability and has developed and produced, and may have weaponized, BW agents in violation of the Convention. Despite the fact that its citizens are starving, the leadership in Pyongyang has spent large sums of money to acquire the resources, including a biotechnology infrastructure, capable of producing infectious agents, toxins, and other crude biological weapons. It likely has the capability to produce sufficient quantities of biological agents for military purposes within weeks of deciding to do so, and has a variety of means at its disposal for delivering these deadly weapons.

In January, I also named North Korea and Iraq for their covert nuclear weapons programs in violation of the Nuclear Non-Proliferation Treaty. This year, North Korea did not meet congressional certification requirements because of its continued lack of cooperation with the International Atomic Energy Agency, its failure to make any progress toward implementing the North–South Joint Denuclearization Declaration as called for under the Agreed Framework, and for proliferating long-range ballistic missiles. Finally, we believe that North Korea has a sizeable stockpile of chemical weapons and can manufacture all manner of CW agents.

Then comes Iran. Iran's biological weapons program began during the Iran–Iraq War and accelerated after Tehran learned how far along Saddam

Hussein had progressed in his own program. The Iranians have all of the necessary pharmaceutical expertise, as well as the commercial infrastructure, needed to produce – and hide – a biological warfare program. The United States believes Iran probably has produced and weaponized BW agents in violation of the Convention. Again, Iran's BW program is complemented by an even more aggressive chemical warfare program, Iran's ongoing interest in nuclear weapons, and its aggressive ballistic missile research, development, and flight testing regimen.

President Bush named these three countries in his State of the Union address earlier this year [2002] as the world's most dangerous proliferators. 'States like these, and their terrorist allies,' he said, 'constitute an axis of evil, arming to threaten the peace of the world. By seeking weapons of mass destruction, these regimes pose a grave and growing danger.'

TROUBLE AHEAD

Beyond the axis of evil, there are other rogue states intent on acquiring weapons of mass destruction – particularly biological weapons. Given our vulnerability to attack from biological agents, as evidenced recently in the anthrax releases, it is important to carefully assess and respond to potential proliferators. Today, I want to discuss three other state sponsors of terrorism that are pursuing or that have the potential to pursue weapons of mass destruction or have the capability to do so in violation of their treaty obligations. While we will continue to use diplomatic efforts and multilateral regimes with these countries, it is important to review the challenges we face and to underline the issues that these states must address. As the President has said, 'America will do what is necessary to ensure our nation's security. We'll be deliberate. Yet time is not on our side. I will not wait on events while dangers gather. I will not stand by as peril draws closer and closer.' First, Libya.

The United States also knows that Syria has long had a chemical warfare program. It has a stockpile of the nerve agent sarin and is engaged in research and development of the more toxic and persistent nerve agent VX. Although Damascus currently is dependent on foreign sources for key elements of its chemical warfare program, including precursor chemicals and key production equipment, we are concerned about Syrian advances in its indigenous CW infrastructure which would significantly increase the independence of its CW program. We think that Syria has a variety of aerial bombs and Scud warheads, which are potential means of delivery of deadly agents capable of striking neighboring countries.

Syria, which has signed but not ratified the BWC, is pursuing the development of biological weapons and is able to produce at least small amounts of biological warfare agents. While we believe Syria would need foreign assistance to launch a large-scale biological weapons program right now, it may obtain such assistance by the end of this decade.

Syria has a combined total of several hundred Scud B, Scud C and SS-21 SRBMs. It is pursuing both solid- and liquid-propellant missile programs and relies extensively on foreign assistance in these endeavors. North Korean and Russian entities have been involved in aiding Syria's ballistic missile development. All of Syria's missiles are mobile and can reach much of Israel, Jordan, and Turkey from launch sites well within the country.

In addition to... Syria, there is a threat coming from another BWC signatory, and one that lies just ninety miles from the U.S. mainland – namely, Cuba. This totalitarian state has long been a violator of human rights. The State Department said last year in its *Annual Report on Human Rights Practices* that 'the Government continued to violate systematically the fundamental civil and political rights of its citizens. Citizens do not have the right to change their government peacefully. Prisoners died in jail due to lack of medical care. Members of the security forces and prison officials continued to beat and otherwise abuse detainees and prisoners... The Government denied its citizens the freedoms of speech, press, assembly and association.' Havana has long provided safe haven for terrorists, earning it a place on the State Department's list of terrorist-sponsoring states. The country is known to be harboring terrorists from Colombia, Spain, and fugitives from the United States. We know that Cuba is collaborating with other state sponsors of terror.

Castro has repeatedly denounced the U.S. war on terrorism. He continues to view terror as a legitimate tactic to further revolutionary objectives. Last year, Castro visited Iran, Syria, and Libya – all designees on the same list of terrorist-sponsoring states. At Tehran University, these were his words: 'Iran and Cuba, in cooperation with each other, can bring America to its knees. The U.S. regime is very weak, and we are witnessing this weakness from close up.'

But Cuba's threat to our security often has been underplayed. An official U.S. government report in 1998 concluded that Cuba did not represent a significant military threat to the United States or the region. It went only so far as to say that 'Cuba has a limited capacity to engage in some military and intelligence activities which could pose a danger to U.S. citizens under some circumstances'. However, then-Secretary of Defense William Cohen tried to add some balance to this report by expressing in the preface his serious concerns about Cuba's intelligence activities against the United States and its human rights practices. Most notably, he said, 'I remain concerned about Cuba's potential to develop and produce biological agents, given its biotechnology infrastructure...'

Why was the 1998 report on Cuba so unbalanced? Why did it underplay the threat Cuba posed to the United States? A major reason is Cuba's aggressive intelligence operations against the United States, which included recruiting the Defense Intelligence Agency's senior Cuba analyst, Ana Belen Montes, to spy for Cuba. Montes not only had a hand in drafting the 1998 Cuba report, but also passed some of our most sensitive information about Cuba back to Havana. Montes was arrested last fall and pleaded guilty to espionage on March 19.

For four decades, Cuba has maintained a well-developed and sophisticated biomedical industry, supported until 1990 by the Soviet Union. This industry is one of the most advanced in Latin America and leads in the production of pharmaceuticals and vaccines that are sold worldwide. Analysts and Cuban defectors have long cast suspicion on the activities conducted in these biomedical facilities.

Here is what we now know: the United States believes that Cuba has at least a limited offensive biological warfare research and development effort. Cuba has provided dual-use biotechnology to other rogue states. We are concerned that such technology could support BW programs in those states. We call on Cuba to cease all BW-applicable cooperation with rogue states and to fully comply with all of its obligations under the Biological Weapons Convention.

CONCLUSION

America is leading in the fight to root out and destroy terror. Our goals are to stop the development of weapons of mass destruction and ensure compliance with existing arms-control and non-proliferation treaties and commitments, which the Bush administration strongly supports, but experience has shown that treaties and agreements are an insufficient check against state sponsors of terrorism. Non-compliance can undermine the efficacy and legitimacy of these treaties and regimes. After all, any nation ready to violate one agreement is perfectly capable of violating another, denying its actual behavior all the while.

And so I close with four fundamental conclusions. First, that global terrorism has changed the nature of the threat we face. Keeping WMD out of terrorist hands must be a core element of our non-proliferation strategy.

Second, the administration supports an international dialogue on weapons of mass destruction and encourages countries to educate their publics on the WMD threat. We must not shy away from truth telling.

Third, the administration will not assume that because a country's formal subscription to UN counter-terrorism conventions or its membership in multilateral regimes necessarily constitutes an accurate reading of its intentions. We call on Libya, Cuba, and Syria to live up to the agreements they have signed. We will watch closely their actions, not simply listen to their words. Working with our allies, we will expose those countries that do not live up to their commitments.

Finally, the United States will continue to exercise strong leadership in multilateral forums and will take whatever steps are necessary to protect and defend our interests and eliminate the terrorist threat.

THE SLOW UNDOING

The Assault on, and Underestimation of, Nationality

George F. Will

Everyone everywhere does not share [what Tony Blair calls]
'our attachment to freedom'... Iraq in its quest for democracy
lacks only — only!... an existing democratic culture... We are, it
seems, fated to learn again the limits of the Wilsonian project.

THE SLOW UNDOING
The Assault on, and Underestimation of, Nationality

GEORGE F. WILL

Man isn't at all one, after all — it takes so much of him to be American, to be French, etc.

Henry James to William Dean Howells, May 17, 1890

Woodrow Wilson was sleepless in Paris.

The President was awake all that night in 1919 because, he told his doctor the next morning, 'My mind was so full of the Japanese–Chinese controversy.' An American president was attending a conference to end a war that began in Belgium and raged mostly within 220 miles of the English Channel. Yet Wilson's sleep was troubled by Sino-Japanese relations. According to historian Margaret MacMillan in *Paris: Six Months that Changed the World*, Wilson was worried about 'what Japan was getting in China, right down to the composition of the railway police in Shantung. (They were to be Chinese with, where necessary, Japanese instructors.)'

'Where necessary'? America's President was struggling to measure the *necessity* of the Japanese component of the Chinese railway police. Such worries were enough to give a man a stroke — and may have done so.

I hope to trouble your sleep with a worry related to what Wilson was doing in Paris. My worry is the assault on the nation-state, which is an assault on self-government — the American project. It is the campaign to contract the sphere of politics by expanding the sway of supposedly disinterested experts, disconnected from democratic accountability and administering principles of universal applicability that they have discovered.

All this is pertinent to today's headlines, for a reason that may, at first blush, seem paradoxical. The assault on the nation-state involves a breezy confidence that nations not only can be superseded by supranational laws and institutions, they can even be dispensed with. Furthermore, nations can be fabricated, and can be given this or that political attribute, by experts wielding universal principles.

The vitality of democracy everywhere is imperiled by the impulse behind the increasingly brazen and successful denial of the importance and legitimacy of nation–states. This denial is most audacious in Europe. But because many of America's political ideas arrive on our shores after auditioning in Europe, Americans should examine the motives and implications of European attempts to dilute and transcend national sovereignty.

When the Cold War ended, my friend [the late New York senator] Pat Moynihan asked me: 'What are you conservatives going to hate, now that you can't hate Moscow?' My instant response was: 'We are going to hate Brussels' – Brussels, because it is the banal home of the metastasizing impulse to transfer political power from national parliaments to supranational agencies that are essentially unaccountable and unrepresentative.

President Kennedy, in his inaugural address, proclaimed America unwilling to permit 'the slow undoing of those human rights to which this nation has always been committed'. Today there is a slow undoing of the elemental human right of self-government, accomplished by the attack on a necessary concomitant of that right – the sovereignty of the nation–state.

Europe's elites – and, increasingly, America's – favor a 'pooling' of sovereignties in institutions insulated from accountability to particular national constituencies. To understand the long, tangled pedigree of this movement, return to Paris in 1919.

Because Wilson, unlike his French, British, and Italian counterparts at the Versailles Peace Conference, was a head of state, he was given a chair a few inches taller than Clemenceau's, Lloyd George's, and Orlando's. Not that Wilson needed that slight physical augmentation of his moral self-confidence. A former college professor, Wilson remained a pedagogue. 'I am,' he had once said, 'going to teach the South American republics to elect good men!'

In Paris, pupils for this professor came from far and wide. Or tried to come. Historian Margaret MacMillan reports, 'The Koreans from Siberia set out on foot in February 1919 and by the time the main part of the Peace Conference ended in June had reached only the Arctic port of Archangel.' However, some pupils were already in Paris when the conference convened – such as a twenty-nine-year-old Vietnamese working in a hotel kitchen: Ho Chi Minh.

Many advocates of subjugated peoples and nascent nations come to Paris, drawn by the magnetism of the central Wilsonian principle: self-determination. What exactly Wilson meant by that was a mystery to, among others, Wilson's Secretary of State, Robert Lansing, who wondered: 'When the President talks of "self-determination" what unit does he have in mind? Does he mean a race, a territorial area, or a community?' Nineteen years later, Hitler championed Sudeten Germans, using Wilsonian language about the right to ethnic self-determination.

There was a vast carelessness – an earnest carelessness – in the Versailles Conference's rearranging of the world. MacMillan, who is Lloyd George's great-granddaughter, says that in 1916 he mused: 'Who are the Slovaks? I can't seem to place them.' Three years later, he was helping place them in a new – and perishable – nation. Not until 1918 had Lloyd George discovered that New Zealand is east of Australia. When, in Paris, he dramatically spoke of the Turks retreating eastward toward Mecca, Lord Curzon sternly corrected him: the retreat, said Curzon, was toward Ankara, not Mecca. Lloyd George breezily replied: 'Lord Curzon is good enough to admonish me on a triviality.'

Laconic [Foreign Secretary] Arthur Balfour, who rarely seemed deeply stirred by anything, was angered by the spectacle of 'all-powerful, all-ignorant men sitting there and partitioning continents'. [Diplomat] Harold Nicolson told his diary: 'How fallible one feels here! A map – a pencil – tracing paper. Yet my courage fails at the thought of the people whom our errant lines enclose or exclude, the happiness of several thousands of people.'

Several thousands? Many millions, actually. The maps were large, the pencils busy. Observers described the Big Four and their experts on their hands and knees crawling on the floor around maps too large to fit on any table.

Turkey was on the conference's agenda but was not promising clay for the experts to mold. Its recent rulers had included one who went mad and another who was so fearful of enemies that, when he desired a cigarette, he had a eunuch take the first puff. In polyglot Turkey, for the dockworkers in Salonika to function, they had to speak half a dozen languages. Never mind. Those experts in Paris, crawling on their hands and knees around those big maps, would fix Turkey in due time.

When French officials invited Wilson to tour the scarred moonscape of the Flanders battlefields, Wilson angrily refused, saying the French were trying to arouse his emotions. Pure reason, he thought, must prevail. Yet Wilson may have included in his Fourteen Points the restoration of Polish independence because at a White House party in 1916 he had been stirred by the pianist Paderewski's rendition of Chopin.

Speaking to Lloyd George's mistress, Frances Stevenson, over a luncheon plate of chicken, Clemenceau said: 'I have come to the conclusion that *force* is right. Why is this chicken here? Because it was not strong enough to resist those who wanted to kill it. And a very good thing too!' What shaped

Clemenceau's dark realism was life on a continent that included such countries as Albania, in parts of which one man in five died in blood feuds.

A story, perhaps apocryphal but certainly plausible, recounts that, when Wilson asked Clemenceau if he did not believe that all men are brothers, Clemenceau exclaimed: 'Yes, all men are brothers – Cain and Abel! Cain and Abel!' Clemenceau did say to Wilson, 'We [Europeans], too, came into the world with the noble instincts and the lofty aspirations which you express so often and so eloquently. We have become what we are because we have been shaped by the rough hand of the world in which we have to live and we have survived only because we are a tough bunch.'

Now, fast forward to today.

Most of the political calamities through which the world has staggered since 1919 have resulted from the distinctively modern belief that things – including nations and human nature – are much more plastic, much more malleable than they actually are. It is the belief that nations are like Tinker Toys: they can be taken apart and rearranged at will. It is the belief that human beings are soft clay that can be shaped by the hands of political artists.

In the eighty-five years since 1919, many more than 100 million people have perished in violence intended to force the world into new configurations. The violence has served ambitious attempts at social engineering – attempts to create racial purity, or a classless society, or the New Soviet Man. Compared to this savagery, today's attempts to produce a new political architecture in Europe may look harmless.

Look again.

Today, European elites believe that Europe's nations are menaced by their own sovereignty. These elites blame Europe's recent blood-soaked history on the nation-state itself – including democratic states. For this reason, the European Union is attempting to turn itself into a single entity without sovereign nations – a federal entity, but a single political entity under a new constitution. The intended effect of the proposed constitution is to dissolve Europe's nation-states, reducing them to administrative departments of a supranational state. Its capital: probably Brussels.

In the hundreds of pages of the EU's proposed constitution, you will find, among much else, the stipulation that 'the physical and moral integrity of sportsmen and sportswomen' should be protected. A sweet thought, that. But what in the name of James Madison is it doing in a constitution?

The proposed constitution guarantees that children shall have the constitutional right 'to express their views freely'. That will make family dinners and bedtime in Europe litigious affairs. The proposed constitution bans discrimination based on birth – but does not say how to square that ban with the existence in the EU of seven hereditary monarchies. The EU's constitution decrees that, to protect the environment, 'preventive action should be taken'. That sentiment may seem merely vapid – until some judge discovers that it requires vast regulatory measures of his devising.

It used to be said that libraries filed French constitutions among periodicals. The EU constitution will someday seem as dated as a yellowing newspaper, because it gives canonical status – as fundamental rights elevated beyond debate – to policy preferences, even to mere fads, of the moment.

The aim of the proposed constitution's more than 400 articles is to put as many matters as possible beyond debate. Beyond the reach of majorities. Beyond democracy.

Article 10 of the EU constitution says: 'The Constitution, and law adopted by the Union's Institutions in exercising competences conferred on it [sic], shall have primacy over the law of the Member States.' Queen Elizabeth has asked for a briefing on the potential implications of the EU constitution for her role as supreme guardian of the British constitution.

British Europhiles simply deny the undeniable. They deny that the EU constitution will accelerate the leaching away of sovereignty from national parliaments. On the continent, enthusiasts of the proposed constitution acknowledge the leaching away – and say it is a virtue. For them, what is called the EU's 'democracy deficit' is not an ancillary cost of progress; it is the essence of progress.

The histories of America and Europe have given rise to markedly different judgments about democracy and nationalism. Americans have cheerful thoughts, and Europeans have dark thoughts, about uniting democracy and nationalism. Hence Americans and Europeans have different ideas of what constitutions should do – ideas that lead to different valuations of international laws and institutions.

Americans believe a democracy's constitution should arise from, and reflect the particularities of, that nation's distinctive political culture. Europeans' quite different idea of constitutions implies a bitterly disparaging self-assessment. Their idea of what constitutions are for is a recoil from the savagery of their twentieth-century experiences. The purpose of their constitutions is to contract radically the sphere of self-government – of democratic politics.

American constitutionalism speaks with a Philadelphia accent, in the language of popular sovereignty: 'We the people of the United States... do ordain and establish…' European constitutionalism speaks with a Parisian accent – the Paris of the eighteenth-century *philosophes*, of timeless and universal truths, defined by intellectuals and given, as gifts from on high, to publics expected to accept them deferentially.

And note well this: the spirit of Europe's trickle-down constitutionalism was the spirit at work in Paris in 1919, where a coterie of experts rearranged the continent – and even the Chinese railway police – according to the coterie's abstract principles and reasoning. The 1919 spirit of trickle-down lawgiving is alive in Europe today. When a European committee wrote a constitution for Kosovo, the committee – which included no member from Kosovo – wrote the constitution after visiting Kosovo for just three days.

Well, what need was there for Kosovars, or for knowledge of Kosovo, if abstract speculation by elites has revealed timeless truths – truths that can gain nothing from being consented to by the masses? Indeed, what need is there for variations among nations, or for experimentation by nations? In fact, what need is there for nations?

So, here comes the supranational entity: Europe. Trouble is, the prerequisites of a real political community include a shared history, culture, and language. Thus the phrase 'European political community' is oxymoronic: there are many democratic nations in Europe, but there is no single European *demos*. How can there be, with soon twenty-five members, twenty-five distinct national memories, more than twenty-five durable ethnicities, twenty-one languages, and annual per capita GDPs ranging from $8,300 in Latvia to $44,000 in Luxembourg?

On the rare occasions when the electorates of European nations are allowed to vote on some step toward a European superstate, they say 'No.' Swedes recently said 'No' regarding replacing their national currency with the euro, and all that implies in terms of the dilution of control of their destinies. Virtually all of Sweden's cosmopolitan classes – the entire political, commercial, and media establishments – advocated a 'Yes' vote.

When Swedes obdurately said 'No', the German newspaper *Die Welt* sniffily blamed 'a certain provincial eccentricity of Swedes'. Well, yes – if to be provincial is to prefer one's own institutions and the traditions, customs, and mores that are both the causes and effects of those institutions.

Denmark has also said 'No' to the proposed extinction of its national currency. The British, if asked, would say 'No', so British elites flinch from permitting a referendum. What do Sweden, Denmark, and Britain have in common? Charles Moore, former editor of the London *Daily Telegraph*, explains that each of the three has a 'well-ordered and continuous historical polity... These,' he says, 'are countries that have a strong belief in the reality of their political culture. They do not have a history in which their whole previous set of arrangements was discredited by war or fascism or revolution.'

In contrast, Germans seek to submerge themselves in Europe to escape German history. The French exalt Europe as something in which to submerge Germany. Italians contemplate the submergence of their political culture and think: good riddance. For Spaniards, the loss of sovereignty to a European superstate is a price willingly paid for a rupture with a past recently stained by Franco, fascism, and civil war.

Democracy and distrust usually are, and always should be, entwined. America's constitutionalism and its necessary corollary, judicial review, amount to institutionalized distrust. But although Americans are said to be suspicious of their government, they actually are less deeply wary of their government than Europeans are of their governments.

Scott Turow, the American lawyer and novelist, sees evidence of this difference in the sharply divergent American and European attitudes about capital punishment. It is, he says, exactly wrong to interpret European opposition to capital punishment as evidence of Europe's higher civility. Rather, says Turow, European democracies have a history of fragility, [and] 'have repeatedly been overwhelmed by dictators'. So 'the day seems far less remote when another madman can commandeer the power of the State to kill his enemies.' In fact, 'American opinion about capital punishment is subtly dependent on the extraordinary stability of our democratic institutions.'

I suggest that there is a similar explanation for the sharp contrast between the European enthusiasm for expanding the reach of international law and institutions at the expense of national sovereignty, and America's more chilly and suspicious stance toward such laws and institutions. It is not quite fair to say that international law is to real law as professional wrestling is to real wrestling. But international law – so frequently invoked; so rarely defined – is an infinitely elastic concept. Who enacts, who construes, who adjudicates, and who enforces this law? Hobbes said: 'Law without the sword is but words.' But law backed by the sword – by coercion – must be legitimized by a political process. Americans wonder: how does that legitimation work for international law?

It is said that international law is the consensus in action of the 'international community'. Well, now.

The attempt to break nations – and especially our nation – to the saddle and bridle of international law founders on the fact that the 'community of nations' is a fiction. Nothing can be properly called a 'community' if it jumbles together entities as different as Saudi Arabia and New Zealand, Japan and Sudan, Italy and Iran, Norway and Libya.

The American Revolution was, at bottom, about the right of a distinctive people, conscious of itself as a single people, to govern itself in its distinctive manner, in nationhood. Here was a great eighteenth-century insight: popular sovereignty is inextricably entwined with nationality.

The nation-state has been a great instrument of emancipation. It has freed people from the idea that their self-government is subject to extranational restraints, such as the divine right of kings or imperial prerogatives or traditional privileges of particular social orders.

Certainly Americans will not passively watch their nation's distinctive ideas of justice be subordinated to any other standards. Most Americans are not merely patriots; they are nationalists, too. They do not merely love their country; they believe that its political arrangements, and the values and understandings of the human condition that those arrangements reflect, are superior to most other nations' arrangements. They believe, but are too polite to say, that American arrangements are not suited to everybody, at least not now. These superior American arrangements are suited to culturally superior people – those up to the demands made by self-government.

And yet, my sleep is troubled by this worry:

There may be a subtle kinship between – a common thread in – two ideas that are currently having large consequences. One is the unAmerican – and increasingly anti-American – idea that the nation-state is both dispensable and dangerous, and therefore that nations should increasingly be subordinated to international laws and arrangements of the 'community of nations'. The other idea – one suddenly central to America's international exertions – is that nations are mechanical, not organic things. And therefore a can-do people with an aptitude for engineering – people like Americans – can build nations.

These ideas share a dangerous lack of respect for the elemental, powerful impulses that produce nations. Both ideas have a Wilsonian flavor. They shaped the American President's participation in Paris in 1919. And they shape the behavior of Wilson's nation eighty-five years later.

Do I seem anxious? Perhaps. But an English skeptic once said he wanted to carve on all the churches of England three cautionary words: 'Important if True.' We must inscribe those words alongside some of today's political utterances.

Last July [2003], Prime Minister Tony Blair, addressing a joint session of the U.S. Congress, said: '[It is a] myth [that] our attachment to freedom is a product of our culture,' and he added: 'Ours are not Western values; they are the universal values of the human spirit. And anywhere, anytime people are given the chance to choose, the choice is the same: freedom, not tyranny; democracy, not dictatorship; the rule of law, not the rule of the secret police.'

That assertion is important. But is it true? Everyone everywhere does not share 'our attachment to freedom'. Freedom is not even understood the same way everywhere, let alone valued the same way relative to other political goods such as equality, security, and piety. Does Blair really believe that our attachment to freedom is not the product of complex and protracted acculturation by institutions and social mores that have evolved over centuries – the centuries that it took to prepare the stony social ground for seeds of democracy?

When Blair says freedom as we understand it, and democracy and the rule of law as we administer them, are 'the universal values of the human spirit', he is not speaking as America's founders did when they spoke of 'self-evident' truths. The founders meant truths obvious not to everyone everywhere but to minds unclouded by superstition and other ignorance – minds like theirs. Blair seems to think: Boston, Baghdad, Manchester, Monrovia – what's the difference? But Blair's argument is true only if it is trivial logic-chopping. That is, when he says 'ordinary' people always choose freedom, democracy, and the rule of law, he must mean that anyone who does not so choose is therefore not ordinary. There are a lot of those people in the world. We are at war with some of them in Iraq.

President Bush recently said something that is important – if true. And perhaps it is even more important if it is not true. He denounced 'cultural condescension' – the belief that some cultures lack the requisite aptitudes for democracy. And the President said: 'Time after time, observers have questioned whether this country, or that people, or this group are "ready" for democracy – as if freedom were a prize you win for meeting our own Western standards of progress.'

Well. Multiculturalists probably purred with pleasure about this president's delicate avoidance of anything as gauche as chauvinism about 'Western standards of progress'. His idea – that there is no necessary connection between Western political traditions and the success of democracy – is important.

But is it true? Today his hypothesis is being tested in Iraq, where an old baseball joke is pertinent. A manager says, 'Our team is just two players away from being a championship team. Unfortunately, the two players are Babe

Ruth and Lou Gehrig.' Iraq is just three people away from democratic success. Unfortunately, the three are George Washington, James Madison, and John Marshall.

Iraq lacks a Washington, a universally revered hero emblematic of national unity and identity. Iraq lacks a Madison, a genius of constitutional architecture, a profound student of what the President calls 'Western standards of progress', and a subtle analyst of the problem of factions and their centrifugal, disintegrative tendencies. Iraq lacks a Marshall, someone who can so persuasively construe a constitution that the prestige of his court, and of law itself, ensures national compliance.

Iraq lacks a Washington, a Madison, a Marshall — and it lacks the astonishingly rich social and cultural soil from which such people sprout. From America's social soil in the fourth quarter of the eighteenth century grew all the members of the Constitutional Convention and of all the state legislatures that created all the conventions that ratified the Constitution.

So, Iraq in its quest for democracy lacks only — only! — what America then had: an existing democratic culture. It is an historical truism that the Declaration of Independence was less the *creation* of independence than the affirmation that Americans had already become independent. In the decades before 1776 they had become a distinct people, a *demos*, a nation — held together by the glue of shared memories, common strivings, and shared ideals. As John Adams said, the revolution had occurred in the minds and hearts of Americans before the incident at Concord bridge.

Now America is engaged in a great exercise in nation-building. America invaded Iraq to disarm a rogue regime thought to be accumulating weapons of mass destruction. After nine months of post-war searching, no such weapons have been found. The appropriate reaction to this is dismay, and perhaps indignation, about intelligence failures — failures that also afflicted the previous American administration and numerous foreign governments.

Instead, Washington's reaction is Wilsonian. It is: never mind the weapons of mass destruction; a sufficient justification for the war was Iraq's non-compliance with various UN resolutions. So a conservative American administration says war was justified by the need — the opportunity — to strengthen the UN, aka the 'international community', as the arbiter of international behavior. Woodrow Wilson lives.

It is counted realism in Washington now to say that creating a new Iraqi regime may require perhaps two years. One wonders: does Washington remember that it took a generation, and the United States army, to bring about, in effect, regime change – a change of institutions and mores – in the American South? Will a Middle Eastern nation prove more plastic to our touch than Mississippi was? Will two years suffice for America – as Woodrow Wilson said of the Latin American republics – to teach Iraq to elect good men? We are, it seems, fated to learn again the limits of the Wilsonian project.

There are those who say: 'Differences be damned! America has a duty to accomplish that project.' They should remember an elemental principle of moral reasoning: there can be no duty to do what cannot be done.

What is to be done in Iraq? As Robert Frost said, the best way out is always through. We are there. We dare not leave having replaced a savage state with a failed state – a vacuum into which evil forces will flow. Our aim should be the rule of law, a quickened pulse of civil society, some system of political representation. Then, let us vow not to take on such reconstructions often.

Four decades ago I arrived at Princeton's graduate school, where I was to spend three happy years. I did not then realize that the 1910 decision to locate the graduate school where it is had been a momentous decision for the twentieth century – and perhaps for the twenty-first as well.

Princeton's decision to locate the graduate school away from the main campus was made against the bitter opposition of the university's president. He often was bitter when others failed to fathom the purity of his motives, his disinterested expertise, and the universality of his principles.

Having lost the argument about locating the graduate school, Woodrow Wilson resigned as Princeton's president and entered politics. Two years later, he was elected America's president. Just nine years after resigning from Princeton, he was sleepless in Paris, troubled by America's responsibility for fine-tuning the Japanese component of the Chinese railway police.

Wilson's spirit still walks the world. That should trouble our sleep.

PART III

NEOCONSERVATIVES AND DOMESTIC POLICY

A CONSERVATIVE WELFARE STATE

Irving Kristol

I shall… assume that the welfare state is with us, for better or worse… What conservatives ought to seek… is a welfare state consistent with the basic moral principles of our civilization and the basic political principles of our nation.

A CONSERVATIVE WELFARE STATE

IRVING KRISTOL

L et me lay down the basic principles – the basic deficiency, some will say – of my approach [to reforming the welfare state]. I shall, to begin with, assume that the welfare state is with us, for better or worse, and that conservatives should try to make it better rather than worse. And I shall pay no attention to the economics of the welfare state, which I regard as a secondary issue. What conservatives ought to seek, first of all, is a welfare state consistent with the basic moral principles of our civilization and the basic political principles of our nation. The essential purpose of politics, after all, is to transmit to our children a civilization and a nation that they can be proud of. This means we should figure out what we want before we calculate what we can afford, not the reverse, which is the normal conservative predisposition. In this respect, public finance differs fundamentally from household economics.

It has long been my opinion that the conservative hostility to social security, derived from a traditional conservative fiscal monomania, leads to political impotence and a bankrupt social policy. Our Social Security System is enormously popular. If the American people want to be generous to their elderly, even to the point of some extravagance, I think it is very nice of them. After all, the elderly are such wonderful, unproblematic citizens. They are patriotic, they do not have illegitimate children, they do not commit crimes, they do not riot in the streets, their popular entertainments are decent rather than degrading, and if they find themselves a bit flush with funds, they happily distribute the money to their grandchildren.

So, in my welfare state, we leave social security alone – except for being a bit more generous, perhaps. Certainly, all restrictions on the earnings of the elderly should be abolished, as a matter of fairness. As for Medicare – well, conservatives believe in honoring thy father and mother, and the Good Book does not say that such honor should be limited only to parents (or grandparents) who are in good health and do not live too long. Medicare's cost is not a conservative problem, except for those conservatives whose Good Book is the annual budget.

As with the elderly, so with children. Ever since World War II, weak-minded and budget-conscious Republican administrations have conspired with liberals to cheat the children of middle-class and working-class households. The income tax deduction for children, now [1993] $2,500, would be $7,500 had it been indexed for inflation. The next Republican administration should address this scandal, giving it the highest priority. The budget consequences are considerable, so perhaps we would want to phase in the indexed increase over a five-year period. But nothing less than that, I would say.

The charms of this reform would, from the conservative point of view, be significant and various. It would be enormously popular, which is no small thing. But it would also be much more than that. These households represent the conservative ideal of the normal household – the household that exemplifies 'family values' – and we wish to encourage such households instead of adding to their financial difficulties, as we have been doing. One could also contemplate unanticipated benefits, instead of the unanticipated ills that are so characteristic of liberal reform. After all, one of the things these parents could do is use the money for the children's education, thereby making 'school choice' an actuality, not merely an advocated possibility.

Now for the more contentious part. It is easy and attractive to discriminate in favor of large sections of the population. It is far less attractive, and makes us all uneasy, to discriminate against any section of the population. Yet such discrimination is absolutely necessary if we are to change the welfare state into something more deserving of that name.

This issue, of 'discriminating against', is most sharply posed when we consider the reform of welfare itself. The problem with our current welfare programs is not that they are costly – which they are – but that they have such perverse consequences for the people they are supposed to benefit. The emergence of a growing and self-perpetuating 'underclass' that makes our cities close to uninhabitable is a demonstrable consequence of the present, liberal-inspired welfare system. The system breeds social pathologies – crime, juvenile delinquency, illegitimacy, drug addiction, and alcoholism, along with the destruction of a once functioning public school system.

The neoliberal response, advocated by Mr. Clinton during his campaign, which calls for 'two years and out' for all able-bodied welfare recipients, is a fantasy. It will not happen. We are not going to see state legislatures and the huge welfare establishment ruthlessly dumping welfare families on to the streets. Public opinion will not stand for it, liberal politicians will not be able to stomach it. It is merely a rhetorical diversionary tactic, and conservatives who are now attracted to it will end up distancing themselves from it as fast as they can. [Irving Kristol was not *always* right, Ed.]

The key to a conservative reform would be (a) to discourage young women from having an illegitimate child in the first place and (b) to discriminate between 'welfare mothers' and 'mothers on welfare'. Such discrimination must have a clear moral basis.

'Mothers on welfare' includes married women with children who have been divorced or widowed or abandoned by their husbands. Most such women have little connection with any kind of underclass. For the most part, they have middle-class aspirations, subscribe to 'family values', and create no intergenerational class of welfare dependents. Their stay on welfare is usually less than two years – they don't like being on welfare. They exit from the welfare population by reason of remarriage or getting a job (sometimes after diligently taking vocational training). They are not a problem population, and deserve our generous assistance as well as our sympathy.

'Welfare mothers', on the other hand, usually end up on welfare as a result of their own actions. Young girls permit themselves to get pregnant, and to bear a child, because the prospect of going on welfare does not frighten them. Welfare permits them to leave homes that are often squalid or worse. It provides them with support, in cash and kind (food stamps, housing allowances, Medicaid), that is in many ways superior to what they could earn working at the minimum wage.

These girls should be made to look upon welfare not as an opportunity, but as a frightening possibility. It follows that they should receive no housing allowance – this is probably the most important change of all. Having your own apartment, in which you can raise your child, can be seen as 'fun'. Living with your child in your parents' home is a lot less alluring. This would especially be the case if the mother received no food stamps and was ineligible for Medicaid. (She would have to rely on the hospital clinic.) The child, on the other hand, would be eligible for food stamps and Medicaid, as well as a children's cash allowance. But the net effect of such reforms would be to reduce the mother's income by 30 per cent to 50 per cent – at which point there is little to be said in favor of welfare, from her point of view. There is, of course, the danger that she won't spend the money on the child. But that is true of the present system as well.

In addition, able-bodied men and mentally healthy men would have no entitlement whatever to welfare. If they are alcoholics or drug addicts or just allergic to responsibilities, they can rely on private charities. (Remember the Salvation Army.) The general rule has to be: if it is your own behavior that could land you on welfare, then you don't get it, or you get very little of it.

Such a reform of welfare as I am proposing will surely be denounced as cruel and 'judgmental'. It would indeed be cruel – and unfair, too – if all those currently on welfare, their situations and characters formed by the current system, were summarily incorporated in the new system. A 'phasing out' procedure would have to be invented. But I would argue that it is crueler to entice people into the blind alley of welfare, where their very humanity is dissipated and degraded, than to sternly warn them off. In social policy, consequences ought always to trump intentions, however benign.

The 'judgmental' issue, however, does get to the heart of the matter. A conservative welfare state should express conservative moral values, just as a liberal welfare state tries to impose liberal moral values upon us. It should discriminate in favor of satisfactory human results, not humane intentions. In the end, the American people will have ample political opportunity to decide what kind of society they wish to live in, what kind of welfare state they wish to live with. But they will never have such a choice if conservatives fail to offer them a conservative vision.

BROKEN WINDOWS
The Police and Neighborhood Safety

James Q. Wilson
and George L. Kelling

We have become accustomed to thinking of the law in essentially individualistic terms... [But] we must return to our long-abandoned view that the police ought to protect communities as well as individuals... [and] recognize the importance of maintaining, intact, communities without broken windows.

BROKEN WINDOWS
The Police and Neighborhood Safety

JAMES Q. WILSON AND GEORGE L. KELLING

In the mid-1970s, the state of New Jersey announced a 'Safe and Clean Neighborhoods Program', designed to improve the quality of community life in twenty-eight cities. As part of that program, the state provided money to help cities take police officers out of their patrol cars and assign them to walking beats. The governor and other state officials were enthusiastic about using foot patrol as a way of cutting crime, but many police chiefs were skeptical. Foot patrol, in their eyes, had been pretty much discredited. It reduced the mobility of the police, who thus had difficulty responding to citizen calls for service, and it weakened headquarters control over patrol officers.

Many police officers also disliked foot patrol, but for different reasons: it was hard work, it kept them outside on cold, rainy nights, and it reduced their chances for making a 'good pinch'. In some departments, assigning officers to foot patrol had been used as a form of punishment. And academic experts on policing doubted that foot patrol would have any impact on crime rates; it was, in the opinion of most, little more than a sop to public opinion. But since the state was paying for it, the local authorities were willing to go along.

Five years after the program started, the Police Foundation, in Washington, D.C., published an evaluation of the foot-patrol project. Based on its analysis of a carefully controlled experiment carried out chiefly in Newark, the foundation concluded, to the surprise of hardly anyone, that foot patrol had not reduced crime rates. But residents of the foot-patrolled neighborhoods seemed to feel more secure than persons in other areas, tended to believe that crime had been reduced, and seemed to take fewer steps to protect themselves from crime (staying at home with the doors locked, for example). Moreover, citizens in the foot-patrol areas had a more favorable opinion of the police than did those living elsewhere. And officers walking beats had higher morale, greater job satisfaction, and a more favorable attitude toward citizens in their neighborhoods than did officers assigned to patrol cars.

These findings may be taken as evidence that the skeptics were right – foot patrol has no effect on crime: it merely fools the citizens into thinking that they are safer. But in our view, and in the view of the authors of the Police Foundation study (of whom Kelling was one), the citizens of Newark were not fooled at all. They knew what the foot-patrol officers were doing, they knew it was different from what motorized officers do, and they knew that having officers walk beats did in fact make their neighborhoods safer.

But how can a neighborhood be 'safer' when the crime rate has not gone down – in fact, may have gone up? Finding the answer requires first that we understand what most often frightens people in public places. Many citizens, of course, are primarily frightened by crime, especially crime involving a sudden, violent attack by a stranger. This risk is very real, in Newark as in many large cities. But we tend to overlook or forget another source of fear – the fear of being bothered by disorderly people. Not violent people, nor, necessarily, criminals, but disreputable or obstreperous or unpredictable people: panhandlers, drunks, addicts, rowdy teenagers, prostitutes, loiterers, the mentally disturbed.

What foot-patrol officers did was to elevate, to the extent they could, the level of public order in these neighborhoods. Though the neighborhoods were predominantly black and the foot patrolmen were mostly white, this 'order-maintenance' function of the police was performed to the general satisfaction of both parties.

One of us (Kelling) spent many hours walking with Newark foot-patrol officers to see how they defined 'order' and what they did to maintain it. One beat was typical: a busy but dilapidated area in the heart of Newark, with many abandoned buildings, marginal shops (several of which prominently displayed knives and straight-edged razors in their windows), one large department store, and, most important, a train station and several major bus stops. Though the area was run-down, its streets were filled with people, because it was a major transportation center. The good order of this area was important not only to those who lived and worked there but also to many others, who had to move through it on their way home, to supermarkets, or to factories.

The people on the street were primarily black; the officer who walked the street was white. The people were made up of 'regulars' and 'strangers'. Regulars included both 'decent folk' and some drunks and derelicts who were always there but who 'knew their place'. Strangers were, well, strangers, and viewed suspiciously, sometimes apprehensively. The officer – call him Kelly – knew who the regulars were, and they knew him. As he saw his job, he was to keep an eye on strangers, and make certain that the disreputable regulars observed some informal but widely understood rules. Drunks and addicts could sit on the stoops, but could not lie down. People could drink on side streets, but not at the main intersection. Bottles had to be in paper bags. Talking to, bothering, or begging from people waiting at the bus stop was strictly forbidden. If a dispute erupted between a businessman and a customer, the businessman was assumed to be right, especially if the customer was a stranger. If a stranger loitered, Kelly would ask him if he had any means of support and what his business was; if he gave unsatisfactory answers, he was sent on his way. Persons who broke the informal rules, especially those who bothered people waiting at bus stops, were arrested for vagrancy. Noisy teenagers were told to keep quiet.

These rules were defined and enforced in collaboration with the 'regulars' on the street. Another neighborhood might have different rules, but these, everybody understood, were the rules for *this* neighborhood. If someone violated them, the regulars not only turned to Kelly for help but also ridiculed the violator. Sometimes what Kelly did could be described as 'enforcing the law', but just as often it involved taking informal or extra-legal steps to help protect what the neighborhood had decided was the appropriate level of public order. Some of the things he did probably would not withstand a legal challenge.

A determined skeptic might acknowledge that a skilled foot-patrol officer can maintain order but still insist that this sort of 'order' has little to do with the real sources of community fear – that is, with violent crime. To a degree, that is true. But two things must be borne in mind. First, outside observers should not assume that they know how much of the anxiety now endemic in many big-city neighborhoods stems from a fear of 'real' crime and how much from a sense that the street is disorderly, a source of distasteful, worrisome encounters. The people of Newark, to judge from their behavior and their remarks to interviewers, apparently assign a high value to public order, and feel relieved and reassured when the police help them maintain that order.

Second, at the community level, disorder and crime are usually inextricably linked, in a kind of developmental sequence. Social psychologists and police officers tend to agree that if a window in a building is broken *and is left unrepaired*, all the rest of the windows will soon be broken. This is as true in nice neighborhoods as in run-down ones. Window-breaking does not necessarily occur on a large scale because some areas are inhabited by determined window-breakers whereas others are populated by window-lovers; rather, one unrepaired broken window is a signal that no one cares, and so breaking more windows costs nothing. (It has always been fun.)

Philip Zimbardo, a Stanford psychologist, reported in 1969 on some experiments testing the broken-window theory. He arranged to have an automobile without license plates parked with its hood up on a street in the Bronx and a comparable automobile on a street in Palo Alto, California. The car in the Bronx was attacked by 'vandals' within ten minutes of its 'abandonment'. The first to arrive were a family – father, mother, and young son – who removed the radiator and battery. Within twenty-four hours, virtually everything of value had been removed. Then random destruction began – windows were smashed, parts torn off, upholstery ripped. Children began to use the car as a playground. Most of the adult 'vandals' were well-dressed, apparently clean-cut whites. The car in Palo Alto sat untouched for more than a week. Then Zimbardo smashed part of it with a sledgehammer. Soon, passers-by were joining in. Within a few hours, the car had been turned upside down and utterly destroyed. Again, the 'vandals' appeared to be primarily respectable whites.

Untended property becomes fair game for people out for fun or plunder, and even for people who ordinarily would not dream of doing such things and who probably consider themselves law-abiding. Because of the nature of community life in the Bronx – its anonymity, the frequency with which cars are abandoned and things are stolen or broken, the past experience of 'no one caring' – vandalism begins much more quickly than it does in staid Palo Alto, where people have come to believe that private possessions are cared for, and that mischievous behavior is costly. But vandalism can occur anywhere once communal barriers – the sense of mutual regard and the obligations of civility – are lowered by actions that seem to signal that 'no one cares'.

We suggest that 'untended' behavior also leads to the breakdown of community controls. A stable neighborhood of families who care for their homes, mind each other's children, and confidently frown on unwanted intruders can change, in a few years or even a few months, to an inhospitable and frightening jungle. A piece of property is abandoned, weeds grow up, a window is smashed. Adults stop scolding rowdy children; the children, emboldened, become more rowdy. Families move out, unattached adults move in. Teenagers gather in front of the corner store. The merchant asks them to move; they refuse. Fights occur. Litter accumulates. People start drinking in front of the grocery; in time, an inebriate slumps to the sidewalk and is allowed to sleep it off. Pedestrians are approached by panhandlers.

At this point it is not inevitable that serious crime will flourish or violent attacks on strangers will occur. But many residents will think that crime, especially violent crime, is on the rise, and they will modify their behavior accordingly. They will use the streets less often, and when on the streets will stay apart from their fellows, moving with averted eyes, silent lips, and hurried steps. 'Don't get involved.' For some residents, this growing atomization will matter little, because the neighborhood is not their 'home' but 'the place where they live'. Their interests are elsewhere; they are cosmopolitans. But it will matter greatly to other people, whose lives derive meaning and satisfaction from local attachments rather than worldly involvement; for them, the neighborhood will cease to exist except for a few reliable friends whom they arrange to meet.

Such an area is vulnerable to criminal invasion. Though it is not inevitable, it is more likely that here, rather than in places where people are confident they can regulate public behavior by informal controls, drugs will change hands, prostitutes will solicit, and cars will be stripped. That the drunks will be robbed by boys who do it as a lark, and the prostitutes' customers will be robbed by men who do it purposefully and perhaps violently. That muggings will occur.

Among those who often find it difficult to move away from this are the elderly. Surveys of citizens suggest that the elderly are much less likely to be the victims of crime than younger persons, and some have inferred from this that the well-known fear of crime voiced by the elderly is an exaggeration: perhaps we ought not to design special programs to protect older persons; perhaps we should even try to talk them out of their mistaken fears. This argument misses the point. The prospect of a confrontation with an obstreperous teenager or a drunken panhandler can be as fear-inducing for defenseless persons as the prospect of meeting an actual robber; indeed, to a defenseless person, the two kinds of confrontation are often indistinguishable. Moreover, the lower rate at which the elderly are victimized is a measure of the steps they have already taken – chiefly, staying behind locked doors – to minimize the risks they face. Young men are more frequently attacked than older women, not because they are easier or more lucrative targets but because they are on the streets more.

Nor is the connection between disorderliness and fear made only by the elderly. Susan Estrich, of the Harvard Law School, has recently gathered together a number of surveys on the sources of public fear. One, done in Portland, Oregon, indicated that three-fourths of the adults interviewed cross to the other side of a street when they see a gang of teenagers; another survey, in Baltimore, discovered that nearly half would cross the street to avoid even a single strange youth. When an interviewer asked people in a housing project where the most dangerous spot was, they mentioned a place where young persons gathered to drink and play music, despite the fact that not a single crime had occurred there. In Boston public housing projects, the greatest fear was expressed by persons living in the buildings where disorderliness and incivility, not crime, were the greatest. Knowing this helps one understand the significance of such otherwise harmless displays as subway graffiti. As Nathan Glazer has written, the proliferation of graffiti, even when not obscene, confronts the subway rider with the 'inescapable knowledge that the environment he must endure for an hour or more a day is uncontrolled and uncontrollable, and that anyone can invade it to do whatever damage and mischief the mind suggests'.

In response to fear, people avoid one another, weakening controls. Sometimes they call the police. Patrol cars arrive, an occasional arrest occurs, but crime continues and disorder is not abated. Citizens complain to the police chief, but he explains that his department is low on personnel and that the courts do not punish petty or first-time offenders. To the residents, the police who arrive in squad cars are either ineffective or uncaring; to the police, the residents are animals who deserve each other. The citizens may soon stop calling the police, because 'they can't do anything'.

The process we call urban decay has occurred for centuries in every city. But what is happening today is different in at least two important respects. First, in the period before, say, World War II, city dwellers – because of money costs, transportation difficulties, familial and church connections – could rarely move away from neighborhood problems. When movement did occur, it tended to be along public-transit routes. Now mobility has become exceptionally easy for all but the poorest or those who are blocked by racial prejudice. Earlier crime waves had a kind of built-in self-correcting mechanism: the determination of a neighborhood or community to reassert control over its turf. Areas in Chicago, New York, and Boston would experience crime and gang wars, and then normalcy would return, as the families for whom no alternative residences were possible reclaimed their authority over the streets.

Second, the police in this earlier period assisted in that reassertion of authority by acting, sometimes violently, on behalf of the community. Young toughs were roughed up, people were arrested 'on suspicion' or for vagrancy, and prostitutes and petty thieves were routed. 'Rights' were something enjoyed by decent folk, and perhaps also by the serious professional criminal, who avoided violence and could afford a lawyer.

This pattern of policing was not an aberration or the result of occasional excess. From the earliest days of the nation, the police function was seen primarily as that of a night watchman: to maintain order against the chief threats to order – fire, wild animals, and disreputable behavior. Solving crimes was viewed not as a police responsibility but as a private one. In the March 1969 *Atlantic*, one of us (Wilson) wrote a brief account of how the police role had slowly changed from maintaining order to fighting crimes. The change began with the creation of private detectives (often ex-criminals), who worked on a contingency-fee basis for individuals who had suffered losses. In time, the detectives were absorbed into municipal police agencies and paid a regular salary; simultaneously, the responsibility for prosecuting thieves was shifted from the aggrieved private citizen to the professional prosecutor. This process was not complete in most places until the twentieth century.

In the 1960s, when urban riots were a major problem, social scientists began to explore carefully the order-maintenance function of the police, and to suggest ways of improving it – not to make streets safer (its original function) but to reduce the incidence of mass violence. Order-maintenance became, to a degree, coterminous with 'community relations'. But, as the crime wave that began in the early 1960s continued without abatement throughout the decade and into the 1970s, attention shifted to the role of the police as crime-fighters. Studies of police behavior ceased, by and large, to be accounts of the order-maintenance function and became, instead, efforts to propose and test ways whereby the police could solve more crimes, make more arrests, and gather better evidence. If these things could be done, social scientists assumed, citizens would be less fearful.

A great deal was accomplished during this transition, as both police chiefs and outside experts emphasized the crime-fighting function in their plans, in the allocation of resources, and in deployment of personnel. The police may well have become better crime-fighters as a result. And doubtless they remained aware of their responsibility for order. But the link between order-maintenance and crime-prevention, so obvious to earlier generations, was forgotten.

That link is similar to the process whereby one broken window becomes many. The citizen who fears the ill-smelling drunk, the rowdy teenager, or the importuning beggar is not merely expressing his distaste for unseemly behavior; he is also giving voice to a bit of folk wisdom that happens to be a correct generalization – namely, that serious street crime flourishes in areas in which disorderly behavior goes unchecked. The unchecked panhandler is, in effect, the first broken window. Muggers and robbers, whether opportunistic or professional, believe they reduce their chances of being caught or even identified if they operate on streets where potential victims are already intimidated by prevailing conditions. If the neighborhood cannot keep a bothersome panhandler from annoying passers-by, the thief may reason, it is even less likely to call the police to identify a potential mugger or to interfere if the mugging actually takes place.

Some police administrators concede that this process occurs, but argue that motorized-patrol officers can deal with it as effectively as foot-patrol officers. We are not so sure. In theory, an officer in a squad car can observe as much as an officer on foot; in theory, the former can talk to as many people as the latter. But the reality of police–citizen encounters is powerfully altered by the automobile. An officer on foot cannot separate himself from the street people; if he is approached, only his uniform and his personality can help him manage whatever is about to happen. And he can never be certain what that will be – a request for directions, a plea for help, an angry denunciation, a teasing remark, a confused babble, a threatening gesture.

In a car, an officer is more likely to deal with street people by rolling down the window and looking at them. The door and the window exclude the approaching citizen; they are a barrier. Some officers take advantage of this barrier, perhaps unconsciously, by acting differently if in the car than they would on foot. We have seen this countless times. The police car pulls up to a corner where teenagers are gathered. The window is rolled down. The officer stares at the youths. They stare back. The officer says to one, 'C'mere.' He saunters over, conveying to his friends by his elaborately casual style the idea that he is not intimidated by authority. 'What's your name?'

'Chuck.'

'Chuck who?'

'Chuck Jones.'

'What'ya doing, Chuck?'

'Nothin'.'

'Got a PO [parole officer]?'

'Nah.'

'Sure?'

'Yeah.'

'Stay out of trouble, Chuckie.'

Meanwhile, the other boys laugh and exchange comments among themselves, probably at the officer's expense. The officer stares harder. He cannot be certain what is being said, nor can he join in and, by displaying his own skill at street banter, prove that he cannot be 'put down'. In the process, the officer has learned almost nothing and the boys have decided the officer is an alien force who can safely be disregarded, even mocked.

Our experience is that most citizens like to talk to a police officer. Such exchanges give them a sense of importance, provide them with the basis for gossip, and allow them to explain to the authorities what is worrying them (whereby they gain a modest but significant sense of having 'done something' about the problem). You approach a person on foot more easily, and talk to him more readily, than you do a person in a car. Moreover, you can more easily retain some anonymity if you draw an officer aside for a private chat. Suppose you want to pass on a tip about who is stealing handbags, or who offered to sell you a stolen TV. In the inner city, the culprit, in all likelihood, lives near by. To walk up to a marked patrol car and lean in the window is to convey a visible signal that you are a 'fink'.

The essence of the police role in maintaining order is to reinforce the informal control mechanisms of the community itself. The police cannot, without committing extraordinary resources, provide a substitute for that informal control. On the other hand, to reinforce those natural forces the police must accommodate them. And therein lies the problem.

Should police activity on the street be shaped, in important ways, by the standards of the neighborhood rather than by the rules of the State? Over the past two decades, the shift of police from order-maintenance to law-enforcement has brought them increasingly under the influence of legal restrictions, provoked by media complaints and enforced by court decisions and departmental orders. As a consequence, the order-maintenance functions of the police are now governed by rules developed to control police relations with suspected criminals. This is, we think, an entirely new development. For centuries, the role of the police as watchmen was judged primarily not in terms of its compliance with appropriate procedures but rather in terms of its attaining a desired objective. The objective was order, an inherently ambiguous term but a condition that people in a given community recognized when they saw it. The means were the same as those the community itself would employ, if its members were sufficiently determined, courageous, and authoritative. Detecting and apprehending criminals, by contrast, was a means to an end, not an end in itself; a judicial determination of guilt or innocence was the hoped-for result of the law-enforcement mode. From the first, the police were expected to follow rules defining that process, though states differed in how stringent the rules should be. The criminal-apprehension process was always understood to involve individual rights, the violation of which was unacceptable because it meant that the violating officer would be acting as a judge and jury – and that was not his job. Guilt or innocence was to be determined by universal standards under special procedures.

Ordinarily, no judge or jury ever sees the persons caught up in a dispute over the appropriate level of neighborhood order. That is true not only because most cases are handled informally on the street but also because no universal standards are available to settle arguments over disorder, and thus a judge may not be any wiser or more effective than a police officer. Until quite recently in many states, and even today in some places, the police make arrests on such charges as 'suspicious person' or 'vagrancy' or 'public drunkenness' – charges with scarcely any legal meaning. These charges exist not because society wants judges to punish vagrants or drunks but because it wants an officer to have the legal tools to remove undesirable persons from a neighborhood when informal efforts to preserve order in the streets have failed.

Once we begin to think of all aspects of police work as involving the application of universal rules under special procedures, we inevitably ask what constitutes an 'undesirable person' and why we should 'criminalize' vagrancy or drunkenness. A strong and commendable desire to see that people are treated fairly makes us worry about allowing the police to rout persons who are undesirable by some vague or parochial standard. A growing and not-so-commendable utilitarianism leads us to doubt that any behavior that does not 'hurt' another person should be made illegal. And thus many of us who watch over the police are reluctant to allow them to perform, in the only way they can, a function that every neighborhood desperately wants them to perform.

This wish to 'decriminalize' disreputable behavior that 'harms no one' – and thus remove the ultimate sanction the police can employ to maintain neighborhood order – is, we think, a mistake. Arresting a single drunk or a single vagrant who has harmed no identifiable person seems unjust, and in a sense it is. But failing to do anything about a score of drunks or a hundred vagrants may destroy an entire community. A particular rule that seems to make sense in the individual case makes no sense when it is made a universal rule and applied to all cases. It makes no sense because it fails to take into account the connection between one broken window left untended and a thousand broken windows. Of course, agencies other than the police could attend to the problems posed by drunks or the mentally ill, but in most communities – especially where the 'deinstitutionalization' movement has been strong – they do not.

The concern about equity is more serious. We might agree that certain behavior makes one person more undesirable than another, but how do we ensure that age or skin color or national origin or harmless mannerisms will not also become the basis for distinguishing the undesirable from the desirable? How do we ensure, in short, that the police do not become the agents of neighborhood bigotry?

We can offer no wholly satisfactory answer to this important question. We are not confident that there *is* a satisfactory answer, except to hope that by their selection, training, and supervision, the police will be inculcated with a clear sense of the outer limit of their discretionary authority. That limit, roughly, is this – the police exist to help regulate behavior, not to maintain the racial or ethnic purity of a neighborhood.

Consider the case of the Robert Taylor Homes in Chicago, one of the largest public-housing projects in the country. It is home for nearly 20,000 people, all black, and extends over ninety-two acres along South State Street. It was named after a distinguished black who had been, during the 1940s, chairman of the Chicago Housing Authority. Not long after it opened, in 1962, relations between project residents and the police deteriorated badly. The citizens felt that the police were insensitive or brutal; the police, in turn, complained of unprovoked attacks on them. Some Chicago officers tell of times when they were afraid to enter the Homes. Crime rates soared.

Today, the atmosphere has changed. Police–citizen relations have improved – apparently, both sides learned something from the earlier experience. Recently, a boy stole a purse and ran off. Several young persons who saw the theft voluntarily passed along to the police information on the identity and residence of the thief, and they did this publicly, with friends and neighbors looking on. But problems persist, chief among them the presence of youth gangs that terrorize residents and recruit members in the project. The people expect the police to 'do something' about this, and the police are determined to do just that.

But do what? Though the police can obviously make arrests whenever a gang member breaks the law, a gang can form, recruit, and congregate without breaking the law. And only a tiny fraction of gang-related crimes can be solved by an arrest; thus, if an arrest is the only recourse for the police, the residents' fears will go unassuaged. The police will soon feel helpless, and the residents will again believe that the police 'do nothing'. What the police in fact do is to chase known gang members out of the project. In the words of one officer, 'We kick ass.' Project residents both know and approve of this. The tacit police–citizen alliance in the project is reinforced by the police view that the cops and the gangs are the two rival sources of power in the area, and that the gangs are not going to win.

None of this is easily reconciled with any conception of due process or fair treatment. Since both residents and gang members are black, race is not a factor. But it could be. Suppose a white project confronted a black gang, or vice versa. We would be apprehensive about the police taking sides. But the substantive problem remains the same: how can the police strengthen the informal social-control mechanisms of natural communities in order to minimize fear in public places? Law enforcement, per se, is no answer. A gang can weaken or destroy a community by standing about in a menacing fashion and speaking rudely to passers-by without breaking the law.

We have difficulty thinking about such matters, not simply because the ethical and legal issues are so complex but because we have become accustomed to thinking of the law in essentially individualistic terms. The law defines *my* rights, punishes *his* behavior, and is applied by *that* officer because of *this* harm. We assume, in thinking this way, that what is good for the individual will be good for the community, and what doesn't matter when it happens to one person won't matter if it happens to many. Ordinarily, those are plausible assumptions. But in cases where behavior that is tolerable to one person is intolerable to many others, the reactions of the others – fear, withdrawal, flight – may ultimately make matters worse for everyone, including the individual who first professed his indifference.

It may be their greater sensitivity to communal as opposed to individual needs that helps explain why the residents of small communities are more satisfied with their police than are the residents of similar neighborhoods in big cities. Elinor Ostrom and her co-workers at Indiana University compared the perception of police services in two poor, all-black Illinois towns – Phoenix and East Chicago Heights – with those of three comparable all-black neighborhoods in Chicago. The level of criminal victimization and the quality of police–community relations appeared to be about the same in the towns and the Chicago neighborhoods. But the citizens living in their own villages were much more likely than those living in the Chicago neighborhoods to say that they do not stay at home for fear of crime, to agree that the local police have 'the right to take any action necessary' to deal with problems, and to agree that the police 'look out for the needs of the average citizen'. It is possible that the residents and the police of the small towns saw themselves as engaged in a collaborative effort to maintain a certain standard of communal life, whereas those of the big city felt themselves to be simply requesting and supplying particular services on an individual basis.

If this is true, how should a wise police chief deploy his meager forces? The first answer is that nobody knows for certain, and the most prudent course of action would be to try further variations on the Newark experiment, to see more precisely what works in what kinds of neighborhoods. The second answer is also a hedge – many aspects of order-maintenance in neighborhoods can probably best be handled in ways that involve the police minimally, if at all. A busy, bustling shopping center and a quiet, well-tended suburb may need almost no visible police presence. In both cases, the ratio of respectable to disreputable people is ordinarily so high as to make informal social control effective.

Even in areas that are in jeopardy from disorderly elements, citizen action without substantial police involvement may be sufficient. Meetings between teenagers who like to hang out on a particular corner and adults who want to use that corner might well lead to an amicable agreement on a set of rules about how many people can be allowed to congregate, where, and when.

Where no understanding is possible – or if possible, not observed – citizen patrols may be a sufficient response. There are two traditions of communal involvement in maintaining order. One, that of the 'community watchmen', is as old as the first settlement of the New World. Until well into the nineteenth century, volunteer watchmen, not policemen, patrolled their communities to keep order. They did so, by and large, without taking the law into their own hands – without, that is, punishing persons or using force. Their presence deterred disorder or alerted the community to disorder that could not be deterred. There are hundreds of such efforts today in communities all across the nation. Perhaps the best known is that of the Guardian Angels, a group of unarmed young persons in distinctive berets and T-shirts, who first came to public attention when they began patrolling the New York City subways but who claim now to have chapters in more than thirty American cities. Unfortunately, we have little information about the effect of these groups on crime. It is possible, however, that whatever their effect on crime, citizens find their presence reassuring, and that they thus contribute to maintaining a sense of order and civility.

The second tradition is that of the 'vigilante'. Rarely a feature of the settled communities of the East, it was primarily to be found in those frontier towns that grew up in advance of the reach of government. More than 350 vigilante groups are known to have existed; their distinctive feature was that their members did take the law into their own hands, by acting as judge, jury, and often executioner as well as policeman. Today, the vigilante movement is conspicuous by its rarity, despite the great fear expressed by citizens that the older cities are becoming 'urban frontiers'. But some community-watchmen groups have skirted the line, and others may cross it in the future. An ambiguous case, reported in *The Wall Street Journal*, involved a citizens' patrol in the Silver Lake area of Belleville, New Jersey. A leader told the reporter, 'We look for outsiders.' If a few teenagers from outside the neighborhood enter it, 'We ask them their business,' he said. 'If they say they're going down the street to see Mrs. Jones, fine, we let them pass. But then we follow them down the block to make sure they're really going to see Mrs. Jones.'

Though citizens can do a great deal, the police are plainly the key to order-maintenance. For one thing, many communities, such as the Robert Taylor Homes, cannot do the job by themselves. For another, no citizen in a neighborhood, even an organized one, is likely to feel the sense of responsibility that wearing a badge confers. Psychologists have done many studies on why people fail to go to the aid of persons being attacked or seeking help, and they have learned that the cause is not 'apathy' or 'selfishness' but the absence of some plausible grounds for feeling that one must personally accept responsibility. Ironically, avoiding responsibility is easier when a lot of people are standing about. On streets and in public places, where order is so important, many people are likely to be 'around', a fact that reduces the chance of any one person acting as the agent of the community. The police officer's uniform singles him out as a person who must accept responsibility if asked. In addition, officers, more easily than their fellow citizens, can be expected to distinguish between what is necessary to protect the safety of the street and what merely protects its ethnic purity.

But the police forces of America are losing, not gaining, members. Some cities have suffered substantial cuts in the number of officers available for duty. These cuts are not likely to be reversed in the near future. Therefore, each department must assign its existing officers with great care. Some neighborhoods are so demoralized and crime-ridden as to make foot patrol useless; the best the police can do with limited resources is respond to the enormous number of calls for service. Other neighborhoods are so stable and serene as to make foot patrol unnecessary. The key is to identify neighborhoods at the tipping point – where the public order is deteriorating but not unreclaimable, where the streets are used frequently but by apprehensive people, where a window is likely to be broken at any time, and must quickly be fixed if all are not to be shattered.

Most police departments do not have ways of systematically identifying such areas and assigning officers to them. Officers are assigned on the basis of crime rates (meaning that marginally threatened areas are often stripped so that police can investigate crimes in areas where the situation is hopeless) or on the basis of calls for service (despite the fact that most citizens do not call the police when they are merely frightened or annoyed). To allocate patrol wisely, the department must look at the neighborhoods and decide, from first-hand evidence, where an additional officer will make the greatest difference in promoting a sense of safety.

One way to stretch limited police resources is being tried in some public-housing projects. Tenant organizations hire off-duty police officers for patrol work in their buildings. The costs are not high (at least not per resident), the officer likes the additional income, and the residents feel safer. Such arrangements are probably more successful than hiring private watchmen, and the Newark experiment helps us understand why. A private security guard may deter crime or misconduct by his presence, and he may go to the aid of persons needing help, but he may well not intervene – that is, control or drive away – someone challenging community standards. Being a sworn officer – a 'real cop' – seems to give one the confidence, the sense of duty, and the aura of authority necessary to perform this difficult task.

Patrol officers might be encouraged to go to and from duty stations on public transportation and, while on the bus or subway car, enforce rules about smoking, drinking, disorderly conduct, and the like. The enforcement need involve nothing more than ejecting the offender (the offense, after all, is not one with which a booking officer or a judge wishes to be bothered). Perhaps the random but relentless maintenance of standards on buses would lead to conditions on buses that approximate the level of civility we now take for granted on airplanes.

But the most important requirement is to think that to maintain order in precarious situations is a vital job. The police know this is one of their functions, and they also believe, correctly, that it cannot be done to the exclusion of criminal investigation and responding to calls. We may have encouraged them to suppose, however, on the basis of our oft-repeated concerns about serious, violent crime, that they will be judged exclusively on their capacity as crime-fighters. To the extent that this is the case, police administrators will continue to concentrate police personnel in the highest-crime areas (though not necessarily in the areas most vulnerable to criminal invasion), emphasize their training in the law and criminal apprehension (and not their training in managing street life), and join too quickly in campaigns to decriminalize 'harmless' behavior (though public drunkenness, street prostitution, and pornographic displays can destroy a community more quickly than any team of professional burglars).

Above all, we must return to our long-abandoned view that the police ought to protect communities as well as individuals. Our crime statistics and victimization surveys measure individual losses, but they do not measure communal losses. Just as physicians now recognize the importance of fostering health rather than simply treating illness, so the police – and the rest of us – ought to recognize the importance of maintaining, intact, communities without broken windows.

PORNOGRAPHY, OBSCENITY, AND THE CASE FOR CENSORSHIP

Irving Kristol

Today... , censorship has to all intents and purposes ceased
to exist... I think the settlement we are living under now, in
which obscenity and democracy are regarded as equals is wrong...
[and] incompatible with any authentic concern for the quality
of life in a democracy.

PORNOGRAPHY, OBSCENITY, AND THE CASE FOR CENSORSHIP

IRVING KRISTOL

B eing frustrated is disagreeable, but the real disasters in life begin when you get what you want. For almost a century now, a great many intelligent, well-meaning, and articulate people – of a kind generally called liberal or intellectual, or both – have argued eloquently against any kind of censorship of art and/or entertainment. And within the past ten years, the courts and the legislatures of most Western nations have found these arguments persuasive – so persuasive that hardly a man is now alive who clearly remembers what the answers to these arguments were. Today, in the United States and other democracies, censorship has to all intents and purposes ceased to exist.

Is there a sense of triumphant exhilaration in the land? Hardly. There is, on the contrary, a rapidly growing unease and disquiet. Somehow, things have not worked out as they were supposed to, and many notable civil libertarians have gone on record as saying this was not what they meant at all. They wanted a world in which *Desire under the Elms* could be produced, or *Ulysses* published, without interference by philistine busybodies holding public office. They have got that, of course; but they have also got a world in which homosexual rape takes place on the stage, in which the public flocks during lunch hours to witness varieties of professional fornication, in which Times Square has become little more than a hideous market for the sale and distribution of printed filth that panders to all known (and some fanciful) sexual perversions. [Times Square has since been transformed into a respectable business district, Ed.].

But disagreeable as this may be, does it really matter? Might not our unease and disquiet be merely a cultural hangover – a 'hang-up', as they say? What reason is there to think that anyone was ever corrupted by a book?

This last question, oddly enough, is asked by the very same people who seem convinced that advertisements in magazines or displays of violence on television do indeed have the power to corrupt. It is also asked, incredibly enough and in all sincerity, by people – for example, university professors and schoolteachers – whose very lives provide all the answers one could want. After all, if you believe that no one was ever corrupted by a book, you have also to believe that no one was ever improved by a book (or a play or a movie). You have to believe, in other words, that all art is morally trivial and that, consequently, all education is morally irrelevant. No one, not even a university professor, really believes that.

To be sure, it is extremely difficult, as social scientists tell us, to trace the effects of any single book (or play or movie) on an individual reader or any class of readers. But we all know, and social scientists know it too, that the ways in which we use our minds and imaginations do shape our characters and help define us as persons. That those who certainly know this are nevertheless moved to deny it merely indicates how a dogmatic resistance to the idea of censorship can – like most dogmatism – result in a mindless insistence on the absurd.

I have used these harsh terms – 'dogmatism' and 'mindless' – advisedly. I might also have added 'hypocritical'. For the plain fact is that none of us is a complete civil libertarian. We all believe that there is some point at which the public authorities ought to step in to limit the 'self-expression' of an individual or a group, even where this might be seriously intended as a form of artistic expression, and even where the artistic transaction is between consenting adults. A playwright or theatrical director might, in this crazy world of ours, find someone willing to commit suicide on the stage, as called for by the script. We would not allow that – any more than we would permit scenes of real physical torture on the stage, even if the victim were a willing masochist. And I know of no one, no matter how free in spirit, who argues that we ought to permit gladiatorial contests in Yankee Stadium, similar to those once performed in the Colosseum at Rome – even if only consenting adults were involved.

The basic point that emerges is one that Walter Berns has powerfully argued: no society can be utterly indifferent to the ways its citizens publicly entertain themselves.[*] Bear-baiting and cockfighting are prohibited only in part out of compassion for the suffering animals; the main reason they were abolished was because it was felt that they debased and brutalized the citizenry who flocked to witness such spectacles. And the question we face with regard to pornography and obscenity is whether, now that they have such strong legal

---

[*] This is as good a place as any to express my profound indebtedness to Walter Berns's superb essay 'Pornography vs. Democracy', in the Winter 1971 issue of *The Public Interest*.

protection from the Supreme Court, they can or will brutalize and debase our citizenry. We are, after all, not dealing with one passing incident – one book, or one play, or one movie. We are dealing with a general tendency that is suffusing our entire culture.

I say pornography *and* obscenity because, though they have different dictionary definitions and are frequently distinguishable as 'artistic' genres, they are nevertheless in the end identical in effect. Pornography is not objectionable simply because it arouses sexual desire or lust or prurience in the mind of the reader or spectator; this is a silly Victorian notion. A great many non-pornographic works – including some parts of the Bible – excite sexual desire very successfully. What is distinctive about pornography is that, in the words of D. H. Lawrence, it attempts 'to do dirt on [sex]... [It is an] insult to a vital human relationship.'

In other words, pornography differs from erotic art in that its whole purpose is to treat human beings obscenely, to deprive human beings of their specifically human dimension. That is what obscenity is all about. It is light years removed from any kind of carefree sensuality – there is no continuum between Fielding's *Tom Jones* and the Marquis de Sade's *Justine*. These works have quite opposite intentions. To quote Susan Sontag: 'What pornographic literature does is precisely to drive a wedge between one's existence as a full human being and one's existence as a sexual being – while in ordinary life a healthy person is one who prevents such a gap from opening up.' This definition occurs in an essay *defending* pornography – Miss Sontag is a candid as well as gifted critic – so the definition, which I accept, is neither tendentious nor censorious.

Along these same lines, one can point out – as C. S. Lewis pointed out some years back – that it is no accident that in the history of all literatures obscene words, the so-called four-letter words, have always been the vocabulary of farce or vituperation. The reason is clear; they reduce men and women to some of their mere bodily functions – they reduce man to his animal component, and such a reduction is an essential purpose of farce or vituperation.

Similarly, Lewis also suggested that it is not an accident that we have no offhand, colloquial, neutral terms – not in any Western European language at any rate – for our most private parts. The words we do use are either (1) nursery terms, (2) archaisms, (3) scientific terms, or (4) a term from the gutter (i.e., a demeaning term). Here I think the genius of language is telling us something important about man. It is telling us that man is an animal with a difference: he has a unique sense of privacy, and a unique capacity for shame when this privacy is violated. Our 'private parts' are indeed private, and not merely because convention prescribes it. This particular convention is indigenous to the human race. In practically all primitive tribes, men and women cover their private parts; and in practically all primitive tribes, men and women do not copulate in public.

It may well be that Western society, in the latter half of the twentieth century, is experiencing a drastic change in sexual mores and sexual relationships. We have had many such 'sexual revolutions' in the past – the bourgeois family and bourgeois ideas of sexual propriety were themselves established in the course of a revolution against eighteenth-century 'licentiousness' – and we shall doubtless have others in the future. It is, however, highly improbable (to put it mildly) that what we are witnessing is the Final Revolution which will make sexual relations utterly unproblematic, permit us to dispense with any kind of ordered relationships between the sexes, and allow us freely to redefine the human condition. And so long as humanity has not reached that utopia, obscenity will remain a problem.

One of the reasons it will remain a problem is that obscenity is not merely about sex, any more than science fiction is about science. Science fiction, as every student of the genre knows, is a peculiar vision of power: what it is really about is politics. And obscenity is a peculiar vision of humanity: what it is really about is ethics and metaphysics.

Imagine a man – a well-known man, much in the public eye – in a hospital ward, dying an agonizing death. He is not in control of his bodily functions, so that his bladder and his bowels empty themselves of their own accord. His consciousness is overwhelmed and extinguished by pain, so that he cannot communicate with us, nor we with him. Now, it would be, technically, the easiest thing in the world to put a television camera in his hospital room and let the whole world witness this spectacle. We do not do it – at least we do not do it as yet – because we regard this as an *obscene* invasion of privacy. And what would make the spectacle obscene is that we would be witnessing the extinguishing of humanity in a human animal.

Incidentally, in the past our humanitarian crusaders against capital punishment understood this point very well. The abolitionist literature goes into great physical detail about what happens to a man when he is hanged or electrocuted or gassed. And their argument was – and is – that what happens is shockingly obscene, and that no civilized society should be responsible for perpetrating such obscenities, particularly since in the nature of the case there must be spectators to ascertain that this horror was indeed being perpetrated in fulfillment of the law.

Sex – like death – is an activity that is both animal and human. There are human sentiments and human ideals involved in this animal activity. But when sex is public, the viewer does not see – cannot see – the sentiments and the ideals. He can only see the animal coupling. And that is why, when men and women make love, as we say, they prefer to be alone – because it is only when you are alone that you can make love, as distinct from merely copulating in an animal and casual way. And that, too, is why those who are voyeurs, if they are not irredeemably sick, also feel ashamed at what they are witnessing. When sex is a public spectacle, a human relationship has been debased into a mere animal connection.

It is also worth noting that this making of sex into an obscenity is not a mutual and equal transaction but rather an act of exploitation by one of the partners – the male partner. I do not wish to get into the complicated question as to what, if any, are the essential differences – as distinct from conventional and cultural differences – between male and female. I do not claim to know the answer to that. But I do know – and I take it as a sign that has meaning – that pornography is, and always has been, a man's work; that women rarely write pornography; and that women tend to be indifferent consumers of pornography.* My own guess, by way of explanation, is that a woman's sexual experience is ordinarily more suffused with human emotion than is man's, that men are more easily satisfied with autoerotic activities, and that men can therefore more easily take a more 'technocratic' view of sex and its pleasures. Perhaps this is not correct. But whatever the explanation, there can be no question that pornography is a form of 'sexism', as the women's liberation movement calls it, and that the instinct of women's liberation has been unerring in perceiving that when pornography is perpetrated, it is perpetrated against them, as part of a conspiracy to deprive them of their full humanity.

But even if all this is granted, it might be said – and doubtless will be said – that I really ought not to be unduly concerned. Free competition in the cultural marketplace – it is argued by people who have never otherwise had a kind word to say for laissez-faire – will automatically dispose of the problem. The present fad for pornography and obscenity, it will be asserted, is just that, a fad. It will spend itself in the course of time; people will get bored with it, will be able to take it or leave it alone in a casual way, in a 'mature way', and,

---

* There are, of course, a few exceptions. *L'Histoire d'O*, for instance, was written by a woman. It is unquestionably the most *melancholy* work of pornography ever written. And its theme is precisely the dehumanization accomplished by obscenity.

in sum, I am being unnecessarily distressed about the whole business. *The New York Times*, in an editorial, concludes hopefully in this vein. 'In the end... the insensate pursuit of the urge to shock, carried from one excess to a more abysmal one, is bound to achieve its own antidote in total boredom. When there is no lower depth to descend to, ennui will erase the problem.' I would like to be able to go along with this line of reasoning, but I cannot. I think it is false, and for two reasons, the first psychological, the second political.

The basic psychological fact about pornography and obscenity is that it appeals to and provokes a kind of sexual regression. The sexual pleasure one gets from pornography and obscenity is autoerotic and infantile; put bluntly, it is a masturbatory exercise of the imagination, when it is not masturbation pure and simple. Now, people who masturbate do not get bored with masturbation, just as sadists do not get bored with sadism, and voyeurs do not get bored with voyeurism.

In other words, infantile sexuality is not only a permanent temptation for the adolescent or even the adult – it can quite easily become a permanent, self-reinforcing neurosis. It is because of an awareness of this possibility of regression toward the infantile condition, a regression which is always open to us, that all the codes of sexual conduct ever devised by the human race take such a dim view of autoerotic activities and try to discourage autoerotic fantasies. Masturbation is indeed a perfectly natural autoerotic activity, as so many sexologists blandly assure us today. And it is precisely because it is so perfectly natural that it can be so dangerous to the mature or maturing person, if it is not controlled or sublimated in some way. That is the true meaning of Portnoy's complaint. Portnoy, you will recall, grows up to be a man who is incapable of having an adult sexual relationship with a woman; his sexuality remains fixed in an infantile mode, the prisoner of his autoerotic fantasies. Inevitably, Portnoy comes to think, in a perfectly *infantile* way, that it was all his mother's fault.

It is true that, in our time, some quite brilliant minds have come to the conclusion that a reversion to infantile sexuality is the ultimate mission and secret destiny of the human race. I am thinking in particular of Norman O. Brown, for whose writings I have the deepest respect. One of the reasons I respect them so deeply is that Mr. Brown is a serious thinker who is unafraid to face up to the radical consequences of his radical theories. Thus, Mr. Brown knows and says that for his kind of salvation to be achieved, humanity must annul the civilization it has created – not merely the civilization we have today, but all civilization – so as to be able to make the long descent backward into animal innocence.

And that is the point. What is at stake is civilization and humanity, nothing less. The idea that 'everything is permitted', as Nietzsche put it, rests on the premise of nihilism and has nihilistic implications. I will not pretend that the case against nihilism and for civilization is an easy one to make. We are here confronting the most fundamental of philosophical questions, on the deepest levels. In short, the matter of pornography and obscenity is not a trivial one, and only superficial minds can take a bland and untroubled view of it.

In this connection, I must also point out, those who are primarily against censorship on liberal grounds tell us not to take pornography or obscenity seriously; while those who are for pornography and obscenity on radical grounds take it very seriously indeed. I believe the radicals – writers like Susan Sontag, Herbert Marcuse, Norman O. Brown, and even Jerry Rubin – are right, and the liberals are wrong. I also believe that those young radicals at Berkeley, some seven years ago, who provoked a major confrontation over the public use of obscene words, showed a brilliant political instinct. And once Mark Rudd could publicly ascribe to the president of Columbia [University] a notoriously obscene relationship to his mother, without provoking any kind of reaction, the SDS [Students for a Democratic Society] had already won the day. The occupation of Columbia's buildings merely ratified their victory. Men who show themselves unwilling to defend civilization against nihilism are not going to be either resolute or effective in defending the university against anything.

I am already touching upon a political aspect of pornography when I suggest that it is inherently and purposefully subversive of civilization and its institutions. But there is another and more specifically political aspect, which has to do with the relationship of pornography and/or obscenity to democracy, and especially to the quality of public life on which democratic government ultimately rests.

Though the phrase 'the quality of life' trips easily from so many lips these days, it tends to be one of those clichés with many trivial meanings and no large, serious one. Sometimes it merely refers to such externals as the enjoyment of cleaner air, cleaner water, cleaner streets. At other times it refers to the merely private enjoyment of music, painting, or literature. Rarely does it have anything to do with the way the citizen in a democracy views himself – his obligations, his intentions, his ultimate self-definition.

Instead, what I would call the 'managerial' conception of democracy is the predominant opinion among political scientists, sociologists, and economists, and has, through the untiring efforts of these scholars, become the conventional journalistic opinion as well. The root idea behind this managerial conception is that democracy is a 'political system' (as they say) which can be adequately defined in terms of − can be fully reduced to − its mechanical arrangements. Democracy is then seen as a set of rules and procedures, and *nothing but* a set of rules and procedures, whereby majority rule and minority rights are reconciled into a state of equilibrium. If everyone follows these rules and procedures, then a democracy is in working order. I think this is a fair description of the democratic idea that currently prevails in academia. One can also fairly say that it is now the liberal idea of democracy par excellence.

I cannot help but feel that there is something ridiculous about being this kind of a democrat, and I must further confess to having a sneaking sympathy for those of our young radicals who also find it ridiculous. The absurdity is the absurdity of idolatry − of taking the symbolic for the real, the means for the end. The purpose of democracy cannot possibly be the endless functioning of its own political machinery. The purpose of any political regime is to achieve some version of the good life and the good society. It is not at all difficult to imagine a perfectly functioning democracy which answers all questions except one − namely, why should anyone of intelligence and spirit care a fig for it?

There is, however, an older idea of democracy − one which was fairly common until about the beginning of this century − for which the conception of the quality of public life is absolutely crucial. This idea starts from the proposition that democracy is a form of self-government, and that if you want it to be a meritorious polity, you have to care about what kind of people govern it. Indeed, it puts the matter more strongly and declares that if you want self-government, you are only entitled to it if that 'self' is worthy of governing. There is no inherent right to self-government if it means that such government is vicious, mean, squalid, and debased. Only a dogmatist and a fanatic, an idolater of democratic machinery, could approve of self-government under such conditions.

And because the desirability of self-government depends on the character of the people who govern, the older idea of democracy was very solicitous of the condition of this character. It was solicitous of the individual self, and felt an obligation to educate it into what used to be called 'republican virtue'. And it was solicitous of that collective self which we call public opinion and which, in a democracy, governs us collectively. Perhaps in some respects it was nervously oversolicitous − that would not be surprising. But the main thing is that it cared, cared not merely about the machinery of democracy but about the quality of life that this machinery might generate.

And because it cared, this older idea of democracy had no problem in principle with pornography and/or obscenity. It censored them – and it did so with a perfect clarity of mind and a perfectly clear conscience. It was not about to permit people capriciously to corrupt themselves. Or, to put it more precisely: in this version of democracy, the people took some care not to let themselves be governed by the more infantile and irrational parts of themselves.

I have, it may be noticed, uttered that dreadful word censorship. And I am not about to back away from it. If you think pornography and/or obscenity is a serious problem, you have to be for censorship. I will go even further and say that if you want to prevent pornography and/or obscenity from becoming a problem, you have to be for censorship. And lest there be any misunderstanding as to what I am saying, I will put it as bluntly as possible: if you care for the quality of life in our American democracy, then you have to be for censorship.

But can a liberal be for censorship? Unless one assumes that being a liberal *must* mean being indifferent to the quality of American life, then the answer has to be yes, a liberal can be for censorship – but he ought to favor a liberal form of censorship.

Is that a contradiction in terms? I do not think so. We have no problem in contrasting *repressive* laws governing alcohol and drugs and tobacco with laws *regulating* (i.e., discouraging the sale of) alcohol and drugs and tobacco. Laws encouraging temperance are not the same thing as laws that have as their goal prohibition or abolition. We have not made the smoking of cigarettes a criminal offense. [Times change, Ed.] We have, however, and with good liberal conscience, prohibited cigarette advertising on television, and may yet, again with good liberal conscience, prohibit it in newspapers and magazines. The idea of restricting individual freedom, in a liberal way, is not at all unfamiliar to us.

I therefore see no reason why we should not be able to distinguish repressive censorship from liberal censorship of the written and spoken word. In Britain, until a few years ago, you could perform almost any play you wished, but certain plays, judged to be obscene, had to be performed in private theatrical clubs, which were deemed to have a 'serious' interest in theater. In the United States, all of us who grew up using public libraries are familiar with the circumstances under which certain books could be circulated only to adults, while still other books had to be read in the library reading room, under the librarian's skeptical eye. In both cases, a small minority that was willing to make a serious effort to see an obscene play or read an obscene book could do so. But the impact of obscenity was circumscribed and the quality of public life was only marginally affected.*

I am not saying it is easy in practice to sustain a distinction between liberal and repressive censorship, especially in the public realm of a democracy, where popular opinion is so vulnerable to demagoguery. Moreover, an acceptable system of liberal censorship is likely to be exceedingly difficult to devise in the United States today, because our educated classes, upon whose judgment a liberal censorship must rest, are so convinced that there is no such thing as a problem of obscenity, or even that there is no such thing as obscenity at all. But, to counterbalance this, there is the further, fortunate truth that the tolerable margin for error is quite large, and single mistakes or single injustices are not all that important.

This possibility of error, of course, occasions much distress among artists and academics. It is a fact, one that cannot and should not be denied, that any system of censorship is bound, upon occasion, to treat unjustly a particular work of art – to find pornography where there is only gentle eroticism, to find obscenity where none really exists, or to find both where its existence ought to be tolerated because it serves a larger moral purpose. Though most works of art are not obscene, and though most obscenity has nothing to do with art, there are some few works of art that are, at least in part, pornographic and/or obscene. There are also some few works of art that are, in the special category of the comic-ironic, 'bawdy' (Boccaccio, Rabelais). It is such works of art that are likely to suffer at the hands of the censor. That is the price one has to be prepared to pay for censorship – even liberal censorship.

But just how high is this price? If you believe, as so many artists seem to believe today, that art is the only sacrosanct activity in our profane and vulgar world – that any man who designates himself an artist thereby acquires a sacred office – then obviously censorship is an intolerable form of sacrilege. But for those of us who do not subscribe to this religion of art, the costs of censorship do not seem so high at all.

---

* It is fairly predictable that someone is going to object that this point of view is 'elitist' – that, under a system of liberal censorship, the rich will have privileged access to pornography and obscenity. Yes, of course, they will – just as, at present, the rich have privileged access to heroin if they want it. But one would have to be an egalitarian maniac to object to this state of affairs on the grounds of equality.

If you look at the history of American or English literature, there is precious little damage you can point to as a consequence of the censorship that prevailed throughout most of that history. Very few works of literature – of real literary merit, I mean – ever were suppressed; and those that were, were not suppressed for long. Nor have I noticed, now that censorship of the written word has to all intents and purposes ceased in this country, that hitherto suppressed or repressed masterpieces are flooding the market. Yes, we can now read *Fanny Hill* and the Marquis de Sade. Or, to be more exact, we can now openly purchase them, since many people were able to read them even though they were publicly banned, which is as it should be under a liberal censorship. So how much have literature and the arts gained from the fact that we can all now buy them over the counter, that, indeed, we are all now encouraged to buy them over the counter? They have not gained much that I can see.

And one might also ask a question that is almost never raised: how much has literature lost from the fact that everything is now permitted? It has lost quite a bit, I should say. In a free market, Gresham's Law[*] can work for books or theater as efficiently as it does for coinage – driving out the good, establishing the debased. The cultural market in the United States today is being pre-empted by dirty books, dirty movies, dirty theater. A pornographic novel has a far better chance of being published today than a non-pornographic one, and quite a few pretty good novels are not being published at all simply because they are not pornographic, and are therefore less likely to sell. Our cultural condition has not improved as a result of the new freedom. American cultural life was not much to brag about twenty years ago; today one feels ashamed for it.

Just one last point, which I dare not leave untouched. If we start censoring pornography or obscenity, shall we not inevitably end up censoring political opinion? A lot of people seem to think this would be the case – which only shows the power of doctrinaire thinking over reality. We had censorship of pornography and obscenity for 150 years, until almost yesterday, and I am not aware that freedom of opinion in this country was in any way diminished as a consequence of this fact. Fortunately for those of us who are liberal, freedom is not indivisible. If it were, the case for liberalism would be indistinguishable from the case for anarchy; and they are two very different things.

---

[*] This 'Law' holds that if two currencies of different quality are allowed to circulate, 'bad money drives out good' as consumers hoard the safer, more valuable currency rather than put it in circulation

But I must repeat and emphasize: what kinds of laws we pass governing pornography and obscenity, what kind of censorship – or, since we are still a federal nation, what kinds of censorship – we institute in our various localities may indeed be difficult matters to cope with; nevertheless the real issue is one of principle. I myself subscribe to a liberal view of the enforcement problem: I think that pornography should be illegal *and* available to anyone who wants it so badly as to make a pretty strenuous effort to get it. We have lived with under-the-counter pornography for centuries now, in a fairly comfortable way. But the issue of principle, of whether it should be over or under the counter, has to be settled before we can reflect on the advantages and disadvantages of alternative modes of censorship. I think the settlement we are living under now, in which obscenity and democracy are regarded as equals, is wrong; I believe it is inherently unstable; I think it will, in the long run, be incompatible with any authentic concern for the quality of life in our democracy.

THE DREAD DEFICIT

Robert L. Bartley

*The deficit is not a meaningless figure, only a grossly overrated
one. It measures something, but it does not measure the
impulse of the economy.*

THE DREAD DEFICIT

ROBERT L. BARTLEY

The deficit is not a meaningless figure, only a grossly overrated one. It measures something, but it does not measure the impulse of the economy – either pushing it up as the Keynesians believe or dragging it down as the flow-of-funds school holds. In particular, the deficit has no detectable effect on interest rates; if it tends to raise interest rates, its effect is swamped by other more important variables. And if it doesn't affect interest rates, it can scarcely affect the sectors of the economy thought to depend on interest rates, investment, for example. Nor is what we call 'the deficit' an appropriate or particularly meaningful measure of the 'burden we are leaving our grandchildren'; the federal government has many other ways of imposing future burdens, which may or may not move in tandem with its direct borrowing.

The fiscal health of the federal government certainly does matter, but the government's impact on the economy is far too large and diffuse to measure by any one number. A decent measure of the federal fiscal condition would have to be something like the change in the net worth of the government; we have no such figure and, given its complications, are not likely to. But it will not help to pretend 'the deficit' is some other figure we do not have, and then to invoke it in place of judgment. The deficit as we measure it is no sort of bottom line.

Yet we have increasingly made 'the deficit' the centerpiece of economic policy, even writing it into law. Both the Gramm–Rudman Act and the 1990 budget deal pretend to control the deficit, or some convoluted version of it. Unable to do the right things on their own, our politicians have conjured the deficit into a bogeyman with which to scare themselves. In symbolizing the bankruptcy of our political process, the deficit has become a great national myth with enormous power. But behind this political symbol, we need to understand the economic reality, or lack of it. Otherwise the symbol may lead us to do dumb things, like trying to fight recessions by increasing taxes.

In the advanced economic literature, the big debate is over whether deficits matter *at all*. Professional economists have noticed that the much-publicized deficits of the 1980s somehow didn't spell the end of the world, or even the end of the economic boom. They understand that the prime rate was 20 to 21.5 per cent in 1981, when the deficit ran 2.6 per cent of GNP, and 7.25 to 8 per cent in 1986, when the deficit was 5.3 per cent of GNP. Unlike politicians or the articulate public, they have tried to adjust their thinking to this empirical reality.

Robert Eisner had the deficit particularly in mind when... he entitled his presidential address to the American Economic Association 'Divergences of Measurement and Theory'. He had many examples of how the statistics we were able to gather did not correspond to the statistical concepts we use in theory and that 'as a consequence, popular discourse, policy-making, and basic principles of economics have suffered inordinate confusion'. But his main dwelling-point was the deficit.

There are of course still plenty of economists who were taught at their major professor's knee that deficits are the center of the universe, as well as plenty of economists invoking the deficit to advance this or that political agenda. The usual theory has been that deficits add to the demand for funds and thus push up interest rates, but falling interest rates with rising deficits leave much to explain. You can of course adjust the interest rate for inflation, and argue that the deficits pushed up the 'real' rate of interest. But if you do this, how can you ignore the fact that inflation also reduces the real value of all debt outstanding? Are trained economists really going to argue seriously that a *nominal* increase in government debt causes a rise in the *real* rate of interest?

This was Eisner's point precisely. You do not run a 'real' deficit unless you borrow enough to offset the effect of inflation on the outstanding debt. This is a large adjustment indeed. At the beginning of fiscal 1979, for example, the public held just over $607 billion in federal debt, and inflation was running at over 11 per cent a year. So just maintaining the real value of federal debt outstanding would require a nominal increase of about $67 billion. In that year, the official deficit was $40.2 billion, and debt held by the public increased $32.7 billion.

Also, Eisner suggested a second large adjustment for the portion of the deficit that went to capital spending by government; most economists would agree that it's entirely appropriate to borrow for capital expenses and pay off the loan over the life of the asset. Eisner remarked, 'These two adjustments, for capital expenditures and for inflation, make such a huge difference in the Federal government budget as to wipe out the much decried "budget deficit".' That is, the two adjustments would move the 1988 federal deficit from its official $155 billion to 'virtual balance'.

These words were uttered, remember, by the man the leading association of academic economists had chosen as its president. Eisner's purpose was grander than defending the Reagan administration. He had in mind nothing less than the resurrection of Keynes. In the statistical confusion, he finds a Keynesian answer to the stagflation of the 1970s; because of the high inflation, the apparent deficits were illusory. The economy stagnated because, in 'real' terms, the government was running surpluses.

In any meaningful economic theory, he argued, 'the deficit' must mean an increase in the government's outstanding debt, since the deficit theoretically induces spending and growth by increasing private assets. He added, 'To have this effect, as the neoclassical argument made clear, the increase in private assets must be real.' In these terms, the federal budget did not go into deficit until late in 1982. With a decline in inflation and a rise in deficits, the Reagan administration staged a Keynesian boom. Eisner remarked, 'It should have been clear — dare I say "perfectly clear"? — that it was the old-fashioned Keynesian stimulus of real budget deficits that has contributed mightily to cutting unemployment in half, from its recession high of almost 11%.'

There is of course a second half to the stagflation puzzle: what caused the inflation? Eisner looked at the then six-year boom and asked, 'Where, I might add, is that supposedly excess-demand "accelerating inflation" we were taught to fear? Perhaps waiting to be confused again with the supply shocks of a new war or oil cartel in the Middle East!' The 1970s inflation, in other words, was caused by OPEC — an 'exogenous shock', like an earthquake, that economic theory is not expected to explain. The inflation was exogenous, and restrictive fiscal policy, measured in 'real' terms, caused the stagnation. Keynes lives.

The way a president of the American Economic Association looks on 'the deficit' is, to underline the point, certainly different from the conventional wisdom we read every day in the headlines. Eisner is an intellectually consistent Keynesian, a refreshing contrast to the sort that in recent years has somehow wanted to increase taxes to fight recession. Yet the Keynes resurrection is likely to seem a bit arch to those of us who associate inflation with monetary policy.

Advanced economists are also debating a second cutting-edge economic theory attempt to deal with the 1980s reality of high deficits, prosperity, and falling interest rates. The theory of 'Ricardian equivalence' has been extensively debated in the economic literature of recent years. Ricardian equivalence holds that deficits are simply irrelevant, or more precisely, in their economic effect indistinguishable from taxes. The theory is named after

David Ricardo (1772–1823), the epitome of classical economists, though in fact Ricardo only toyed with these ideas. The modern theory is identified with Robert Barro of Harvard, one of the leading 'new classical' economists, and also a contributing editor of *The Wall Street Journal*. Ricardian equivalence traces to [Barro's] exquisitely timed 1974 article, entitled 'Are Government Bonds Net Wealth?'

The question seems an arcane curiosity, but is actually an Exocet aimed at the heart of the Keynesian universe. For if the government borrows now and promises to pay back later, a public sector with rational expectations would not feel itself wealthier. It would spend no more freely, and the deficit would have no effect.

Indeed, a perfectly rational public sector would recognize that in the future it would be taxed to repay the bonds it now receives, and would set aside some savings for that purpose. That is, government saving would decrease through the deficit, public savings would increase, total national savings would be unaffected; so nothing would change because the government chose to tax later instead of sooner.

Ricardian equivalence has been the subject of a wide-ranging debate on both theoretical and empirical grounds; in a 1989 reassessment, Barro cited more than fifty articles, nearly all directly on points he raised in 1974. Details of the debate include intergenerational altruism, the smoothing of the income tax, glitches in the loan markets, and other esoterica.

While the theory remains controversial, by 1989 Barro was able to assert, '[I]t is remarkable how respectable the Ricardian approach has become in the last decade. Most macroeconomists now feel obligated to state the Ricardian position, even if they then go on to argue that it is either theoretically or empirically in error. I predict this trend will continue and that the Ricardian approach will become the benchmark model for assessing fiscal policy.' That is, 'I would not predict that most analysts will embrace Ricardian equivalence in the sense of concluding that fiscal policy is irrelevant. But satisfactory analyses will feature explicit modeling of elements that lead to departures from Ricardian equivalence, and the predicted consequences of fiscal policies will flow directly from these elements.'

Ricardian equivalence has also fared surprisingly well in studies trying to relate deficits and interest rates. As Barro put it, 'Overall, the empirical results on interest rates support the Ricardian view. Given these findings it is remarkable that most macroeconomists remain confident that budget deficits raise interest rates.'

At Eureka College in the 1930s they taught classical economics, and the Eureka College economist Ronald Reagan said things like he didn't understand why borrowing crowded out investment but taxes didn't. The heirs of Michael I* would say that both taxing and borrowing take real resources from the private sector, and that any difference would depend on second-order effects (like which took resources at a lower marginal rate). On the whole, the schools of thought represented by Eisner and Barro show that professional economists have been becoming increasingly ambivalent about the deficit. At the same time, of course, politicians and public have been turning it into an idol.

The lack of a correlation between deficits and interest rates is less surprising if you understand that the deficit is a curious figure from the standpoint of accounting. I remember sharing garden-party cocktails with Paul Volcker one summer night when he was approached by the CEO of a highly successful regional retailer, demanding how the government could go deeper and deeper into debt everywhere. He was quite right in looking to Volcker for support of his view, but Paul mischievously turned to me and said, 'You answer that, Bob,' then grinned and ambled away leaving me with a worked-up CEO. Well, I asked, doesn't your company add to its debt every year? I guess it does, he responded, but that's different.

It sure is. Corporations have Generally Accepted Accounting Principles. The government has the National Income Accounts. If you are going to speculate about the economic impact of 'the deficit', you have to have some sense of the differences among accrual accounting, cash accounting, and government accounting.

If a corporation borrows $200 million to build a shopping center, this will be reflected in its balance sheet. It will have $200 million in liabilities for the debt, and $200 million in assets for the shopping center. But in its annual income accounts, it will not charge the entire $200 million as an expense. Instead of 'expensing' the sum in the first year, it will 'depreciate' it. That is, it will charge some portion of it as an expense against income each year over the assumed useful life of the shopping center.

Similarly, if a family takes out a $400,000 mortgage to buy a home, it recognizes that it has gone $400,000 in debt. But in trying to match income with outgo, it does not consider the $400,000 but the monthly or yearly

---

* Michael I, a restaurant, is described by Bartley as 'a restaurant for Wall Street wannabees [and]… the site of extraordinary seminars in economics', Ed.

payment to amortize the mortgage. Both corporations and households consider it entirely appropriate to borrow to buy capital items, and pay off the loan as the asset is used. As former Citicorp chairman Walter Wriston put it, 'The familiar refrain that every family must balance its budget, so why can't the federal government, has a nice ring to it, but no family I know of expenses its home.' In the federal budget, he added, 'All in all, capital expenditures totaled 13.2% of total outlays, a not inconsiderable amount to expense, and if funded in a capital budget would produce near balance in the operating budget.'

So too with state and local governments. Typically they are required by law to 'balance' their operating budgets, but this does not include bond issues for capital items, which usually must be approved by voters at referendum. Most foreign governments also have distinct capital budgets, if only for help in deciding how much yearly deficit may be sustainable. Not so the U.S. federal budget; indeed, Treasury Secretary Donald Regan was nearly laughed out of Washington for suggesting the government needs a capital budget.

So 'the deficit' may be borrowing to pay welfare benefits or farm subsidies, or it may be borrowing to pay for a highway or an airplane. We have constructed our accounts to make it impossible to tell the difference. Partly this is because we don't trust our politicians to be honest in designating capital projects. Some state and local governments, New York City in particular, got into financial trouble by cheating on their capital budgets – by designating more and more operating expenses as capital expenses for which it was legitimate to borrow.

Even more importantly, the National Income Accounts reflect a Keynesian view of the world. Keynes felt that the depression was caused by a shortfall in aggregate demand because saving was too high and investment too low. The point of 'investment' was to borrow the excess savings and spend them, thus boosting total demand. Whether the investments would pay for themselves economically made no difference whatever; indeed, worrying about waste could only be counterproductive.

In *The General Theory*, for example, Keynes suggests that the Treasury should stuff old bottles with banknotes and bury them in abandoned coal mines, then lease the rights to the mines, and 'leave it to private enterprise on well tried principles of laissez faire to dig the notes up again'. This would boost demand and eliminate unemployment. He added:

> The analogy between this expedient and the gold mines of the real world is complete. At periods when gold is available at suitable depths experience shows that the real wealth of the world increases rapidly; and

when but little of it is available, our wealth suffers stagnation or decline. Thus gold mines are of the greatest value and importance to civilization. Just as wars have been the only form of large-scale loan expenditure which statemen have thought justifiable, so gold mining is the only pretext for digging holes in the ground which has recommended itself to bankers as sound finance; and each of these activities has played its part in progress – failing something better.

Little wonder that accounts designed when such attitudes held sway would fail to distinguish between government consumption and government investment. If we pretend that accounts set up to answer some other question answer our questions today, we only confuse ourselves.

That the deficit does not account for capital spending is the good news, however. The bad news is that it also does not account for the government's future liabilities. One night in 1980, Congress increased federal deposit insurance from $40,000 an account to $100,000. This one act increased the liabilities of the U.S. government by some $150 billion, half the cost of bailing out the savings and loan accounts insured by the government. But it did not change the 1980 deficit a penny. The recorded 1980 deficit was $73.8 billion; the unrecorded liability of the deposit insurance boost amounted to twice the borrowing for all the government's on-the-book activities.

That's an example of why 'the deficit' does not measure anything that could realistically be called 'the burden we are leaving our grandchildren'. What the federal debt represents is government bonds outstanding, or to put it plainly, that portion of future liabilities on which the government has chosen to pay interest.

The actual liabilities are far larger, so much so that changes in them can swamp changes in the official deficit; the deficit numbers can go up while the burden to our grandchildren goes down, or vice versa. In terms of the burden for our grandchildren, the elephant in the room is the social society system. At the end of fiscal 1981, in the midst of Ronald Reagan's first year in office, federal debt held by the public amounted to $785 billion. The unfunded liabilities of the social security system, however, came in at $5.9 *trillion*. The pension liabilities for federal personnel, at $842 billion, were themselves larger than the cumulative 'deficits' over two centuries.

In the National Income Accounts these numbers do not count, of course; they are not relevant to the current year's aggregate demand. They are highly relevant, though, to the burden on our grandchildren. Is the government any more likely to default on a social security payment than it is on a Treasury bond? The danger to the latter is that its value will be inflated away, but under current law social security payments are indexed to inflation, while future benefits are linked to future wage levels, increasing with both inflation and real advances in the standard of living.

It is somehow not surprising that an administration that cuts taxes would also compile a better record on the government's off-budget liabilities. Also, slower inflation and more real growth make the fiscal climate easier, since figures like social security liabilities depend on estimates of future economic performance. The 1983 Greenspan Commission dealt with the social security deficit, in no small way by advancing previously scheduled increases in the payroll tax. With the economy performing better than expected during that reform, social security looks healthier, at least in the short term.

Thomas E. Daxon, a certified public accountant and former state auditor in Oklahoma, calculated the burden to future taxpayers in a 1989 article in *Policy Review*. His calculation included interest-bearing debt, social security, personal pensions, and a variety of other liabilities and offsetting assets. He concluded that the burden to future taxpayers was $7.185 trillion at the end of fiscal 1981, and $7.952 trillion at the end of fiscal 1987. As a percentage of GNP, it declined from 241 per cent to 180 per cent.

Such calculations need to be taken with a grain of salt, of course. We do not know which contingent liabilities may explode the way deposit insurance did with the savings and loan associations [thrifts, in the UK, Ed.]. Government has assumed much of the liability for medical care for the elderly, for example, and seems poised to assume more. The Greenspan Commission fix of social security really only pushed the problem into the future; if we want to reduce the burden on our grandchildren, the first thing we should do is reduce the incomes we expect to claim when we retire.

At the same time, government accounting takes no notice of the government's asset position. We know that federal debt held by the public is now some $2.7 trillion. But how does this liability compare with the asset of, say, federal land holdings – nearly all of Alaska and Nevada, for example, and much of California?

The deficit is not much of a measure of any of these issues. It seems likely that during the 1980s even as the deficit grew, other burdens on our grandchildren declined. Deposit insurance of course clouds the picture, and it's not easy to assess responsibility for these enormous costs... Even so, it's possible that during the 1980s the net worth of the government, if we could measure it, may have gone up rather than down. This is perhaps a hidden secret of the Seven Fat Years...

If we want a fiscal policy that speeds economic growth, we know what needs to be done with or without a deficit number: hold government spending to essentials, keep marginal tax rates as low as possible, keep the dollar sound, let the price mechanism work, avoid imposing unnecessary regulation and unnecessary costs. Preoccupation with 'the deficit' was a hindrance the Reagan administration had to overcome in implementing the program that produced the Seven Fat Years, and in the 1990s the danger is that the same preoccupation will lead us away from these fundamentals.

Meanwhile, the deficit becomes less and less attached to reality. In the 1990 budget agreement, the surpluses of the social security system have been taken out of the calculation, apparently to make the deficit a bigger and better bogeyman.

NEOCONSERVATIVE ECONOMIC POLICY

Virtues and Vices

Irwin Stelzer

The neoconservatives' objection to making a balanced budget the
centerpiece of economic policy has [considerable] support...
[But] deficits that loom large relative to a nation's
ability to produce wealth do matter.

NEOCONSERVATIVE ECONOMIC POLICY
Virtues and Vices

IRWIN STELZER

The neoconservatives' contribution to economic policy receives far less attention than does their contribution to foreign policy. Which is understandable. After all, policies that are complicit in justifying a war are more likely to attract front-page headlines than anything so seemingly arcane as microeconomic and macroeconomic policies. Yet, long after the war in Iraq has been concluded, the effects of neoconomics will endure.

Start with what has come to be called 'Reaganomics', shorthand for the reforms that Ronald Reagan introduced on the supply side of the economy. These included creating a presumption against new regulations, the costs of which exceed any benefits they might bring; a revival of entrepreneurs' willingness to invest by persuading the nation that its best days were ahead, not behind it; and a revision of the tax structure so as to reduce marginal tax rates from levels that discourage work and risk-taking. At minimum, the enduring contribution of neoconservative Reaganomics has been to shift the burden of proof from those who want to encourage entrepreneurship to those who espouse tax and regulatory policies that have the opposite effect.

Then there is the neoconservative approach to fiscal policy. As in so many other areas, Irving Kristol led the charge against the conservative notion that a balanced budget is a policy goal in and of itself, and that all government initiatives must be subordinated to the achievement of that balance of receipts and outlays. John Maynard Keynes, of course, had earlier and famously objected to conservatives' slavish adherence to balanced budgets, but his was an objection based on his claim that deficit spending could be used to stimulate demand in times of recession. Neocons have rather different reasons for considering the desire to balance budgets an old-fashioned fetish, held only by those who have not thought deeply about what goes into national budgets.

The first is a rather cold-blooded, or practical – depending on your point of view – calculation that balanced budgets are not a rallying cry likely to win favor with voters, no matter what they tell pollsters – especially when the opposition has on offer a variety of expensive but attractive 'goodies'. One neoconservative is fond of joking that the advantage of neocon deficits is that 'they leave us free to spend what we like when in power, and force the Democrats to raise taxes when their turn at the White House comes around'.

The second practical-political reason for denigrating the importance of deficits was a desire to liberate Ronald Reagan to pursue victory in the Cold War by spending whatever was necessary to persuade the Soviet Union that it simply could not compete with America in an ongoing arms race. Viewed in the context of the West's victory in the Cold War, the deficits incurred by President Reagan to increase military spending were investments that were (sooner rather than later, as it turned out) repaid in the form of a 'peace dividend' – the reduction in military spending made possible by the collapse of the Soviet Union. Surely, the neocons can claim that their liberation of Reagan from concern with deficits resulted in the liberation of millions of people in Eastern Europe from Soviet oppression. They can also point out that European critics of Reagan's deficits rushed to carve themselves a share of the peace dividend by reducing their defense spending.

The third reason neoconservatives downplay the role of deficits is a deep suspicion of the ability of 'bean counters' to determine the state of a nation's fiscal health, and an even deeper suspicion of the ability of economic forecasters to predict the course of the nation's budget for even a few years into the future.

The neoconservatives' objection to making a balanced budget the centerpiece of economic policy has support from (a) the frequent and major revisions of what Irving Kristol recently called 'those majestic but ghostly figures' that represent estimates of economic output, government outlays, and other macroeconomic variables; (b) the fact that a deficit or surplus is a tiny number derived from subtracting one very large number, outlays, from another very large number, tax receipts, meaning that very small errors in either receipts or outlays result in very large errors in the estimated deficit or surplus; and (c) the fact that government budgets do not distinguish between expenses such as bureaucrats' wages, and capital expenditures, such as outlays to add to the nation's infrastructure. Worrying about a deficit recorded because the costs of long-lasting assets such as roads, schools, and hospitals are counted as expenses in the year incurred is the equivalent of worrying that a family faces ruin because its purchase of a house throws its household finances into the red if the entire outlay is charged against one year's income. As Bartley puts it,

'Government accounting takes no notice of the government's asset position.'
Well, U.S. government accounting at any rate. But in Great Britain the neocon
distinction between expenses and investment – the need to take notice of the
government's asset position – has been adopted by a Labour chancellor,
perhaps proving that good ideas can, in the right circumstances, cross
ideological lines.

Neocons also won a victory in the battle over the correct way to measure
the cost of tax cuts. Bartley and others of a neocon persuasion convinced most
policy-makers that reduced tax rates, especially lower marginal tax rates, will
in many instances encourage people to work harder, engage in less elaborate
avoidance schemes, and take increased risks in response to the opportunity of
keeping more of the rewards. These are the famous 'supply-side' effects that all
sensible governments now take into account in developing tax policy. Those
behavioral responses to reduced tax rates, neocons contend, reduce the revenue
loss resulting from lower rates, and might even produce higher total revenues
for the Treasury than would higher rates of tax.

But – and this is bad news for unsophisticated neocon supply-siders so much
in favor with free-spending politicians – experience and empirical studies teach
that although tax cuts do change behavior on the supply side of the economy,
and do encourage greater output, the revenues generated by tax cuts in most
instances will not fully compensate for the revenues lost by reducing tax rates.
Tax cuts cannot miraculously turn a flood of red ink to black.

Irving Kristol, for one, never said they could. He argues that *over time*
economic growth, propelled by tax cuts, will result in ever-smaller deficits.
These deficits will be sufficiently small, relative to the enhanced size of the
economy, to permit markets to decide that they do not threaten to cause
inflation, raise interest rates, or incite a run on the dollar.

Unfortunately, liberation from concern about *some* deficits has liberated free-
spending politicians from concern about *all* deficits, no matter how large they
are and threaten to become. Neoconservatives will have to find some way of
overcoming the apparent failure of elected officials to agree on spending
reductions, or swallow hard and apply their minds and models to devising tax
increases that have no – or only very minor – negative effects on productivity.
The urgency of this demand on their creativity will increase as the demographic
fuse on the pension time bomb burns down to near-explosive length.

Irving Kristol may be right that deficits don't matter, if kept to sensible
proportions and viewed in the long run; Bartley may be right that they do not
have the negative economic consequences that budget-balancers in the

traditional conservative camp and, lately, in the Bill Clinton–Robert Rubin wing of the Democratic Party contend; and President George W. Bush may be right when he shows his disregard for deficits with the flippant, 'It is clearly a budget. It's got lots of numbers in it.'

I rather doubt it. In the end, deficits on the scale that America now confronts do matter, and will be among the factors affecting interest rates, the value of the dollar, and other variables that record the state of the economy. But the neocons can claim victory for showing the complexity of the relationship between tax rates, tax revenues, and economic performance, and for broadening acceptance of the proposition that it is better to reduce deficits by cutting inefficient government spending than by raising incentive-destroying taxes.

So there we have it: neoconservatives have made an enduring contribution to policies that have made the supply side of the economy more flexible, and to a more nuanced approach to deficits and tax policy. But they have also handed the politicians an excuse for ignoring the fact that, sooner or later, deficits that loom large relative to a nation's ability to produce wealth do matter, especially if that nation intends to water with cash the democratic values it intends to plant in desert sands.

PART IV

THE ORIGINS OF NEOCONSERVATISM

PHILOSOPHIC ROOTS, THE ROLE OF LEO STRAUSS, AND THE WAR IN IRAQ

Kenneth R. Weinstein

Straussians and their fellow travelers have been able to play a significant role in the public policy arena because of their ability to think through fundamental questions, distilling them to their essence.

PHILOSOPHIC ROOTS, THE ROLE OF LEO STRAUSS, AND THE WAR IN IRAQ[1]

KENNETH R. WEINSTEIN

In the aftermath of the Iraq War, no intellectual was as vilified in either the mainstream European media or the left-wing American media as University of Chicago political philosopher Leo Strauss. Strauss was characterized as the force behind the war, the behind-the-scenes intellectual elitist who preached the politics of force and deception, and the philosopher-king of the neoconservative movement. As Mary Wakefield, assistant editor at the *Spectator*, put it in the *Daily Telegraph* earlier this year,[2] after accusing Tony Blair and Paul Wolfowitz of lying:

> I am prepared to consider the possibility that Blair had altruistic motives [for lying]... Perhaps, like Paul Wolfowitz and other neo-conservatives, he is a disciple of the political philosopher Leo Strauss. Strauss was a champion of the 'noble lie' – the idea that it is practically a duty to lie to the masses because only a small elite is intellectually fit to know the truth.
>
> Politicians must conceal their views, said Strauss, for two reasons: to spare the people's feelings and to protect the elite from possible reprisals. It's a version of the Moonie philosophy of truth: falsehood is OK as long as it is used to convert unbelievers to the Unification Church. As Byron's Don Juan puts it: 'And, after all what is a lie? 'Tis but the truth in masquerade.'

This hitherto obscure philosopher is now more or less famous not only in the British press but, of all places, on the New York stage. Actor and activist Tim Robbins' off-Broadway play, *Embedded*, even featured a character, Pearly White, based on former Defense Policy Board Chairman Richard Perle, who fulminated publicly for the war in moral terms, while openly declaring that 'In the words of Leo Strauss: "Moral virtue only exists in popular opinion where it serves the purpose of controlling the unintelligent majority."'

What is remarkable about this Strauss obsession is that Leo Strauss never held an opinion on Saddam Hussein. In fact, Leo Strauss has been dead for more than three decades. And, as critic Terry Teachout noted shortly after *Embedded* opened, the views of 'Pearly White' – Perle actually never studied with Strauss – were at no time offered by Strauss as his own, but seem to emanate from an article published by the organization run by conspiracy theorist, convicted felon, and perennial presidential candidate Lyndon H. LaRouche, Jr, which paraphrases the work of Shadia Drury, a professor of political theory at the University of Calgary, who has made it her life's work to attack Strauss.

Strauss (1899–1973), the author of fifteen books, was, for the most noted portion of his professional life, a professor of political science at the University of Chicago, where he taught political philosophy. He was, by all accounts, a gifted teacher who drew some of the best minds in academia to his classroom. How Strauss came to be seen as allied with a movement of public intellectuals such as the neoconservatives is indeed paradoxical. Strauss was never involved in the policy movements of his day and never engaged in public policy research. Moreover, Strauss viewed intellectuals as somehow akin to the sophists of the ancient city: men less concerned with the quest for wisdom than with the prestige or power that accompany well-stated ideas. Readers interested in an overview of his philosophy and its roots might find the note appended to this essay (p. 207) of interest.

Straussians and their fellow travelers have been able to play a significant role in the public policy arena because of their ability to think through fundamental questions, distilling them to their essence. Their ability to make reasoned policy arguments on behalf of restraints on behavior – which is hard to do, especially as the right becomes increasingly market- and hence choice-oriented – and to make them replete with appeal to America's founding documents, have made them powerful complements to traditional conservatives less able to produce secular arguments, but able to understand such issues through the prism of faith.

Strauss's concern that the politics of liberty could degenerate into a libertinism that poses a danger to the republican character of the American regime, and his rejection of the language of values for that of virtues, have played a significant role in debates over the past few years on drug policy, welfare reform, and education. Among the Straussians who have reinvigorated such debates in the Bush administration are Leon Kass, MD, Professor of Social Thought at the University of Chicago, who chairs the President's Commission on Bioethics; John P. Walters, who serves in President Bush's cabinet as director of the Office of National Drug Control Policy; and Eugene W. Hickok, formerly Professor of Government of Dickinson College, who serves as Deputy Secretary of Education. Straussians have also served in significant positions in Democratic administrations, though in fewer numbers. Professor William Galston of the University of Maryland served as Deputy Assistant to President Clinton for Domestic Policy, and played a key role in shaping social policies.

But it is in the area of foreign policy that Straussianism and Straussians have attracted the most attention of late. Straussians came to hold significant roles in American foreign policy during the Reagan administration, handling portfolios for public diplomacy and human rights. Professor Nathan Tarcov of the political science department of the University of Chicago served on the policy planning staff of the Department of State, while Carnes Lord, now on the faculty of the Naval War College, was director of international communications and information policy for the National Security Council. Charles Fairbanks, now on the faculty of the Paul H. Nitze School for Advanced International Affairs at Johns Hopkins University, served as Deputy Assistant Secretary of State for Human Rights and Humanitarian Affairs; and Mark Blitz, now Fletcher Jones Professor of Political Philosophy at Claremont McKenna College, was associate director of the U.S. Information Agency. Through their knowledge of how America was founded as a regime dedicated to liberty and inalienable rights, these Straussians and others were able to offer a compelling and principled case for American anti-communism, which explains why so many Straussians served in the Reagan administration – more, even, than serve President George W. Bush.

British and American mainstream publications – the *Daily Telegraph*, *The New York Times, Harper's*, among others – see a nefarious role for Straussians in President George W. Bush's administration and in the run-up to the Iraq War. Much has been made of the fact that Deputy Secretary of Defense Paul Wolfowitz studied as an undergraduate with Allan Bloom at Cornell (as immortalized by the character Philip Gorman in Saul Bellow's 2000 novel about Bloom, *Ravelstein*), and with Leo Strauss as a graduate student at the University of Chicago. Just how influential Strauss was on Wolfowitz we do not know. But we do know, from James Mann's *Vulcans: The Rise of Bush's War Cabinet*, that Wolfowitz took only two courses with Strauss in graduate school; his doctoral dissertation, on the challenges of nuclear-powered desalting stations in the Middle East, was written with deterrence strategist Albert

Wohlstetter. Others who can be reasonably classified as Straussians who played a role in arguing for the war include William Kristol, Editor of *The Weekly Standard*, Gary Schmitt, Executive Director of the Project for the New American Century (PNAC), and Abram Shulsky of the Office of Special Plans at the Pentagon.

Mary Wakefield is not the only commentator to have argued that, just as Plato used the noble lie of the republic, somehow Straussians promoted a myth of weapons of mass destruction in Iraq in order to manipulate support for the war. (The noble lie, in Book III of the *Republic*, seeks to convince the city's warriors to accept their station as selfless spear-carriers for the regime by persuading them of the naturalness of the regime and its clear hierarchy of souls – gold for rulers, silver for warriors, and bronze for artisans.) The charge made by Wakefield and others does not do justice to the dignity with which Strauss treats either the citizen or the challenges of democratic statesmanship. Indeed, this claim fails to pass the laugh test. Hussein was unique among contemporary tyrants for having used chemical weapons against his own people. Every major intelligence agency believed Iraq had some weapons of mass destruction programs. Moreover, the war had other justifications: to free Iraqis from a brutal tyrant; to begin the transformation of the Middle East; and to free American forces from the need to be in Saudi Arabia to protect that regime from Saddam.

The distinctly Straussian elements of support for the war seem to have had several intellectual bases in Strauss's thought. First, Strauss sought to revive awareness of the dangers of tyranny, both for the dangers it posed and to challenge 'value free social science', which, in its neutral, scientific methodology, could not offer a critique of such regimes. Second is the notion of 'regime change' as a means of bringing fundamental change. Like Aristotle, Strauss stressed the primacy of the regime to shaping the way of life of the city. Steven Lenzner and William Kristol argue that 'President Bush's advocacy of "regime change" [is] a not altogether unworthy product of Strauss's rehabilitation of the notion of regime.'[3] Aside from a focus on the regime, a third Straussian element seems to be the recognition that, in a clash with totalitarian or authoritarian states, liberal democracies need to act, as it were, against character and be constantly vigilant.

Though many prominent Straussians supported the Iraq War in some fashion, a number of Straussians expressed doubts, both privately and publicly. In fact, there seem to be numerous theoretical justifications in Strauss's own understanding of politics to think that the anti-utopian Strauss might have been skeptical of parts of the enterprise of the war – especially the notion that regime change would help, as some of the more exuberant supporters of the war believed, to bring democracy to Iraq.

Here, a focus on Aristotle's *Politics* may be helpful. Needless to say, any extrapolation from a particular text is fraught with difficulty, but Aristotle's basic account of the role of the regime is essential. The regime is the primary fact about politics, but, as Aristotle notes, it is not the only fact of politics. Aristotle compares the founder of a regime, the man who gives it order, to a sculptor who gives form to matter. But that matter has distinct limitations as to what form it can take, whether through a founding or a 'refounding' after wartime.[4] Moreover, Strauss's own knowledge of the fragility of democracy, as he portrayed its rise in early modern political philosophy against theological claims to political sovereignty, might have served as a warning of the enormous challenges that lie ahead.

In sum, those who oppose the war in Iraq, and who would blame the influence of a relatively obscure philosopher on the Bush administration's neocon contingent, would do well to look elsewhere: perhaps even to Strauss himself and the classics he revived for support for their view that there are distinct limitations to the form that a post-Saddam Iraq might take.

A note on the philosophy of Leo Strauss

Strauss's life was dedicated to liberal education in the broadest sense through the continuous study of fundamental questions. His basic insight was that the greatest minds of the past offered the clearest gateway to understanding our contemporary situation, free of the jargon and inherited frameworks which shape our horizons and, hence, limit our understanding. By seeking to understand the great minds, Strauss believed that man could come to a better comprehension of the permanent problems.

His books, which include *Natural Right and History* (1953), *Thoughts on Machiavelli* (1958), and *The City and Man* (1964), therefore, appear as commentaries on the most important writers in the Western tradition. As the late Allan Bloom (1930–92), a Strauss student who wrote the 1987 best-seller

The Closing of the American Mind, noted: 'His writings were tentative but ever surer steps toward understanding writers as they understood themselves and thereby toward making the fundamental alternatives again clear to men whose choices had become impoverished.' Strauss's writings, in short, are philosophic inquiries and have nothing of the dogma of a political movement. His thought culminates in no political program, no slogans or 'cookie cutter' approaches to public policy. His focus, instead, is on how to read books. As commentaries, his writings do not put Strauss in the limelight, but rather focus on the thought of others.

For Strauss, perhaps the best image of the human dilemma is the image of the cave in Book VII of Plato's *Republic*. That image, of men in a cave, shackled so they can only see the shadows of images projected on the wall, is a metaphor for the ancient city, for the notion that men are bound to horizons shaped in some sense by the dominant opinions of their day. Strauss tried to escape the cave and turn his soul to the blinding light of the sun, through the meticulous study of the great minds of the past.

Though the political situation may in some sense approximate Plato's cave, Strauss thought that there were clear differences between regimes that made some far superior to others. He viewed himself as a friend of liberal democracy, both on a practical and a theoretical level. He saw the ravages of fascism first-hand in his native Germany, and was deeply grateful to America for the refuge it afforded him from the Nazis. More importantly, he recognized that liberal democracy was the only decent and just alternative for modern man.

But Strauss saw liberalism threatened theoretically by the philosophically informed belief, developed in modernity, that unaided human reason could not find permanent principles. Hitherto, Western thought had been shaped by what Strauss characterized as the tension between the two most compelling alternatives for developing a comprehensive account of the whole: reason and revelation, or, as Strauss put it figuratively, Athens and Jerusalem. Though Strauss left the Orthodox Judaism in which he was raised as a youth, he took the Bible seriously, saw revelation as offering the firmest foundation for morality, and criticized the atheism of the Enlightenment's more strident figures.

After early modern political philosophy, especially in the Enlightenment, unmasked the claims of revelation in the name of reason, late modernity took to unmasking the claims of reason. The growing importance ascribed to history in philosophy since Jean-Jacques Rousseau (1712–78) meant that nature was no longer a standard for man. The rise of historical consciousness was especially a threat to the U.S., a regime based on the unalienable rights ascribed to man by

America's Founding Fathers. Radical historicism, as seen in the writings of Friedrich Nietzsche (1844–1900) and Martin Heidegger (1889–1976), made the defense of intellectual rationalism and democratic republicanism increasingly difficult. Nietzsche's view that beliefs are values, mere human creations, paved the way to cultural relativism as well as to nihilism.

In the face of the crisis of the West, in particular, historicism and relativism, Strauss turned to the great authors of the past. In contrast to most of his contemporaries, Strauss sought to understand these thinkers as they understood themselves, not assuming that their ideas were shaped or limited by the times in which they lived. It is, in part, this rejection of standard operating scholarly procedure in political theory that has led Strauss to be disliked by much of his profession.

His work on the medieval philosophers, especially the Islamic philosopher al Farabi (circa 870–950), led him to uncover the technique of reading for which he has become most famous, a careful attention to esotericism, the method by which philosophers would hide their most unconventional thoughts, and exotericism, the way philosophers would present their teachings as salutary. In his commentary on Plato, Farabi noted that Plato did not feel the need to expose his fullest teaching to everyone, choosing instead to hide his most important ideas. Strauss saw that esotericism, employed by Farabi, had been likewise used by the Jewish medieval philosopher Moses Maimonides (1135–1204), who himself learned the technique from the ancient political philosophers.

Philosophers used exoteric writing to offer desirable or conventional opinions that often hid esoteric thoughts that were true but could not be publicly stated. The need for exotericism, for rhetoric to defend philosophy publicly, could be seen when Athens sentenced Socrates to death for impiety and corrupting the youth. Exotericism had multiple purposes: to prevent the persecution of philosophers, to avoid the damage to society and its conventions that might result from public philosophic reasoning, and, finally, to train the few philosophical minds capable of careful reading. The dialogue form, in which Plato wrote, lends itself well to esotericism since numerous factors, such as dramatic setting, actions, and variety of characters, provide a backdrop against which the author's intent can be gauged. Though Strauss certainly brought greater attention to both esotericism and exotericism than any modern philosopher, he certainly did not discover it; its presence and practice was of great interest to the seventeenth-century freethinkers and the eighteenth-century authors of the *Encyclopédie*, among others.

Strauss's rediscovery of classical political philosophy deepened his understanding of the modern dilemma. For the ancients, the ordering of the city through the regime (in Greek, the *politeia*) determined the way of life of its citizens, directing them toward a certain type of virtue through its understanding of justice. The city sought to promote this virtue through its laws and conventions. Classical political philosophy rejected the belief that the city's virtue is the highest virtue for man, instead looking beyond the city to the life in accordance with reason as highest.

Modern political philosophy, beginning with Machiavelli, rejected both the ancient city and classical political philosophy as setting too high a standard for man, and thereby leaving man prey to the vicissitudes of fortune. Rather than seeking the best possible political order, or what ought to be, modern political philosophy focuses on what is attainable. Key to modern political philosophy is the modern scientific project; as Francis Bacon (1561–1626) understood it, 'the conquest of nature to ease man's estate'.

Strauss understood the moderns as having lowered the standard for what politics can achieve. Rather than believing, as the ancient city did, that it could speak for the best possible way of life and the promotion of virtue, modern liberalism sought to assure the preconditions for life, liberty, and the pursuit of happiness.

Though Strauss is attacked for defending the ancient city against the modern state, Strauss showed how the American republic, in fact, had the potential to incorporate some of the best features of the ancient world. As Aristotle evinces in the *Politics*, though politics in the ancient sense is architectonic, each city's claim to justice is somehow incomplete. Ancient democracy, which featured selection of rulers randomly through lots – was far more egalitarian in key ways than modern liberal democracy, which features election of officials who make claims to rule. Ancient aristocracy, based on conventional claims to excellence, often failed to have due regard for the claims of the average man. Strauss saw America as a mixed regime, incorporating, as had some of the best existing ancient regimes, claims to excellence through election – a reflection, in some sense, of aristocracy, with representation as a replacement for direct democracy.

Strauss saw America as a democratic republic, a regime needing attention to some form of civic virtue and self-sacrifice, to maintain itself most effectively. This civic virtue, in turn, was threatened by liberalism's propensity toward more immediate self-interest and libertinism.

Like Aristotle, Strauss understood the role of the political scientist to see the regime from the perspective of the citizen, to assess its strengths and weaknesses, especially those based on the partial understanding of the claims it makes, and, cautiously, to broaden the regime's self-understanding when possible. Strauss and his students, therefore, pay special attention to the claims made by the founders of the American regime in the Declaration of Independence, *The Federalist Papers*, and the Constitution. Deepening an appreciation for Jefferson, Hamilton, and Madison, Strauss and his students, most notably the late Herbert Storing and Martin Diamond, defended the American regime as a modern, commercial, democratic republic, against those on the left who held America to be a plutocracy or those on the right who claimed its origins in religious principles.

In line with his sober appreciation of what modern politics can achieve, Strauss paid special heed to the threats to democratic republicanism from both liberal self-interest run amuck, and radical egalitarianism. Strauss and his students became central to the rediscovery of Alexis de Tocqueville (1805–59), the great aristocrat whose *Democracy in America* (1835) offered the first thorough study of how the democratic principle of equality shapes every aspect of life in a democratic age – and how the democratic age's tendency toward tyranny can be corrected.

Perhaps the key political lesson Strauss imparted to his students was the limits of utopianism. This, Strauss claims, was central to understanding Plato's *Republic*. Most scholarly interpretations understand the *Republic* literally, especially its proposal for the rule of the philosopher-king, as the best way to order the city and the only way to end the ills; they tend to denounce Plato as totalitarian. But Strauss argues that Plato never intended the rule of philosophers as a realistic possibility since the life of philosophy requires the type of constant questioning that would lead to detachment from the city and its interests. Instead, Strauss argues that the *Republic* is designed to teach the limits of what politics can achieve.

After the defeat of fascism, Strauss's main political concern was the danger of tyranny, of a universal tyranny under the guise of Marxist philosophy. His concern with this tyranny becomes most clear in his exchange with Alexandre Kojeve, the left–Hegelian philosopher turned Common Market technocrat, who viewed his life's work as bringing into existence a universal, rational state as the embodiment of the inevitable march of history. Strauss, by contrast, rejected the notion of the universal, rationalist state, dismissing world government because of the possibility that it might succumb to the danger of modern tyranny, which, thanks to modern technology, was able to wreak horrors far worse than those seen in the city-states of old.

Strauss was uniquely disturbed that economic theorists and historians denied the dignity of politics by insisting that non-human forces, such as markets, are the primary drivers of history. Strauss saw this tendency among historians of a democratic age, as Tocqueville had warned, to deny that public-spirited individuals can make a profound difference in shaping man's destiny. Strauss, instead, praised great democratic statesmen, such as Abraham Lincoln, who protected the Union and defended the principles of the American Revolution, and Winston Churchill who recognized and led the struggle against fascist and communist dictatorships. For Strauss, Churchill offered the greatest living embodiment of the statesman.

1   The argument draws on Thomas Pangle and Nathan Tarcov, 'Epilogue: Leo Strauss and
      the History of Political Philosophy', in History of Political Philosophy, edited by Leo Strauss
      and Joseph Cropsey (Chicago: The University of Chicago Press, 1987), pp. 907–38;
      Allan Bloom, 'Leo Strauss: September 20, 1899–October 18, 1973', in Bloom, Giants and
      Dwarfs (New York: Simon and Schuster, 1990), pp. 235–55; and Mark Blitz, 'Government
      Practice and the School of Strauss', in Kenneth L. Deutsch and John A. Murley (eds),
      Leo Strauss, The Straussians, and the Study of the American Regime (Lanham, MD: Rowman
      and Littlefield, 1999), pp. 439–46. I am grateful to, among others, Hillel Fradkin,
      Montgomery Brown, Mark Blitz, and William Schambra for sharing their insights.
      I am also very grateful to Matthew Rosenberg for providing research assistance.

2   January 9, 2004.

3   Steven Lenzner and William Kristol, 'What was Leo Strauss Up to', The Public Interest,
      Fall 2003.

4   Cf. Leo Strauss, The City and Man (Chicago and London: University of Chicago Press,
      1964), p. 46.

CONSERVATIVES AND NEOCONSERVATIVES

Adam Wolfson

*Those who see in modernity admirable principles
but also worrisome tendencies, their persuasion will be
neoconservatism... Recognizing this fact about American life –
that almost everything is up for grabs and in continual flux –
neoconservatives believe... that we should aim at educating
and directing democracy.*

CONSERVATIVES AND NEOCONSERVATIVES

ADAM WOLFSON

Neoconservatism has become the topic of the day. But does neoconservatism really exist, and if so what is it? What exactly is 'new' in neoconservatism, and how does it differ from other strands of conservative thought in America? And finally, what kind of political influence does neoconservatism wield today? Of course, it is this last question that is nowadays on everyone's mind. Yet one can hardly begin to weigh the influence of neoconservatism on the [George W.] Bush White House without first reaching some understanding of what it is, and how it differs from the old conservatism.

Until quite recently, neoconservatism was thought to be a spent force. Few intellectuals anymore identified themselves as 'neocons', and the label rarely surfaced in political conversation and debate or in the news media. The two leading spokesmen for neoconservatism had themselves concluded that the term had outlived its usefulness. In his 1995 book *Neoconservatism: The Autobiography of an Idea*, Irving Kristol asked, 'Where stands neoconservatism today?' to which he answered: 'It is clear that what can fairly be described as the neoconservative impulse... was a generational phenomenon, and has now been pretty much absorbed into a larger, more comprehensive conservatism.' A year later, in an address before the American Enterprise Institute, Norman Podhoretz emphatically declared that 'neoconservatism is dead'.

Over the last year or so, however, and especially during the run-up to the Iraq War, the label of neoconservatism made its way back into our public discussions and political debates. 'It is neocons... who are the brains behind Bush's push to expel Hussein,' wrote Jacob Heilbrunn in the *Los Angeles Times*. 'Without them there would be no war talk.' He was not alone in singling out the neocons. It has become the label of choice for left- and right-wing war critics. Though John Judis and Patrick Buchanan may have little in common, though Christopher Matthews and Paul Craig Roberts may not agree on much else, they all agree that the war in Iraq was somehow an outgrowth of neoconservative ideology. And the fascination with neoconservatism has hardly abated: 'Neocons on the Line' blared a recent headline in *Newsweek*; 'The Neocons in Charge' read another in *The New York Review of Books*. Presidential hopeful Howard Dean declared on the campaign stump that President Bush has 'been captured by the neoconservatives around him'. And now that the war in Iraq is not going so well, some critics speak of a neoconservative 'crack-up'.

The sudden and unexpected return of the neocon label could be attributed to conspiracy mongering by the left or as the convenient shorthand of journalists to describe apparent fault lines within the Bush administration. Both explanations have merit, but it is also the case that neoconservatism never quite went away as claimed. Neoconservatism may in fact constitute not a generational phenomenon but one of several fundamental alternatives within conservatism taken as a whole. Generally, the neoconservative label has been applied to a particular group of intellectuals who moved from what might be called a neo-liberal politics in the 1960s and 1970s to what became known as neoconservatism. It now seems more likely that something like neoconservatism represents a natural conservative response to modernity, at least in America, one with its own distinctive qualities, its own style and substance, its own strengths and weaknesses.

Today, it is simply assumed that neoconservatism is mainly about foreign policy and stands for something like Wilsonianism-on-steroids – a unilateralist, even utopian, democracy-promoting foreign policy. Yet, historically speaking, as Irving Kristol has noted, neoconservatism was more concerned with the possibilities and limits of the free-enterprise system than with the 'free world' as such. And so it is here, on the domestic side of things, if you will, that we must begin if we are to understand neoconservatism.

The basic contours of neoconservatism most readily emerge against the backdrop of its two main conservative rivals: libertarianism and traditionalism. (I will have little to say of religious conservatives and Straussians, since they are frequently allied with neocons and have moreover helped shape the neocon impulse.) These three conservative approaches – traditionalism, libertarianism, and neoconservatism – first began to take the form we recognize today shortly after World War II. However, each also has deeper historical and philosophic roots. Generally speaking, traditionalists look to Edmund Burke, libertarians to Adam Smith or (more so today) to Friedrich Hayek, and neocons to Alexis de Tocqueville. Each might also be said to find its origins in something more elemental and immediate. Any one of us can't help but have a gut feeling about modernity and modern American life in particular – its possibilities and limits, whether it is humane and decent or alienating and corrupting. Those of us who regret much of modern American life and find solace in old, inherited ways will cling to traditionalism. Others, who celebrate the new freedoms and new technologies, will turn to libertarianism. As for those who see in modernity admirable principles but also worrisome tendencies, their persuasion will be neoconservatism.

THE TRADITIONALISTS

In the post–World War II period, a number of exceptional thinkers sought to adapt a traditionalist, Burkean conservatism to American public life. They became known as the 'new conservatives'. The most prominent of them was Russell Kirk, who authored in 1953 the best-seller *The Conservative Mind*. An overly simple but for our purposes accurate enough way of characterizing Kirk's achievement would be to say that he initiated a turn among American conservatives away from a bourgeois Lockean philosophy and toward a mildly aristocratic Burkean one. A typical American 'conservative' in the pre–World War II period was in fact a nineteenth-century liberal – a believer in laissez-faire, scientific improvements, and progress more generally. The Burke revival that Kirk helped spark in the 1950s lent to American conservatism a very different voice. No longer would it settle for being the party of 'big business' or an apologist for bourgeois society. The traditionalists joined Burke in his lament that 'the age of chivalry is gone', and concurred in his denunciations of the 'new conquering empire of light and reason'.

To the new conservatives, the problem was modern rapaciousness generally, as the following passage from Kirk's classic illustrates: 'The modern spectacle of vanished forests and eroded lands, wasted petroleum and ruthless mining, national debts recklessly increased until they are repudiated, and continual revision of positive law, is evidence of what an age without veneration does to itself and its successors.' And in Kirk's romantic description of the town of Beaconsfield where Burke was buried, traditionalism's unease with modern mass society is clearly evident:

> Little has changed here: the good old houses of four centuries, the tidy half-timbered inn, the great oaks and the quiet lanes are as they were in Burke's day, though the villadome and new-housing-scheme expanses of London bite deep into Buckinghamshire, and light industry is

invading the neighboring towns. At Stoke Poges, only a few miles distant, a tremendous and hideous housing estate of unredeemed monotony has shouldered right against Gray's country churchyard. But Beaconsfield Old Town is an island of ancient England in an industrial and proletarian sea of humanity.

Kirk's project was less about public policy than philosophic definition and cultural recovery. With Burke as his touchstone, Kirk aimed at explaining to an American audience what it meant to be conservative and to think conservatively. In *The Conservative Mind*, he surveyed a kaleidoscope of conservative thinkers, from John Adams to Tocqueville, and from Disraeli to Henry Adams. It had been a long time since Americans had been taught to take these thinkers seriously, and Kirk's prolific writings changed the face of American conservatism. In its early years, the *National Review* was heavily influenced by traditionalist modes of thought, and for a while Kirk wrote a column for the magazine. The magazine's opening statement of purpose, authored by William F. Buckley in 1955, was a neo-Burkean call to arms in which it was declared that the *National Review* 'stands athwart history, yelling Stop'.

The desire to stop, reflect, reconsider, and perhaps go back remains alive within conservative circles. It can be seen in the conservative defense of the traditional family, and in its cultivation of the older virtues and a religious sensibility. Most practically it is evident in the traditionalist view that the federal government has usurped the prerogatives of localities. Such conservatives look back, almost wistfully, to an America of small towns and close-knit communities, and they have become increasingly critical of what they view as President Bush's 'Big Government conservatism'.

The influence of traditionalism in America, however, largely stops at the doorway of practical politics. There are today no real 'traditionalist' politicians in America, in quite the same way that there are, for example, identifiable neoconservative, or paleoconservative, or libertarian politicians and policy-makers. In part this was by design: traditionalist intellectuals in America tended to be more interested in culture, as well as the cultivation of a certain sensibility, than they were in 'mere' party politics. To be sure, they expected to have an influence on politics, but more by indirection, and for the most part they did not actively pursue a public policy agenda. Their lack of a strong political presence can also be traced a bit further. It has long been understood that the United States from its origins is thoroughly (though, of course, not entirely) liberal and Lockean. Americans were born democrats, as Tocqueville pointed out, and never had an aristocratic tradition to which they might recur. This desideratum, if it can be called that, puts a traditionalist style of politics at a decisive disadvantage in America.

THE PALEOCONSERVATIVES

This is the place to digress for a moment and say a word about the paleoconservatives, as they have been labeled. Commonly thought to be the heirs of Kirk and the traditionalists, paleoconservatives in fact dissent from what Kirk considered true conservative principles. They are not conservatives so much as reactionaries or pseudo-radicals. The paleos can fairly be said to despise much of contemporary American life and would like somehow to move beyond the modern American political debate.

Paleoconservatives were largely unknown to the general public until the 1990s when Patrick Buchanan championed many of their ideas in his efforts to remake the Republican Party. Buchanan's goal was not to restore an older conservative ideal but to initiate a right-wing reformation instead. In 2000, he made his radical intentions clear by bolting from the Republican Party and running as the Reform candidate. 'With this campaign,' he declared, 'I intend to redefine what it means to be a conservative.' Buchananism stood for anti-free trade and anti-globalism in economic policy; anti-immigration and pro-life in social policy; and isolationism in foreign policy. Yet despite his strong pro-life position and frequent religious appeals, Buchanan was rejected by rank-and-file religious conservatives and their leadership. He may have declared a 'religious war' for the heart and soul of the nation, but religious conservatives did not buy it. They sided in the Republican primaries with President [George H. W.] Bush in 1992 and Senator Robert Dole in 1996 – neither of whom was known to be strongly supportive of the religious right's agenda. The media largely missed the salience of these alliances, which greatly damaged Buchanan's electoral viability. The paleos' agenda, as it turns out, is more quixotic than anyone quite realized, and the religious right more bourgeois than is generally supposed.

The very term paleoconservative is misleading. Unlike the traditionalists, the paleocons contend that we have become irrevocably cut off from a living, sustainable tradition. In their view, the acids of modernity have left us entirely disinherited from old customs and ways, and conservatism's project of conservation is but a glittering illusion. They have thus gone in search of new gods. Thomas Fleming, editor of the paleoconservative journal *Chronicles: A*

Magazine of American Culture, has looked to sociobiology, evolutionary theory, and anthropology – hardly traditional conservative guides – for a new beginning. Paul Gottfried, another influential paleo theoretician, has sought solutions in the philosophy of Carl Schmitt as well as varieties of historicist ideology. In his book *The Search for Historical Meaning*, he has spoken sympathetically of a return to 'spiritual heroes who enhance civilization by further illuminating the ground of being'. Meanwhile, Samuel Francis, political editor for *Chronicles*, has simply called for 'radical opposition to the regime'.

In another of his books, *The Conservative Movement*, Gottfried has summed up the paleos as follows:

> Above all they raise issues that the neoconservatives and the Left would both seek to keep closed, for instance, questions about the desirability of political and social equality, the functionality of human rights thinking, and the genetic basis of intelligence. In all these assaults on liberal and neoconservative pieties, paleoconservatives reveal an iconoclastic exuberance rarely found on the postwar intellectual Right. Their spirit is far more Nietzschean than neo-Thomistic, and like Nietzsche they go after democratic idols, driven by disdain for what they believe dehumanizes.

THE LIBERTARIANS

In contrast to the paleoconservative and the traditionalist, the libertarian is entirely at home in today's world. He takes his bearings from John Locke, Adam Smith, John Stuart Mill, and such twentieth-century social thinkers as Friedrich Hayek. The libertarian spirit is neither backward-looking nor meliorative. It is progressive, and aims at expanding economic freedom and individual choice ever-forward. Libertarians oppose almost all regulation, whether of markets or morals.

It is arguable whether libertarianism is in fact a variety of conservative thought. Hayek once wrote an essay explaining why he was not a conservative, and Milton Friedman has always insisted that he is a nineteenth-century liberal, not a conservative. But there is at this late date no point in playing semantics and quibbling over labels and definitions. From the 1950s to the present, libertarianism has been an important and influential – arguably the most influential – stream of thought on the right, informing both Republican policy-making and conservative ideology more generally.

Nowhere is the libertarian influence more discernible than in the conservative opposition to Big Government. And here the influence of the writings of Hayek, and in particular his 1944 best-seller *The Road to Serfdom*, looms large. The book was written in response to the rise of Nazi and Soviet totalitarianism, but also to the growing popularity of economic planning and socialist thought generally in the West at the time. Hayek warned, 'We have progressively abandoned that freedom in economic affairs without which personal and political freedom has never existed in the past.' His main target was socialism, of course, but the breadth of his argument was sweeping. In the book's 1956 and 1976 prefaces, he argued that the expanding welfare states of the United States and Western Europe would also lead, necessarily, to the eclipse of liberty. Indeed, the very notion of 'the general welfare' was suspect to Hayek, and in *The Road to Serfdom* he denounced it as a smokescreen behind which totalitarianism marches.

Traditionalists also look upon the modern welfare state with great skepticism, but it is the less romantic, more analytical and policy-oriented libertarian critique that holds sway today at such Washington D.C. think tanks as the Cato Institute, the American Enterprise Institute, and the Heritage Foundation. Their concern for economic efficiency and individual liberty predominates, not the traditionalist's desire to preserve the moral ethos of small-town life. Newt Gingrich rose to Speaker of the House of Representatives in 1994 largely on his libertarian campaign to rein in government regulation and spending. It was libertarianism's greatest political triumph. The preamble to the 'Contract with America' pledged the Republican Party to bring about 'the end of government that is too big, too intrusive, and too easy with the public's money'. In his inaugural speech as Speaker of the House, Gingrich urged his fellow congressmen to 'learn from the private sector... from Ford, IBM, from Microsoft'. In this we catch a glimpse of the libertarian's love affair with the new technologies: they would like to modernize government by e-technology as well as enhance the human pursuit of happiness by biotechnology.

THE NEOCONSERVATIVES

My brief overview of traditionalism and libertarianism hardly does justice to the complexity and richness of each, or to the profound impact they have had on American public life. Yet even so the puzzle of their political alliance over the decades should be readily apparent. Of course, they are both opposed to much government regulation and spending, but beyond this they might seem to share little in common. Their fundamental outlooks are quite at odds, and indeed it was the great project of conservatives in the 1950s and 1960s to find a way of reconciling the two – *National Review* writer Frank Meyer had called his solution 'fusionism'. However, at a deeper level traditionalism and libertarianism do find common cause, and it is here where their differences from neoconservatism first emerge. For both the traditionalist and the libertarian, and in contrast to the neoconservative, politics is of secondary significance. The traditionalist believes that culture or history is the primary factor in human affairs; for the libertarian it is economics. And thus, not surprisingly, they can oftentimes seem to have little affinity for modern democratic life. It is in neoconservatism's appreciation for politics generally and the politics of democracy in particular that its unique characteristics can be seen.

Nostalgia for a pre-industrial, pre-Enlightenment past, as found in traditionalism, is largely absent from neoconservatism. It is not that neoconservatives are proponents of the unregulated market or are without appreciation for our moral and spiritual inheritance as are libertarians. Instead, the neoconservative faults Kirk's neo-Burkean project for its sheer futility. Appeals to tradition as an authoritative guide in American life or as a brake on change and innovation are more than likely to fall on deaf ears. True enough, we have our traditions in America, but these tend to be liberal-democratic ones, such as our reverence for individual rights or our veneration of health and well-being. One need not have lived through our recent cultural upheavals to glean this truth about American democracy. From his visit to America in the 1830s, Tocqueville observed that Americans 'treat tradition as valuable for information only'.

Not from such American materials is a Burkean politics made. Recognizing this fact about American life – that almost everything is up for grabs and in continual flux – neoconservatives believe, to paraphrase Tocqueville, that we should aim at educating and directing democracy, rather than seeking to overcome it, or just as inadvisably, as some more literary conservatives in fact do, scorning it. It was a political axiom of Burke's that 'when ancient opinions and rules of life are taken away, the loss cannot possibly be estimated. From that moment we have no compass to govern us.' This goes too far for the neoconservative. Without siding with the Enlightenment's faith in reason as our only true compass, the neocon recognizes that in democratic times ancient opinions cannot rely on their own authority but must defend themselves in open debate, and that old rules must find some other basis than what is known as prescription if they are to flourish. The loss is, of course, considerable, but rather than retreating in defeat or condemning democracy outright, neoconservatives seek democratic substitutes for these older modes of living. Neoconservatives understand that tradition and custom, in themselves, can have little hold on a democratic people, and thus they look to other means to restrain democracy from its worst instincts.

At least here if nowhere else neocons and paleos are in partial agreement: both share in opposition to traditionalists a sense that much of the past is irretrievable. The question is, where does one go from here? The lamentation for a lost tradition leads paleoconservatives in search of new gods, new heroes, and new myths. Full of disdain for what they consider the democratic idols of equality and commodious living, they seek not to rescue democracy from itself but to expedite its collapse, to make way for a postmodern, post-democratic age. In contrast, neocons seek to refurbish America's founding principles, its constitutional forms, and its democratic way of life. They are aware of democracy's shortcomings – its frequently low aspirations and dehumanizing tendencies – but they also recognize the fundamental justice of democratic equality. Neoconservatives seek to secure a genuine human freedom and dignity in the age in which we live *now*, the democratic age, rather than in some futurist utopia.

LIBERTY AND DESPOTISM

Neoconservatism's political realism, its insistence that we begin our reflections with how life is actually lived by democratic peoples, has never meant simple boosterism for democratic capitalism. 'Two cheers for capitalism,' Irving Kristol once famously remarked – not three. The fault line between neoconservatism and libertarianism is to be found here.

Consider again the question of Big Government. Neoconservatives have also been highly critical of the welfare state, and in particular of the left's exaggerated hopes in it, but their arguments have been more limited in scope than the libertarian's. Neoconservatism's hostility toward the welfare state has never extended, as it does for libertarianism, to the idea of the public good itself. Where libertarians worry that Big Government is liable to stamp out nearly all personal liberty, neoconservatives see things quite differently. In their view, democracies tend to encourage the pursuit of private interests to the neglect of all else, and thus it is the general welfare that is more likely to wither.

The Hayekian analysis of Big Government has always seemed to the neoconservative overly simplistic as well as somewhat naive. The dangers of soft (or hard) despotism against which Hayek warned are at once more distant than he realized and more insidious than he imagined. Most modern democracies have lived with more extensive welfare states and highly socialized economies than the United States, without somehow reaching a 'tipping point' whereupon they tumble into totalitarianism. There is in fact no road to serfdom through the welfare state.

But this good news is overshadowed by a far deeper problem, one that Hayek and his libertarian followers do not see with sufficient acuity, but [which] was well delineated by Tocqueville. Their oversight is in some ways surprising, since Hayek claimed the French philosopher as the inspiration for *The Road to Serfdom*. But Hayek to some extent misunderstood Tocqueville's argument about the threats to liberty in a democracy, while he lacked his predecessor's evident solicitousness for the public realm. As Tocqueville explained, it is democracy itself that fosters the growth of government and threatens liberty. The origins of Big Government are several: democratic peoples have neither the inclination nor the time to engage in public business (being too preoccupied with their own business) – and so in their apathy they leave matters of governing to the State. Their otherwise admirable pride in their independence also feeds the State's growth. Unlike the power exercised by a family patriarch, a local magistrate, or a religious minister, governmental authority, being more anonymous, is less likely to offend, and is thus more easily tolerated in a democracy. Democratic capitalism also plays a role. In times of equality, the middle class increases and eventually predominates. Their aspirations for comfort and ease become society's, as does their strong aversion to whatever might upset their pursuit of well-being, and so increasingly the State is looked to for security and public order. For all of these various reasons, concluded Tocqueville, men in democratic times 'naturally love the central power and willingly extend its prerogatives'.

Big Government is, as it were, written into the political DNA of democracy. Recognizing this, neoconservatives view the struggle against it as almost, though certainly not entirely, beside the point. The important task is to distinguish those expansions of government that are degrading from those that are a natural response to the middle class's feelings of insecurity. The problem of the welfare state has less to do with political liberty than with the specter of moral corruption. Thus neoconservatives tended to oppose Aid to Families with Dependent Children (AFDC), which was rescinded with the reform of welfare in 1996, but are generally supportive of something like social security. It became clear that AFDC discouraged work and inflicted considerable damage on the family and marriage, while despite its larger expense social security can hardly be considered detrimental to seniors. Of course, the form such entitlements take is of great importance in terms of national saving and investment and economic efficiency.

Neoconservatives object not only to the libertarian critique of Big Government but also to its cramped understanding of liberty. Libertarians rise to the defense of every conceivable freedom but that of self-government; they typically tend to be pro-abortion, pro-drug legalization, pro-human cloning, and so on. Their goal, also ardently advanced by the postmodern left, is the expansion of individual choice. But the 'right to choose' has generally been secured in contemporary America only by enacting a judicial prohibition, one that forbids individuals from acting together to determine what laws they shall live under.

Now, neoconservatives are hardly a moralistic lot. On some of these contentious cultural issues, they are as likely to be on the 'pro' as on the 'anti' side. Moreover, their analysis tends toward the urbane – perhaps too urbane given what is morally at stake. Religious conservatives not infrequently become impatient with what they see as the softness of many neoconservatives on these vital issues. However, dispassion should not be mistaken for approval or naivety about what is on the line. Neoconservatism, after all, came into its own in reaction against the left's nihilistic revolt against conventional morality and religion. Moreover, neoconservatives are in agreement in their condemnation of the high-handed manner in which the libertarian agenda is enacted. Democratic discussion is circumvented, and 'we the people', as the phrase would have it, are disenfranchised. To the neoconservative, the true road to serfdom lies in the efforts of libertarian and left-wing elites to mandate an anti-democratic social policy all in the name of liberty. But it is a narrow, privatized liberty that is secured. An active and lively interest in public affairs is discouraged as a result. Everything is permitted – except a say in the shaping of the public ethos. Libertarian ideology would turn citizens into foreigners who live happily, if indifferently, in their country.

THE NEOCONS IN CHARGE?

So wherein lies neoconservatism's political influence, and especially its impact on U.S. foreign policy? George W. Bush's politics and policies, it must be admitted, have, as did Ronald Reagan's, a certain neoconservative resonance.

During the primaries, Bush criticized the libertarian approach, declaring that 'economic growth is not the solution to every problem', and he rejected its core belief that 'if government would only get out of our way, all our problems would be solved'. He also dissented from the traditionalist or paleoconservative view of America: 'Too often,' said Bush, 'my party has painted an image of America slouching toward Gomorrah.' Against these conservative views, Bush advanced the idea of 'compassionate conservatism', which he defined as 'the creed of aggressive, persistent reform. The creed of social progress.' The compassionate conservative, not unlike the neoconservative, is sobered by the difficult problems and peculiar delusions of the modern age, but cautiously optimistic in the good that can still be achieved. Several of Bush's domestic policies, from his faith-based initiatives to his establishment of a commission on bioethics, are quite congenial to neoconservatism.

But more than anything else it is the war in Iraq that brought back the neoconservative moniker. Critics say that neocons have seized control of Bush's foreign policy. This is, at the very least, a surprising claim. Neoconservatism has tended to find its focus in the possibilities of our public life, and has never produced a single approach to foreign policy. (It is, as should by now be clear enough, not an ideology with party-like planks on every issue of the day but an intellectual disposition.) Many of neoconservatism's representative thinkers – to name but a few, Irving Kristol, Nathan Glazer, Daniel Patrick Moynihan, Norman Podhoretz, and Jeane Kirkpatrick – had rather different views on the foreign-policy issues of the day. The claim is surprising for another reason as well. Before the 2000 election, support for George W. Bush among those who would later be labeled as 'neocons' was tepid. The editors of The Weekly Standard, for example, strongly backed Senator John McCain in the primaries, and criticized candidate Bush's foreign-policy positions for being too narrowly 'realist'. The mutual hostility continued well after the election, when Vice President Dick Cheney, who had been asked about criticisms leveled by the Standard's editors, retorted, 'They have to sell magazines. We have to govern.'

Yet much has changed since the September 11 attacks, and there is at least something to the claim that Bush's foreign policy is in part informed by neoconservatism. However, in approaching this complicated question of influence, one salient fact should be noted at the outset: the charge of influence – or, really, it is a charge of conspiratorial, nefarious influence – originated with the Bush administration's most resolute critics. It was the paleoconservatives and the far left who first raised the bogey of a neocon conspiracy. Both camps are notoriously hostile toward neoconservatism, and both are obviously also no friends of George W. Bush. Only later did the charge trickle down to the general media. Most conservatives themselves have rejected the idea that Bush's foreign policy is a neoconservative one, as opposed to a conservative one plain and simple. The accusation of neocon influence should thus be seen for what it is: less an objective analysis of Bush's foreign policy and its intellectual sources than an effort by ideological opponents of the left and right to bloody an administration they loathe.

A more accurate, less biased reading of neoconservatism in U.S. foreign policy might be attained by turning momentarily to the foreign-policy debates of the previous decade. In the 1990s those eventually known as neoconservatives essentially split into two camps. Neoconservatives as a whole opposed the neo-isolationism of Buchanan, the amoral realism of Secretary of State James Baker and the first President Bush, as well as the cosmopolitan humanitarianism of the Clinton administration. But they were divided on the alternatives. Some, like William Kristol, Robert Kagan, and Lawrence Kaplan, held that America's national interests are best served by the spread of democracy throughout the world. They favored a vigorous American response to the crises in Kosovo, Rwanda, and elsewhere, and to some extent one could say they are 'democratic evangelists'. But only up to a point. Unlike liberal Wilsonians, their promotion of democracy is not for the sake of democracy and human rights in and of themselves. Rather, democracy promotion is meant to bolster America's security and to further its world pre-eminence; it is thought to be pragmatically related to the U.S. national interest. The principles of these neocons are universalistic, but not so their policy, which steers clear of international organizations and is nationalist and unilateralist. They also have certain domestic concerns of the Tocquevillian variety, such as the belief that democracies are impatient and fickle in the conduct of foreign affairs. In their view, only a principled foreign policy premised on advancing democracy can sustain the American public's interest in foreign affairs for the long haul.

Meanwhile, a second, smaller band of neoconservatives, whose most prominent spokesman is *Washington Post* columnist Charles Krauthammer, has put forth a slightly different vision. They also favor a principled and proactive foreign policy but are less inclined to see America's national interests as perfectly coinciding with democracy promotion abroad. Krauthammer, for instance, opposed American involvement in Kosovo and Liberia because the connection between these conflicts and our national interest, however broadly the latter might be conceived, was in his view tenuous. To these neoconservatives, the ambition to spread democracy worldwide or to make democracy's tastes and predilections those of every other state is unachievable. They also believe, contrary to their neocon allies, that purely humanitarian missions, such as Kosovo, are more likely to turn Americans off from foreign affairs and foster isolationist sentiment at home. At the same time, these neocons agree that America's interests are necessarily those of a great and powerful democracy. Moreover, these interests cannot be defined, in their view, in strictly strategic terms, encompassing instead an affirmation of our core democratic beliefs – and no more so than when these beliefs are under attack. Pride in our democratic way of life requires no less of us.

More generally, neoconservatives argued that the world's leading and oldest constitutional republic, as well as its lone superpower, has no choice but to be involved in the world. It is less a question of whether the United States should be interventionist and unilateralist, but whether we will manage our new (and largely) unavoidable responsibilities well and effectively or merely reactively and haphazardly. When it was suggested by some – whether by friends or critics of the United States – that what was being proposed was an American Empire, most neoconservatives tended, however, to take exception. As followers of Tocqueville, neocons are generally too aware (or at least should be) of America's fundamentally bourgeois and democratic character to dream of empire. Some have spoken of 'hegemony' (Kagan), others of a 'unipolar moment' (Krauthammer), while still others of 'American Greatness' (David Brooks). Perhaps these writers and thinkers were groping toward something like a more far-reaching, updated Monroe Doctrine.

Now, little of this neocon foreign-policy analysis seemed to have made much of an impression on George W. Bush or his advisors at the time – either during the election or in the early months of his administration. Before the election Bush had vocally called for a more 'humble' foreign policy. But then September 11 came. It seems clear that the President and his closest advisors by temperament prefer to take the initiative, rather than be reactive. They are also philosophically of the view that the executive branch ought to be energetic, especially in its conduct of foreign affairs, and are unapologetic American nationalists. Faced by an unprecedented crisis, they found in neoconservatism a marriage of minds as well as a strategy. In a 1996 article for *Foreign Affairs*, William Kristol and Robert Kagan had supported 'actively pursuing policies – in Iran, Cuba, or China, for instance – ultimately intended to bring about a change of regime'. No mention of Iraq or pre-emptive war here, but Kristol and Kagan's argument for regime change and democracy promotion had a new audience in the White House after September 11.

It must be said, however, that the neocon influence on the Bush administration can be easily exaggerated and often is by hostile critics for their own purposes. The roots of the Bush Doctrine can be as easily traced to positions taken over the years by the conservative *National Review* as by the neoconservative *Commentary* magazine. *The Washington Post's* liberal editorial board has almost as steadfastly supported the Iraq War as has *The Wall Street Journal's* conservative board. Indeed, the roots of Bush's foreign policy may not be, in the strictest sense, conservative at all. In their recent book on American conservatism, *The Right Nation*, John Micklethwait and Adrian Wooldridge make the point that Bush's foreign policy 'is harder to depict as straightforwardly "right-wing" than his stance on some domestic issues'. A distinctively conservative influence is much more apparent, for example, in Bush's firm opposition to abortion, gay marriage, and stem-cell research, or in his strong support of the death penalty and tax-cutting. In contrast, his post-9/11 foreign policy arguably transcends ideological labels and represents something exceptionally American.

In his recent, widely acclaimed book *Surprise, Security, and the American Experience*, Yale historian John Lewis Gaddis traces the historical lineage of Bush's foreign policy to none other than John Quincy Adams. In response to an earlier surprise attack on American soil – the British burning of the White House in 1814 – Adams formulated a policy of unilateralism, pre-emption, and the aim of hegemony. This grand strategy lasted, Gaddis points out, until Franklin D. Roosevelt's multilateralist turn in the midst of World War II. But even before the surprise attacks of September 11, the multilateralist strategy that had guided the United States through much of the Cold War was showing signs of strain. And after September 11 the venerable approach of Adams, which says Gaddis lay deeply 'embedded in our national consciousness', came to the fore. 'Deep roots do not easily disappear,' concludes Gaddis. 'Despite some obvious differences in personality, John Quincy Adams and George W. Bush would not have much difficulty, on matters of national security, in understanding one another.'

The roots of Bush's foreign policy might arguably be traced even deeper. Pre-emption is a prominent feature of a Lockean liberal politics generally. Consider John Locke's *Second Treatise*, for example, where it is argued that, in their defense, people must take action before 'it is too late, and the evil is past

Cure', and that to be 'secure from Tyranny' people must 'have not only a Right to get out of it, but to prevent it'. A Lockean mode of politics is almost hypervigilant against tyranny. Throughout America's history we have, in the Lockean fashion, sought to build 'fences' around our rights, and have tended to see in 'a long train of abuses' plots of enslavement. Americans prefer to act before the danger is upon them – which is roughly the approach taken by the Bush administration to what it considered the 'gathering' threat posed by Iraq. One might suggest, admittedly at the risk of some overgeneralization, that, in moving against Iraq, the Bush administration simply reflected aspects of the political psychology embodied in Locke's *Second Treatise*.

As with Big Government in domestic affairs, unilateralism in foreign policy is perhaps written into our political DNA. Certainly, it would seem to be an enduring feature of American politics. Neocons have tended, for better or worse, to affirm these aspects of the American character more readily than other conservatives. But however we describe the sources of the Bush Doctrine, this much is clear: it is a policy still in the making, with many political factions in the administration fighting over its ultimate meaning and scope. If the decision to go to war in Iraq was supported by many neoconservatives (certainly, not all), the way the war has been fought thus far, and how the occupation managed, have been harshly criticized by neoconservatives and are not reflective of their overall strategic thinking. Neoconservatives have been similarly critical of U.S. strategy in Afghanistan. As for the Bush administration, it is obviously learning as it goes and has been improvising considerably. Where it will end up is hardly clear.

POLITICAL REGIMES

More often than not political labels distract us from what is truly important, and in the hands of pundits and politicians, they can become merely a way of scoring points against the opposition. Such labels are useful only if they further our understanding of political reality. The public's rediscovery of neoconservatism is thus to be welcomed, for it returns us to certain fundamental and unresolved quarrels within conservatism. Contrary to general impression, neoconservatism never was subsumed into a broader conservative intellectual movement. This was in fact unlikely to happen, since neoconservatism represents less a mere reaction against the 1960s counter-culture than a recurrent conservative impulse in our democratic age, possibly its most vital. Conservatism's other strands are strangely anti-democratic.

Traditionalists pine for aristocracy; libertarians look to limited government by technocracy; while paleoconservatives dream vaguely of postmodern utopias. Only neoconservatism among contemporary conservative modes of thought has made its peace with American democracy. That also might be considered a serious weakness, but would be a subject for another day.

NEOCONSERVATISM
AS A RESPONSE TO THE
COUNTER-CULTURE

Jeane Kirkpatrick

*As long as the United States was perceived as a virtuous society,
policies that enhanced American power were also seen as virtuous.*

NEOCONSERVATISM AS A RESPONSE TO THE COUNTER-CULTURE

JEANE KIRKPATRICK

I think I was first called a neoconservative sometime after 1972 – that is after the culture wars had been raging for a decade in the Democratic Party. Those wars split the party and led directly to the nomination of George McGovern as the Democratic presidential candidate for 1972 and the founding of a Democratic faction called CDM (the Coalition for a Democratic Majority). This was about the time I moved to New York to head the U.S. delegation to the United Nations, that is, January 1981.

The 'neoconservative' designation puzzled me. I had never thought of myself as a conservative of any kind. What is a neoconservative? I asked my friend, Irving Kristol, who was widely described as the godfather of the neoconservative movement. He responded without hesitation that a neoconservative was a liberal who had been mugged by reality. That is, I thought, a person with a liberal past. It was the liberal past that distinguished a neoconservative from a traditional conservative, say Russell Kirk or Bill Buckley and all the others who had begun their political lives as traditional conservatives. The neocon had embraced liberal values and quite possibly never abandoned them, but was unhappy with the political turns taken by many in liberal ranks. Voilà, I thought, the neoconservative was born from a reaction to the counter-culture that dominated American politics through the sixties and seventies.

The extremes of this counter-culture had disappeared by 1976, but the residue was more lasting. Its effects on what has been called liberal politics were profound. The counter-culture was much broader than the anti-war movement with which it was associated and, I believe, constituted a sweeping rejection of traditional American attitudes, values, and goals. The counter-culture subjected virtually all aspects of American life and culture to criticism and repudiation.

The cultural revolution under way in American society was also under way in the United Nations, whose activities and membership had been transformed by the wave of decolonization that liberated many colonies of the formerly colonial powers in Africa, Asia, and the Middle East, thus transforming the membership of the United Nations and dramatically strengthening the voice and votes of the formerly colonial states.

One result was a revolution in the issues that rather quickly came to dominate the agenda of the United Nations General Assembly and other United Nations agencies, including UNESCO, UNDP, ECOSOC, among others.

The cultural revolution swept through American cities, campuses, and newsrooms, challenging basic American beliefs and transforming American institutional practices. This was a time when a leading columnist of the *New York Times* wrote: 'The United States is the most dangerous and destructive power in the world.' It was a time when the president of a leading university asserted: 'In twenty-six years since waging a war against the forces of tyranny, fascism, and genocide in Europe we have become a nation more tyrannical, more fascistic, and more capable of genocide than was ever conceived or thought possible two decades ago. We conquered Hitler but we have come to embrace Hitlerism.' This was the period when a nationally known cleric stated, 'The reason for the paroxysm in the nation's conscience is simply that Calley★ is all of us. He is every single citizen in our graceless land.' Well.

If the United States was 'the most destructive power in the world', if we are 'capable of genocide', if we are a 'graceless land', then defense of our national interest could not be integrally linked to the defense of human rights or any other morally worthy cause.

As long as the United States was perceived as a virtuous society, policies that enhanced American power were also seen as virtuous. Morality and American power were indissolubly linked in the traditional conception. But with the U.S. defined as an essentially immoral society, valuing and/or enhancing power were perceived as immoral. Morality now required transforming our deeply flawed society, not enhancing its power.

Michael Novak, theologian, scholar, friend, newly appointed U.S. Commissioner on Human Rights, wrote to me from the Geneva meeting of the UN Human Rights Commission in February 1981. 'As matters stand, we are just a few short years from being a pariah nation. Rhetorically, we already are.

★ Lt. William Calley was convicted of slaughtering innocents at the village of My Lai during the Vietnam War, and was sentenced to life imprisonment at hard labor [Ed.].

Swedish observers, Australian junior delegates, and some Western Europeans already think of us as the enemy.' Novak was deeply shocked at almost the daily assault on the United States (and Israel) in the United Nations Commission on Human Rights, shocked by the reaction and lack of reaction of our allies, shocked at the success that the Soviet Union and the socialist nations had already had in redefining and capturing the key concepts of liberal democracy.

He was not the first to notice that the UN had become the scene of continuing attacks on the values and institutions of liberal democracy. William F. Buckley had written about it after his stint as a public delegate to the General Assembly. The late Daniel Patrick Moynihan had noticed this phenomenon during his tenure as Permanent Representative in 1975. I was already beginning to notice it in New York.

Novak was stunned by the extent to which the redefinition of the political world had already taken place, and the UN had become a cognitive universe dominated by language, values, and understandings hostile to our own. Moynihan had noticed that too; even before he went to the United Nations, he had written a famous article in *Commentary* magazine, advocating that the United States confront this challenge to the values and institutions of liberal democracy and defend ourselves.

I had read Buckley, Moynihan, Conor Cruise O'Brien, and Chaim Herzog on the UN but still was not aware of the extent of the revolution that had taken place there.

Harold Lasswell, a friend and a brilliant American social scientist, had written that a revolution is a marked change in the vocabulary and composition of the elite.

In the United Nations a revolutionary change in the composition and vocabulary of the ruling elite had occurred more than a decade before Ronald Reagan went to the White House, or I went to the UN, or Michael Novak arrived in Geneva for the meeting of the UN Commission on Human Rights, but we did not yet understand it.

Before the revolution, the representatives of democratic governments had had a dominant influence on the agenda, the administration, and the policies of the United Nations. The original language of the UN was that of the UN Charter, an idealistic internationalist version of liberal democracy. But, the democratic structure of the UN guaranteed that the views and values of dozens of new nations entering the UN would be quickly reflected in the organization. And many of those views and values were very different. The language of the new governments was largely nationalist, socialist, and 'non-aligned'. Established in 1961 by Tito, Nasser, and Nehru [the leaders of Yugoslavia, Egypt, and India, respectively], the Non-aligned Movement (NAM) was in the beginning what it was intended to be, an organization of states 'non-aligned' with either the democratic or the communist worlds. Then, the NAM itself was transformed. The Non-aligned Movement was itself progressively captured by states linked to Moscow. By 1968, the NAM failed to condemn the Soviet invasion of Czechoslovakia. A decade later the NAM met the invasion of Afghanistan with what one member called a 'deafening silence'. By the time that Cuba became chairman of the NAM in 1979, the movement was regularly and effectively manipulated by a group of its members that regularly threw its support behind the foreign policy of the Soviet Union. During Cuba's chairmanship the efforts to formally align the NAM with the Soviet Union were pushed hard by the Cuban chair who argued that the Soviet Union and the socialist bloc were 'the natural allies' of the non-aligned countries.

Despite Cuba's persistent efforts, the NAM declined to formally commit its members to the 'natural allies' doctrine. However, the language and the positions of the NAM were simultaneously nationalist, socialist, and hostile to democratic values, alliances, and interests. More important, the language of NAM communiqués, and the positions they advocated, continued to reflect a global orientation and a cognitive universe that was in many ways antithetical to those of a democratic world in which 'self-determination' reflects the choices of citizens, 'national independence' reflects the position of fully independent countries, and 'restructuring the world economy' means redistributing the 'world's' wealth.

The world of the NAM paid lip-service to 'the sovereign equality of states', but regularly treated some states and groups as much more equal than others. And Israel as the least equal of all.

Let me be clear. Soviet satellites did not control the NAM. Neither did the Third World states that constituted an overwhelming majority of the non-aligned movement. Moreover, NAM communiqués were finally forced to take some timid notice of the invasion and continuing occupation of Afghanistan and Kampuchea, and some of its most violent attacks on the U.S. were moderated. But the affinity of Soviet client states in the NAM gave them what the Italian Marxists called 'hegemony'.

I am not saying that Soviets controlled everything that happened at the UN. They did not. I am saying that for various reasons – including ideological affinity and organizational manipulation – the priorities, assumptions, and terms of discourse of UN proceedings became much closer to Soviet conceptions than American. But not only UN proceedings. The counter-culture had progressively radicalized the intellectual life of America.

In the media, in universities, in public debates and demonstrations, large numbers of Americans engaged in scathing, ongoing self- and mutual-criticism sessions in which our collective life was attacked. The enemy was always us.

Authorities – parents, policemen, presidents, judges, lawyers, governors – were attacked with a vehemence and violence it is hard to remember. American Red Guards attacked professors, politicians, policemen, and public officials with mobs, rocks, obscenities, and sometimes guns. At Columbia, Berkeley, Harvard, Kent State [universities], and dozens of imitating institutions, fundamentals of traditional liberalism and democracy were repudiated, and their proponents attacked in the classroom and in the streets.

Although it was generally asserted that resistance to the Vietnam War spawned the counter-culture, I believed the reverse was true. I believed the ideological assault on authority symbols and structures preceded the anti-war movement and made it possible.

Lionel Trilling's analysis of the 'adversary culture' – which antedated the anti-war movement – explained how attitudes hostile to traditional American values spread from the avant-garde to progressively larger audiences. The questions and negations of the counter-culture made possible middle-class resistance to the demands of the anti-war movement.

The central aspect of the anti-war movement was less its rejection of the Vietnam War than its rejection of the United States. The argument was less that the war was unwise or unnecessary than that the United States was immoral – a 'sick society' guilty of racism, materialism, imperialism, and murder of Third World people in Vietnam.

This passionate rejection – less of what the U.S. did than of what it was – constituted a wholesale assault on the legitimacy of American society. *I believe this assault became the foundation of the opposing neoconservative position.* Neoconservatives were not fundamentally alienated from American life and society.

The old liberalism – which stood for an inclusive welfare state in domestic affairs and was internationalist in foreign affairs – affirmed the need for military strength, and resisted the Soviet aggression and subversion of independent nations.

George McGovern's presidential campaign was a principal carrier of counter-cultural attitudes and approaches in the presidential politics of 1972.

The McGovern campaign not only advocated immediate withdrawal of the U.S. from the Vietnam War, thus announcing itself indifferent to the spread of communist power in Vietnam and south-east Asia, it adopted as its own a revisionist interpretation of the post-World War II period. In that revisionist view (first propounded by Henry Wallace in 1948), the United States had major responsibility for the Cold War and Soviet expansion.

Traditional liberals believed that, while not perfect, the U.S. was a successful society, which provided freedom and decent standards of living to most of its citizens. We did not doubt that American society could be improved but we believed it first had to be preserved. We believed moreover that there were important differences between democracy and dictatorship, and that the greatest differences of all were between democracy and totalitarianism. We could not therefore be indifferent to the spread of Soviet power or to the human consequences of seeing new tyrannies established.

Like mainstream conservatives, Republicans, and mainstream liberals, which in those years we thought we were, we worried about abandoning the people of South Vietnam to the mercies of North Vietnam, and we worried about the vulnerability of Vietnam's neighbors to victorious North Vietnamese armies. We were right to worry. Hundreds of thousands of South Vietnamese were sent for re-education to slave labor camps in the North; many thousands of boat people risked sharks, security police, drowning, and pirates to escape precisely the tyranny we feared for them.

I believe the new politics had from the start been marked by a persistent tendency to blame America first and most, and to extend to others 'understanding' and tolerance denied the United States. I still feel an affinity to traditional liberalism, but a more powerful aversion to counter-cultural liberalism. That, I suppose, makes me a neoconservative.

As such, I agree with Irving Kristol that the welfare state is, and should be, here to stay, and with those who share with me a healthy skepticism toward some multinational organizations.

THE
NEOCONSERVATIVE
CABAL

Joshua Muravchik

On September 11... the neoconservatives, who had been warning for years that terror must not be appeased, stood vindicated... They... stood ready with proposals for what to do now... If... the policies succeed, then the world will have been delivered from an awful scourge.

THE
NEOCONSERVATIVE CABAL

JOSHUA MURAVCHIK

Over the last months, the term 'neoconservative' has been in the air as never before in its thirty-year career. Try entering it in *Nexis*, the electronic database of news stories. Even if you were to restrict the request to stories containing 'Iraq' and 'Bush', the search will abort; the number of entries exceeds the program's capacity. Seven years after Norman Podhoretz, the conductor of the neocon orchestra, pronounced the demise of the movement in these pages,[*] neoconservatives are seen to be wielding more influence than ever before. For it is they who, notoriously, are alleged to have transformed George W. Bush beyond all recognition. At their hands, the President who as a candidate had envisioned a 'humble' America – one that would reduce foreign deployments and avoid nation-building – became a warrior chieftain who has already toppled two foreign governments and has laid down an ultimatum to others warning of a similar fate.

'The neoconservatives... are largely responsible for getting us into the war against Iraq,' observes Elizabeth Drew in *The New York Review of Books*. 'The neocon vision has become the hard core of American foreign policy,' declares *Newsweek*. 'They have penetrated the culture at nearly every level from the halls of academia to the halls of the Pentagon,' frets *The New York Times*, adding that 'they've accumulated the wherewithal financially [and] professionally to broadcast what they think over the airwaves to the masses or over cocktails to those at the highest levels of government.' 'Long before George W. Bush reached the White House, many of these confrontations [with other nations] had been contemplated by the neoconservatives,' reveals the *National Journal*.

Overseas, where the policies attributed to the neocons are far more controversial than here, the tone is commensurately hotter. A six-page spread in the French weekly *Le Nouvel Observateur* described *'les intellectuels néoconservateurs'* as the 'ideologues of American empire'. The article ran under a banner headline: 'After Iraq, the World'. In England, the British Broadcasting

---

[*] 'Neoconservatism: A Eulogy', *Commentary*, March 1996.

Company (BBC) aired an hour-long television special that began: 'This is a story about people who want the world run their way, the American way, [and]... scare the hell out of people.' *The Times* of London anxiously urged close British cooperation with the U.S. if only to gain the leverage needed to 'spike the ambitions of U.S. neoconservatives'.

Who makes up this potent faction? Within the administration, Deputy Secretary of Defense Paul Wolfowitz is usually identified as the key actor, together with Richard Perle, a member and until recently the chairman of the Defense Advisory Board. A handful of other high-level Bush appointees are often named as adherents of the neocon faith, including Under Secretary of Defense Douglas Feith, Under Secretary of State John Bolton, National Security Council staff member Elliott Abrams, and vice-presidential aide Lewis 'Scooter' Libby. The American Enterprise Institute (AEI, where I work), *The Weekly Standard* magazine, and William Kristol's Project for the New American Century – all three rent offices in the same building – are often described as constituting the movement's Washington command center. And then, of course, there is this magazine, crucible of so much neoconservative thought.

The history of neoconservatism is less sensational than its current usage implies. The term came into currency in the mid-1970s as an anathema – pronounced, by upholders of leftist orthodoxy, against a group of intellectuals, centered mostly in *Commentary* and the quarterly *The Public Interest*, who then still thought of themselves as liberals but were at odds with the dominant thinking of the left. One part of this group consisted of writers about domestic policy – Irving Kristol, Daniel Patrick Moynihan, James Q. Wilson, Nathan Glazer – who had developed misgivings about the programs of the New Deal or Lyndon Johnson's Great Society. The other main contingent focused on foreign policy, and especially on the decline of America's position vis-à-vis the Soviet Union in the wake of the Vietnam War. The names here included, among others, Podhoretz, Jeane Kirkpatrick, and Eugene V. Rostow. Although, at first, most of these people resisted the label neoconservative, eventually almost all of them acquiesced in it.

Today, many who are called neoconservatives are too young to have taken part in these debates, while others, although old enough, followed a different trajectory in arriving at their political ideas. This would hardly matter if neoconservatism were an actual political movement, or if there were general agreement about its tenets. But few of those writing critically about neoconservatism today have bothered to stipulate what they take those tenets to be. For most, the term seems to serve as a sophisticated-sounding synonym for 'hawk' or 'hardliner' or even 'ultraconservative'.

For others, however, it is used with a much more sinister connotation. In their telling, neoconservatives are a strange, veiled group, almost a cabal, whose purpose is to manipulate U.S. policy for ulterior purposes.

Thus, several scribes have concentrated on laying bare the hidden wellsprings of neoconservative belief. These have been found to reside in the thinking of two improbable figures: the immigrant American political philosopher Leo Strauss (1899–1973)* and the Bolshevik military commander Leon Trotsky (1879–1940). 'Who runs things?', *The New York Times* asked, concluding that 'it wouldn't be too much of a stretch to answer: the intellectual heirs of Leo Strauss' with whom the Bush administration is 'rife'. The *Boston Globe* ran a 3,000-word article claiming that 'we live in a world increasingly shaped by Leo Strauss', while in a sidebar to its own feature story on the neocons, *Le Nouvel Observateur* introduced French readers to 'Leo Strauss, their Mentor'.

Michael Lind, an American who writes for the British leftist magazine *New Statesman*, has been the most insistent voice invoking the name of Trotsky, or rather 'the largely Jewish-American Trotskyist movement' of which, Lind says, 'most neoconservative defense intellectuals... are products'. Jeet Heer, who expounded the Straussian roots of neoconservatism in the *Boston Globe*, went on to disclose the Trotsky connection in Canada's *National Post*. ('Bolshevik's Writings Supported the Idea of Pre-emptive War', ran the subhead.) Others agreed about this dual connection. William Pfaff, in the *International Herald Tribune*, contributed one column on the influence of Leo Strauss and another linking Bush's foreign policy to the 'intellectual legacy of the Trotskyism of many of the neoconservative movement's founders'. In particular, in Pfaff's judgment, administration policy 'seems a rightist version of Trotsky's "permanent revolution"'.

Actually, neither line of genealogical inquiry is new. Eight years ago, in *Foreign Affairs*, John Judis derided my advocacy of 'exporting democracy' as a kind of 'inverted Trotskyism'. As for Strauss, it was noticed as far back as the Reagan administration that a small number of the philosopher's former students had taken policy positions in the State and Defense departments. But the prize for the recent resuscitation of Strauss's name would seem to belong to the crackpot political agitator Lyndon LaRouche, who began to harp on it in speeches and publications months before any of the references I have cited above. LaRouche,

---

* See the essay by Kenneth Weinstein, Ed.

who ceased using the pseudonym Lyn Marcus (a conscious derivation of Lenin Marx) when he vaulted from the far left to the far right, and who has served time in a federal penitentiary on charges of gulling elderly people out of their savings in order to finance his political movement, has fingered Strauss 'along with Bertrand Russell and H. G. Wells' as the parties responsible for 'steering the United States into a disastrous replay of the Peloponnesian war'.

This preoccupation with ancestor-hunting may seem of secondary interest, but since it is typical of the way most recent 'analysis' of neoconservative ideas has been conducted, it is worth pausing over for another moment.

For one thing, the sheer sloppiness of the reporting on the alleged Strauss–Trotsky connection is itself remarkable. Thus, *The New York Times* claimed extravagantly that AEI consists in its entirety of Straussians, whereas a little checking yields, out of fifty-six scholars and fellows, exactly two who would count themselves as Straussians and a third who would acknowledge a significant intellectual debt to Strauss; none of the three is in the field of foreign policy. *The New York Times* also identified Perle as a Straussian – which is false – while erroneously stating that he was married to the daughter of the late military strategist Albert Wohlstetter, whom it likewise falsely labeled a Straussian. Even after an initial correction (explaining that Perle had merely studied under Wohlstetter at the University of Chicago and had not married his daughter) and a second correction (acknowledging that Perle had never studied under Wohlstetter *or* attended the University of Chicago), the paper still could not bring itself to retract its fanciful characterizations of either Perle's or Wohlstetter's ties to Strauss. The paper also mischaracterized Podhoretz as an 'admirer' of Strauss, which is true only in a very loose sense. Similar errors have infected the stories in other publications.

And Trotsky? Lind in his disquisition on 'the largely Jewish-American Trotskyist movement' instanced seven pivotal neocon figures as the Bolshevik revolutionary's acolytes: Wolfowitz, Feith, Libby, Bolton, Abrams, James R. Woolsey, and Perle. This was too much for Alan Wald, a student of political ideas and himself a genuine Trotskyist, who pointed out that none of these men 'ever had an organizational or ideological association with Trotskyism'.* Even more

---

* In a shrill rejoinder to Wald, Lind named me as an exemplar of neocon Trotskyism, calling me a 'Schachtmannite' [*sic*] to boot. Although I did know Max Shachtman, who was a member of the Socialist Party when I was active in its youth arm in the 1960s, I was never a Shachtmanite, and Shachtman himself had ceased to be a Trotskyite about a decade before I met him.

ludicrously, Lind characterized a series of open letters to the President published by the Project for the New American Century as 'a PR technique pioneered by their Trotskyist predecessors'; whatever Lind may have had in mind by this phrase, genuine Trotskyists would be less interested in sending petitions to the President than in hanging him from the nearest lamppost.

In truth, I can think of only one major neocon figure who did have a significant dalliance with Trotskyism, and that was Irving Kristol. The dalliance occurred during his student days some sixty-odd years ago, and whatever imprint it may have left on Kristol's thought certainly did not make him a neoconservative on foreign policy, for in that area his views have been much more akin to those of traditional conservatives. During the 1980s, for example, Kristol opposed the 'Reagan Doctrine' of support for anti-communist guerrillas and belittled the idea of promoting democracy abroad.

But that brings us to the actual ideas of these two presumed progenitors of neoconservatism. Strauss, according to Jeet Heer, emerges from a close reading as a 'disguised Machiavelli, a cynical teacher who encouraged his followers to believe that their intellectual superiority entitles them to rule over the bulk of humanity by means of duplicity'. Similarly, Pfaff: 'An elite recognizes the truth... and keeps it to itself. This gives it insight and implicitly power that others do not possess. This obviously is an important element in Strauss's appeal to American conservatives... His real appeal to the neoconservatives, in my view, is that his elitism presents a principled rationalization for policy expediency, and for "necessary lies" told to those whom the truth would demoralize.'

Neither Heer nor Pfaff offers a clue as to where in Strauss's corpus one might find these ideas, giving one the impression that they learned what they know of him from a polemical book by one Shadia Drury, who holds a chair in 'social justice' at a Canadian university and who finds Strauss to be a 'profoundly tribal and fascistic thinker'. In any event, although Strauss did write about restrictions on free inquiry, notably in *Persecution and the Art of Writing*, his point was not to advocate persecution but to suggest a way of reading philosophers who had composed their work in unfree societies. Far from the authoritarian described by Heer and Pfaff, Strauss, a refugee from Nazi Germany, was a committed democrat whose attachment and gratitude to America ran deep and who, in the words of Allan Bloom (perhaps his most famous student), 'knew that liberal democracy is the only decent and just alternative available to modern man'.

Both Heer and Pfaff make Strauss out to be a Machiavellian, but both have the story upside down. If there is a single core point in Strauss's teachings, including his book on Machiavelli, it concerns the distinction between ancients and moderns; his own affinity – perhaps eccentric, certainly 'conservative' – lay with the thought of the former, who were devoted to knowing the good, in contradistinction to the latter who were more exclusively concerned with practical things. In this understanding, it was Machiavelli who initiated the philosophical break with the Platonic/Aristotelian tradition, a development that Strauss regarded as baneful. But reading political counsel into Strauss is altogether a misplaced exercise. He was not a politico but a philosopher whose life's work was devoted to deepening our understanding of earlier thinkers and who rarely if ever engaged in contemporary politics.

If Strauss's writing is abstruse, Trotsky by contrast is easy to understand, at least if one knows the basic formulas of Marxism. Nonetheless, those who invoke him as another dark influence on neoconservatism are no better informed than those who invoke Strauss. Lind, Pfaff, and Judis all refer portentously to Trotsky's theory of 'permanent revolution', apparently under the impression that by it Trotsky must have intended a movement to spread socialism from one country to another in much the same violent and revolutionary manner that neocons supposedly aim to disseminate their own brand of democracy around the world.

But the theory of permanent revolution was about other matters entirely. According to the late nineteenth- and early twentieth-century Marxists, the socialist revolution could unfold only some years *after* capitalism and the bourgeoisie had triumphed over feudalism; in undeveloped countries like Russia, this meant that socialists had no choice but to support capitalism until it ripened and set the stage for revolution. From this prospect of deadly boredom, Trotsky rescued the movement by arguing for an immediate seizure of power in hopes of somehow telescoping the bourgeois and socialist revolutions into one seamless sequence. That was 'permanent revolution'.

As is the case with the Strauss-hunters, it is far from evident what any of this has to do with Iraq, terrorism, or promoting democracy. The neocon journalist Arnold Beichman put it sardonically and well: 'STOP THE PRESSES: Trotsky... wouldn't have supported the Iraq war.' On second thought, he probably would have – on Saddam's side.

Finally, if the attempts to link neoconservatives to Strauss and Trotsky are based on misidentification and misconstruction, the fact that *both* linkages have been made – in some cases by the same writer – is stranger still. For it would be hard to come up with a more disparate pair of thinkers. Strauss's mission was to take us back by means of contemplation to the nearly lost past of classical antiquity. Trotsky's was to lead mankind by means of violent action to an unprecedented new society. The one aimed to rescue philosophy from ideology; the other was the consummate ideologue. How, exactly, does neoconservatism bear the earmarks of both of these projects simultaneously? No one has attempted to explain.

There is, however, one thing that Strauss and Trotsky did have in common, and that one thing may get us closer to the real reason their names have been so readily invoked. Both were Jews. The neoconservatives, it turns out, are also in large proportion Jewish – and this, to their detractors, constitutes evidence of the ulterior motives that lurk behind the policies they espouse.

Lind, for example, writes that neocons 'call their revolutionary ideology "Wilsonianism"... , but it is really Trotsky's theory of the permanent revolution mingled with the far-right Likud strain of Zionism'. Lind's view was cited at length and with evident approval by the *National Journal*, which noted that he 'isn't alone':

> Commentators from surprisingly diverse spots on the political spectrum [agree] that neocons took advantage of the attacks on the World Trade Center and the Pentagon to advance a longstanding agenda that is only tangentially related to keeping the United States safe from terrorism. In this view, America's invasion of Iraq and threatening of Syria have little to do with fighting terrorism, eliminating weapons of mass destruction, or promoting democracy. Instead, those actions largely have to do with settling old grievances, putting oil-rich territory into friendly hands, and tilting the balance of power in the Middle East toward Israel.

Elizabeth Drew made a similar point, if more opaquely:

> Because some... of the neoconservatives are Jewish and virtually all are strong supporters of the Likud party's policies, the accusation has been made that their aim to 'democratize' the region is driven by their desire to surround Israel with more sympathetic neighbors. Such a view would explain the otherwise puzzling statements by Wolfowitz and others before the [Iraq] war that 'the road to peace in the Middle East goes through Baghdad.' But it is also the case that Bush and his chief political adviser Karl Rove are eager both to win more of the Jewish vote in 2004 than Bush did in 2000 and to maintain the support of the Christian Right, whose members are also strong supporters of Israel.

Drew's use of the word 'but' at the head of the last sentence was no doubt designed to distance her from the accusation that the neocons' motive is to serve the interests of Israel, even as the words that follow the 'but' only seem to confirm the charge.

More explicit, and more egregious, was the hard-left historian Paul Buhle, who wrote in *Tikkun* that 'It is almost as if the anti-Semitic *Protocols of Zion*, successfully fought for a century, have suddenly returned with an industrial-sized grain of truth' – that 'truth' being, of course, that the hawkish policies of the neoconservatives are indeed tailored for Israel's benefit.

Perhaps the most dramatic effort to expose the hidden Jewish interest underlying neocon ideas was the BBC-TV special on America's 'war party'. It was aired on the program *Panorama*, which touts itself as the British equivalent of CBS's *60 Minutes*, and the lead-in announced: 'Tonight: Will America's Superhawks Drag us into More Wars against their Enemies?' It did not take long for the meaning of the phrase *'their* enemies' to become apparent. First, however, viewers were introduced to a rogues' gallery of neoconservative interviewees, each of them filmed at an unusually close angle with the head filling the entire screen for an eerie, repulsive effect. Freeze-frame stills of the subjects were also shown, shifting suddenly from color into the look of white-on-black negatives, while in the background one heard sound effects appropriate to a line-up on a police drama. By contrast, the interviewer, Steve Bradshaw, and a number of guests hostile to the neocons were shown mostly in appealing poses.

On the show itself, Perle was introduced as 'the neocons' political godfather', a suggestive term whose implication was reinforced by a question put separately to him and another guest: 'Are you a mafia?' As the camera panned over the building that houses AEI and the other arms of this 'mafia', we heard from the announcer that here was where the 'future is being plotted'.

And what exactly *is* being 'plotted'? The answer was foreshadowed early on when an unidentified woman in the street said of the war in Iraq: 'It seems like there's… another agenda that we're not really privy to and that is what concerns me most.' Several minutes later, Bradshaw returned to the same motif: 'We picked up a recurrent theme of insider talk in Washington. Some leading neocons, people whisper, are strongly pro-Zionist and want to topple regimes in the Middle East to help Israel as well as the U.S.' To shed light on this 'highly sensitive issue', he then turned to Jim Lobe, identified as a 'veteran neocon watcher and long-standing opponent of anti-Semitism'.

Lobe was used repeatedly as the show's resident expert. A reporter with the 'alternative' media who prides himself on being a nemesis of neoconservatives, he has no special credentials as an 'opponent of anti-Semitism', but the gratuitous compliment was there for a purpose – namely, to inoculate him and his hosts against the obvious charge of Jew-baiting. For that is indeed what came next. Bradshaw posed the leading question: 'You think it's legitimate to talk about the pro-Israeli politics of some of the neoconservatives?' And Lobe, looking as Jewish as his name sounds, replied: 'I think it's very difficult to understand them if you don't begin at that point.' A few moments later, in a simulacrum of journalistic balance, Bradshaw allowed the Middle East specialist Meyrav Wurmser to deny any special neoconservative fidelity to Israel. Wurmser is an immigrant to the United States from Israel, and looks and sounds the part; she could not have been chosen with more care to verify the charge she was brought on to deny – that the neoconservatives are indeed a Jewish mafia, dragging both America and Britain into war after war for the sake of Israel.

If there is an element of anti-Semitism at work in some of the attacks on the neoconservatives – and there manifestly is – to call it such is not, alas, enough. Even outright canards need to be rebutted, tedious and demeaning though the exercise may be. So let us ask the question: is it true that neoconservatives are mostly Jews, and are they indeed working to shape U.S. policy out of devotion to the interests of the 'Likud Party' or of Israel?

Many neoconservatives are in fact Jews. Why this should be so is not self-evident, although part of the answer is surely that Jews, whenever and wherever they have been free to indulge it, exhibit a powerful attraction to politics and particularly to the play of political ideas – an attraction that is evident all across the political spectrum but especially on the left. Indeed, the disproportionate presence of Jews in early communist movements in Eastern and Central Europe became grist for the Nazis and other far-right movements that portrayed Bolshevism as a Jewish cause whose real purpose was (yes) to serve Jewish interests. In reality, Trotsky and Zinoviev and the other Jewish communists were no more concerned about the interests of the Jewish people than were Lenin and Stalin – which is to say, not at all.

As it happens, the Jewish affinity with the left may be one reason why neoconservatism boasts so many Jewish adherents: it is a movement whose own roots lie in the left. But the same affinity is to be seen at work in many of the insinuations *against* Jewish neocons by leftists who are themselves Jews, or who profess some Jewish connection. Michael Lind, for one, has gone out of his way to assert his own Jewish 'descent', and *Tikkun* is in some self-professed sense a Jewish magazine. Even the BBC's assault on the neocons featured a Jewish critic in the starring role. So passionate are these Jews in their opposition to neoconservative ideas that they have not hesitated to pander to anti-Semitism in the effort to discredit them. What about *their* ulterior motives, one wonders?

It may sound strange in light of the accusations against them, but in fact the careers of leading neoconservatives have rarely involved work on Middle East issues. The most distinctive of Richard Perle's many contributions to U.S. policy lie in the realm of nuclear-weapons strategy. Elliott Abrams made his mark as a point man for President Reagan's policies toward Central America. Paul Wolfowitz's long career in government includes not only high office in the State and Defense Departments but also a stint as ambassador to Indonesia during which he pressed for democratization harder than any of his predecessors.

These three, as well as the rest of the neocon circle, are and were hardliners toward the USSR, China, Nicaragua, and North Korea. Is it any wonder that they held a similar position toward Saddam Hussein's Iraq? If Israel did not exist, which of them would have *favored* giving Hans Blix's team still more time, or leaving the whole matter in the hands of the UN? Are we to believe that the decades-long neoconservative campaign against communism and anti-Americanism was a fantastically far-sighted Rube Goldberg machine programmed to produce some benefit for Israel somewhere down the line?

The BBC claimed to have found a smoking gun, one that others have pounced on as well. Bradshaw: 'In 1996, a group of neocons wrote a report intended as advice for incoming Israeli Prime Minister Benny [*sic*] Netanyahu. It called for... removing Saddam Hussein from power, an important Israeli strategic objective in its own right.' Perle and Douglas Feith, the latter now a high official in Bush's Defense Department, were among those who had 'contributed' to this paper.

Yet even if the BBC had characterized the document accurately, it would not imply what the BBC (and not the BBC alone) suggested it did. The Americans whose names appeared on the paper had long sought Saddam's ouster, an objective that was already, in 1996, the declared policy of the *Clinton* administration. It would thus make more sense to say that, in preparing a paper for Netanyahu, they were trying to influence Israeli policy on behalf of American interests than the other way around. Indeed, most Israeli officials at that time viewed Iran, the sponsor of Hezbollah and Hamas, as a more pressing threat to their country than Iraq, and (then as later) would have preferred that *it* be given priority in any campaign against terrorism.

To make matters worse, the BBC fundamentally misrepresented the nature of the document. Contrary to Bradshaw's claim, no 'group of neocons' had written it. Rather, it was the work of a rapporteur summarizing the deliberations of a conference, and was clearly identified as such. The names affixed to it were listed as attendees and not as endorsers, much less authors.

In any case, although it is true that many neocons are Jews, it is also true that many are not. [Jeane] Kirkpatrick, [James R.] Woolsey, Michael Novak, Linda Chavez, William J. Bennett – all are of pure neocon pedigree, while other non-Jews figuring prominently in current foreign-policy debates and today called neocons include Libby, Bolton, AEI president Christopher DeMuth, and Gary Schmitt of the Project for the New American Century. These Gentile neocons are no less strong in their support of Israel than are Jewish neocons, which suggests a stance growing not out of ethnic loyalty but out of some shared analysis of the rights and wrongs of the Arab–Israel conflict.

Just as it is undeniable that many neoconservatives happen to be Jews, it is undeniable that America's war against terrorism will redound to Israel's benefit as the biggest victim of terrorism. But the attacks on the World Trade Center and the Pentagon, taking at a stroke 3,000 lives, pushed America pretty high up on the list of terror's victims. That blow, and the certain knowledge that the terrorists would try for even greater carnage in the future, drove us to war in 2001 just as Pearl Harbor had done in 1941.

That earlier decision by the United States suffused Winston Churchill with joy, for England was then on the front lines with the Nazis just as Israel is today on the front line with terrorists. At the time, there were those who said we were going to war for the sake of England. For that matter, there were some who said we were going to war for the sake of the Jews: the subject is perennial. Then, as now, they were wrong.

If any single episode exposes the fatuousness of the charge that neoconservative policies amount to Jewish special pleading, it was the 1990s war in Bosnia – the same conflict that served to crystallize a post-Cold War approach to foreign policy that might fairly be described as neoconservative. It had been in large part as a response to the Soviet challenge that neoconservatism took shape in the first place, so it is only natural that the end of the Cold War should have invited the question Norman Podhoretz raised in 1996: was there anything left of neoconservatism to distinguish it from plain, unprefixed conservatism?

One answer to this question may have come as early as 1992, when hostilities first broke out in Bosnia and then-President George H. W. Bush dismissed them as a 'hiccup', while Secretary of State James Baker declared: 'We have no dog in that fight.' These two were not heartless men, but they were exemplars of a traditional conservative cast of mind. The essence of the matter, as they saw it, was that Bosnia engaged little in the way of American interests, which in the conventional view meant vital resources, or strategic geography, or the safety of allies.

Then a movement coalesced in opposition to American inaction. Its leaders, apart from a handful of young foreign-service officers who had resigned from the State Department in protest and who carried no ideological labels, were almost all from neoconservative ranks. Perle, Wolfowitz, Kirkpatrick, and Max Kampelman were among those in the forefront. So ardent was I myself on the issue that Bosnia was the chief of several points impelling me to support Bill Clinton against Bush in 1992, a choice over which I would sing my regrets in these pages when Clinton turned out to care not a whit more about Bosnia than had the elder Bush.[*]

It bears recalling that the Bosnian cause was championed by international Islamists, and that the Bosnians themselves had been part of the Croatian fascist state during World War II, infamous for its brutality toward Jews. Logically, then, if there was any 'Jewish interest' in the conflict, it should have led to support for the Bush–Clinton position. But as the bloodletting wore on, neoconservatives, Jewish and non-Jewish alike, were much more likely than traditional conservatives to support intervention. Despite the occasional, prominent exception – neoconservative columnist Charles Krauthammer was an opponent of intervention, conservative Senator Bob Dole a supporter – the prevailing division on Bosnia demonstrated that a distinctive neoconservative sensibility, if not ideology, endured, or perhaps had been reborn, after the end of the Cold War. It centered on the question of the uses of American power, and it was held even by some who had not made the whole journey from liberalism with the original neocons.

What is that sensibility? In part it may consist in a greater readiness to engage American power and resources where nothing but humanitarian concerns are at issue. In larger part, however, it is concerned with national security, sharing with traditional conservatism the belief that military strength is irreplaceable and that pacifism is folly. Where it parts company with traditional conservatism is in the more contingent approach it takes to guarding that security.

---

[*] 'Lament of a Clinton Supporter', *Commentary*, August 1993.

Neoconservatives sought action in Bosnia above all out of the conviction that, however remote the Balkans may be geographically and strategically, allowing a dictator like Serbia's Slobodan Milošević to get away with aggression, ethnic cleansing, and mass murder in Europe would tempt other malign men to do likewise elsewhere, and other avatars of virulent ultranationalism to ride this ticket to power. Neoconservatives believed that American inaction would make the world a more dangerous place, and that ultimately this danger would assume forms that would land on our own doorstep. Thus it had happened throughout the twentieth century; and thus, in the fullness of time, it would happen again on September 11 of the first year of the twenty-first.

In addition to their more contingent approach to security, neoconservatives have shown themselves more disposed to experiment with unconventional tactics – using air strikes against the Serbs, arming the Bosnians or, later, the Iraqi National Congress. By contrast, conservatives of traditional bent are more inclined to favor the use of overwhelming force or none at all, and to be more concerned with 'exit strategies'. Still another distinguishing characteristic is that neoconservatives put greater stock in the political and ideological aspects of conflict.

A final distinction may reflect neoconservatism's vestigial links with liberalism. This is the enthusiasm for democracy. Traditional conservatives are more likely to display an ambivalence toward this form of government, an ambivalence expressed centuries ago by the American founders. Neoconservatives tend to harbor no such doubts.

With this in mind, it also becomes easier to identify the true neoconservative models in the field of power politics: Henry 'Scoop' Jackson, Ronald Reagan, and Winston Churchill. These were tough-minded men who were far from 'conservative' either in spirit or in political pedigree. Jackson was a Democrat, while Reagan switched to the Republicans late in life, as Churchill did from the Liberals to the Tories. All three were staunch democrats and no less staunch believers in maintaining the might of the democracies. All three believed in confronting democracy's enemies early and far from home shores; and all three were paragons of ideological warfare.

Each, too, was a creative tactician. Jackson's eponymous 'amendments' holding the Soviet Union's feet to the fire on the right of emigration and blocking a second unequal nuclear agreement put a stop to American appeasement. Reagan's provocative rhetoric, plus his arming of anti-communist guerrillas, paved the way to American victory in the Cold War.

Churchill's innovative ideas, which rightly or wrongly had won him disrepute in the First World War, were essential to his nation's survival in the Second. Could this element in neoconservatism help explain why the cause of Israel, an innovative, militarily strong democracy, is embraced by all neoconservatives, non-Jews as well as Jews?

But this brings us back at last to the question of the neocons' alleged current influence. How *did* their ideas gain such currency? Did they 'hijack' Bush's foreign policy, right out from under his nose and the noses of Richard Cheney, Colin Powell, Donald Rumsfeld, and Condoleezza Rice – all members of the same team that, to hear the standard liberal version, was itself so diabolically clever that in the 2000 election it had stolen the presidency itself?

The answer is to be found not in conspiracy theories but in the terrorist outrage of September 11, 2001. Though it constituted a watershed in American history, this event was novel not in kind but only in scale. For roughly thirty years, Middle Eastern terrorists had been murdering Americans in embassies, barracks, airplanes, and ships – even, once before, in the World Trade Center. Except for a few criminal prosecutions and the lobbing of a few mostly symbolic shells, the U.S. response had been inert. Even under President Reagan, Americans fled in the wake of the bombing of the Marine barracks in Beirut, then the largest single attack we had suffered.

Terrorism, we were told, was an accepted way of doing politics in the Middle East. More than a handful of the region's governments openly supported it, and the PLO, an outfit steeped in terror, was the poster child of the Arab cause. Any strong response to this scourge would serve only to make the people of the region angrier at us, and generate still more terrorists.

On September 11, we learned in the most dreadful way that terrorists would not be appeased by our diffidence; quite the contrary. We saw – they themselves told us – that they intended to go on murdering us in ever larger numbers as long as they could. A sharp change of course was required, and the neoconservatives, who had been warning for years that terror must not be appeased, stood vindicated – much as, more grandly, Churchill was vindicated by Hitler's depredations after Munich.

Not only did the neocons have an analysis of what had gone wrong in American policy, they also stood ready with proposals for what to do now: to wage war on the terror groups and to seek to end or transform governments that supported them, especially those possessing the means to furnish terrorists with the wherewithal to kill even more Americans than on September 11.

Neocons also offered a long-term strategy for making the Middle East less of a hotbed of terrorism: implanting democracy in the region and thereby helping to foment a less violent approach to politics.

No neoconservative was elevated in office after September 11, as Churchill had been to prime minister after the collapse of the Munich Agreement, but policies espoused by neoconservatives were embraced by the Bush administration. Was this because Bush learned them from the likes of Wolfowitz and Perle? Or did he and his top advisors – none of them known as a neocon – reach similar conclusions on their own? We may have to await the President's memoirs to learn the answer to that narrow question, but every American has reason to be grateful for the result.

If these policies should fail, for whatever reason – including a recurrence of national faint-heartedness – then neoconservative ideas will no doubt be discredited. But this matters hardly at all compared with what we will have lost. For, if they fail, either we will then be at the mercy of ever more murderous terrorism or we will have to seek alternative methods of coping with it – methods that are likely to involve a much more painful and frightening course of action than the admittedly daunting one that still lies before us.

If, however, the policies succeed, then the world will have been delivered from an awful scourge, and there will be credit enough to go around – some of it, one trusts, even for the lately much demonized neoconservatives.

PART V

THE FUTURE OF NEOCONSERVATISM

NEOCONSERVATIVES AND THE COURT OF PUBLIC OPINION IN AMERICA

Karlyn Bowman

Neocons' optimism is clearly in sync with that of most Americans... Many of their ideas have a substantial following.

NEOCONSERVATIVES AND THE COURT OF PUBLIC OPINION IN AMERICA

KARLYN BOWMAN

Hardly anyone doubts the influence of the neoconservatives in Washington, D.C. But have they made their case to the broader U.S. public? Should we expect them to? If we use Irving Kristol's definition of neoconservatism as a 'persuasion' and not a movement, it's unreasonable to expect the neocons to have a national following. Scores of questions have been asked over the past thirty years in the U.S. about mainstream ideological identification. More people consistently describe themselves as conservatives rather than liberals, but most feel comfortable in the middle. When asked by Gallup, CNN, and *USA Today* interviewers in July 2004 to describe their political views, 39 per cent of those surveyed described themselves as conservatives, 20 per cent as liberals, and 38 per cent as moderates. As for the neoconservatives, not a single question appears in the public polls about them.

In an essay in *The Weekly Standard* in 2003 (reproduced in this volume), [Irving] Kristol described beliefs that differentiate neoconservatives from traditional conservatives, but they can also be used as benchmarks to compare neocons and the general public. The neoconservative temperament, Kristol says, is more optimistic than that of traditional conservatives. Neoconservatives focus on economic growth, he says, with particular attention to cutting tax rates. As for the role of the state, Kristol tells us that neoconservatives don't feel the alarm that traditional conservatives do about 'the growth of the state in the past century'. The neocons and traditional conservatives share a concern about 'the steady decline in our democratic culture'. Kristol says there is no set of conservative beliefs concerning foreign policy, only a set of attitudes that include a deep love of country, a suspicion of world government, a clear-headed view of friends and enemies, a commitment to a muscular defense, and a willingness to come to terms with and project America's unique power in the world. This essay looks not at differences among conservatives, but at the areas where American public opinion collides and connects with the neoconservative persuasion Kristol has described.

As for temperament, neocons' optimism is clearly in sync with that of most Americans. Virtually every polling question in the literature shows that Americans expect to be better off in the future than they are today. An April 2004 Harris Poll illustrates the point. Harris found that 68 per cent of those surveyed expected their personal situation to improve in the course of the next five years. Only 6 per cent expected it to get worse. Harris data collected in 2003 showed that Americans were far more optimistic and had much higher life satisfaction than Europeans. Large majorities of Americans of all colors and creeds continue to say they believe in the American Dream. Many think it will be harder to achieve than in the past, but the idea is alive and well. In May 2004, 62 per cent of those surveyed by ABC News and *The Washington Post* said they were optimistic about the situation in Iraq, and this after the dark days of Fallujah and the abuse of Iraqi prisoners by U.S. soldiers at Abu Ghraib.

One could argue, in looking at recent presidential elections, that the candidate with the more hopeful or optimistic persona has always won. Ronald Reagan's sunny optimism was a stark contrast to Jimmy Carter's malaise and Walter Mondale's meditations on the need for higher taxes. George H. W. Bush seemed more upbeat than the dour Dukakis, but, four years later, the man from Hope exuded the quality and sent him packing. Bob Dole had sterling qualities, but many Americans felt that he looked back and not ahead, and he went down to defeat. As for George W. Bush and Al Gore, both men seemed like a breath of fresh air after President Clinton's indiscretions. On Election Day in 2000, 48 per cent of voters said they would be excited or optimistic if Gore won, and 49 per cent felt that way about a Bush victory.

Kristol notes that neoconservatives focus on economic growth and especially on cutting tax rates. In this, they follow the path carved by traditional Republican conservatives such as congressmen William Steiger and Jack Kemp, and Senator William Roth, who changed their party's orientation on taxes in the late 1970s. The painful stagflation of the time made Americans receptive to their new arguments when candidate Ronald Reagan articulated them, and Americans supported the President's tax cuts as a way to get the economy moving again.

Like traditional and neo-conservatives, the American people have always been more interested in making the economic pie grow than in dividing it.

Even though they would like to see money and wealth more evenly distributed among more people, they reject the idea that the federal government knows how to do this. When asked by the National Opinion Research Center in 2000 whether it was the responsibility of government to reduce the differences between people with high incomes and those with low ones, a plurality disagreed. A plurality of people in every income category above $20,000 said this wasn't the government's job. Polls show that even those who might benefit from a redistribution of wealth, people in the lowest income categories, have never been very enthusiastic about the idea.

Kristol argues that neoconservatives are less alarmed by big government than traditional conservatives are. It is difficult to know precisely what Americans think about the size of the federal government for they have long been of two minds about it. They want and expect government to do many things for them, especially in the areas of old-age assistance and health care. At the same time, they see big government as a big problem. It's wasteful, intrusive, and inefficient. The polling evidence from the post-World War II period to the mid-sixties suggests that Americans equated federal government activity with progress. Starting in the mid-1960s, at about the time Lyndon Johnson launched the Great Society project, doubts about big government began to surface. In a question asked twenty-five times since 1965, Americans have told the pollsters that big government and not big business or big labor will be the biggest threat to the country in the future. Even after the business scandals of late 2001 and 2002, 47 per cent said big government represented the biggest threat, 38 per cent big business, and just 10 per cent big labor.

Despite these worries, there is some evidence in the polls today that indicates that Americans are either comfortable with, or perhaps simply inured to, the current size of the federal government. In 2003, for the first time since 1950, more Americans told Gallup that the amount of federal taxes they paid was 'about right' instead of the more familiar response, 'too high'. Today Americans tell the pollsters they are more concerned about their property taxes than their federal income taxes. George W. Bush is clearly more comfortable with the size of the federal government than his Republican predecessors. To give just one example, Ronald Reagan wanted to shutter the Education Department. George W. Bush has expanded it. Americans liked the idea of a substantial new federal government entitlement – a prescription drug benefit – even if they didn't have a clue about how to pay for it. But the public still resists some expansions of federal government activity. The President's proposal in January 2004 for a new manned space program sank like a stone. This expensive ambitious program just didn't make sense to them while the country was fighting a war in Iraq and a war on terrorism. As for the deficits, Americans have almost always said that large ones are a problem and that they are serious, but they have never had much intensity politically.

Kristol argues that traditional conservatives and neocons (but not libertarians) are equally alarmed by cultural trends in divorce, out-of-wedlock births, crime, drugs, and declining social mores. Fox News and Opinion Dynamics regularly ask Americans whether the United States is generally headed in the right direction or whether it is off on the wrong track. Americans' responses are optimistic or pessimistic depending on conditions. But the polling team also asks a second question about the moral climate of the U.S. Americans almost always say the country is on the wrong track in terms of the moral climate. When you care deeply about something, as most Americans do about the cultural moorings of their nation, you tend to worry about its loss. There's an element of nostalgia here, but nonetheless, most Americans are deeply concerned about their culture.

Finally, Kristol says that traditional conservatives have had difficulty adjusting to the idea of the United States as uniquely powerful, a new reality in foreign affairs. Americans are generally not aware of the debates swirling in intellectual circles on foreign policy. They bring a set of fairly clear beliefs to their thinking about America's place in the world, and they have been remarkably consistent in them. First and foremost, they are internationalists, albeit cautious or reluctant ones. In a question asked since 1947, no more than 36 per cent have ever said that it is better for the future of the United States for us to stay out of world affairs, and usually only about a quarter give that response. Two-thirds or more have consistently said that it is better for us to play an active role. After 9/11, Americans have been even more certain of the necessity of international involvement.

Americans have always preferred to act with allies or with international organizations – when it is possible. They know that it is not always possible. They are often cranky about the costs of international involvement, tired of shouldering what seems to them to be a disproportionate share of the costs. They tell the pollsters they prefer to devote resources and attention to problems at home. While they are not eager to spend vast sums on defense, they believe it is important to have a defense that is second to none. They worry about long-term foreign engagements, but they also realize these are sometimes necessary. They supported U.S. government policy in the Cold War for forty years. These general attitudes underlie their responses to each new administration.

Americans give their leaders considerable latitude in foreign affairs once they trust them. George H. W. Bush had significant experience in foreign affairs, and Americans felt comfortable with him in this area from the start. Other recent presidents haven't had foreign policy résumés, and they have had to work to build public confidence. Some have been more successful than others. Doubts about Jimmy Carter's stewardship of foreign affairs grew over the course of his presidency and contributed to his defeat in 1980. It took many Americans some time to feel comfortable that Ronald Reagan would not get the country into World War III after some of his fellow Republicans and many Democrats tried to raise doubts about him on that score. Despite considerable activity around the globe, Bill Clinton wasn't able to establish a strong foreign policy profile. People weren't confident in George W. Bush initially, but after 9/11, they rallied to him. Americans want their presidents to define objectives clearly and prosecute them successfully. They don't follow day-to-day foreign policy developments, and they don't usually second-guess decisions. Although President Bush has articulated major new foreign policy directions, it's not clear how much Americans have thought about a doctrine of pre-emption or a Greater Middle East Peace Initiative.

Americans believe strongly in the ideals that have defined their nation and they see their nation as a force for good in the world. They hope others can enjoy the benefits of democracy. More than 80 per cent tell pollsters that their system of government is the best in the world, whatever its faults. A majority, 56 per cent, told Gallup in 2003 that the United States had a responsibility to help other countries rid themselves of dictators and become democracies, while 38 per cent demurred. Still, they are wary of imposing their ideas on others. A question asked by CBS News five times in 2003 and 2004 finds between 48 per cent and 62 per cent saying we should stay out of other countries' affairs. No more than 29 per cent in these polls said that we should try to change dictatorships to democracy where we can.

Americans supported President Bush's decision to go to war in Iraq. Poll after poll showed that they thought that the peace would be more difficult than the war. Throughout it all, their optimism has shown through. After the hot phase of the war, in May of 2003, 63 per cent were confident that the United States could establish a stable democratic government in Iraq over the long term. In April 2004, after numerous setbacks and difficulties, 50 per cent gave that response. People believe that a stable democratic Iraq would help in the war on terrorism. Americans are eager for the Iraqis to take over responsibility for their government, which comports well with their long-held views of our responsibilities at home and abroad.

It's unlikely that many Americans have heard the term neoconservative. Nor have many people read the articles or books that have been written by or about them. That is to be expected in a vibrant heterogeneous democracy like the United States. The neoconservative banner may not exist in the court of public opinion, but many of their ideas have a substantial following.

THE VERY BRITISH ROOTS OF NEOCONSERVATISM AND ITS LESSONS FOR BRITISH CONSERVATIVES

Michael Gove

Insofar as neoconservatism is a philosophy for foreign policy, it is one with deep roots in British state thinking and practice... it speaks directly to the needs of twenty-first-century British, and European, conservatism... If Canning, Palmerston, or Churchill were alive today they would recognize their policies, being carried on by Paul Wolfowitz, Donald Rumsfeld, and George Bush.

THE VERY BRITISH ROOTS OF NEOCONSERVATISM AND ITS LESSONS FOR BRITISH CONSERVATIVES

MICHAEL GOVE

America's neoconservatives did not invent pre-emption. Nor reliance on intelligence services. Nor the use of 'self-preservation' and the need to 'rescue the world' from tyranny as justifications for pre-emptive strikes.

In August 1807 the British Foreign Secretary, George Canning, launched an audacious pre-emptive strike. Britain, at that time, stood alone in opposition to Napoleon Bonaparte and his plans for European domination. Bonaparte had concluded a treaty with the last of his continental enemies, Tsar Alexander I, in July of that year and with Russia subdued only Britain stood against the tyrant.

Canning was very far from the conventional model for a Tory Foreign Secretary of the early nineteenth century. He was neither well born nor smoothly diplomatic. The son of an actress and the possessor of an acid tongue, he discomfited many of the party's traditional leaders. But Canning also had formidable gifts, not least confidence in himself, his nation, and his principles as well as a first-class intelligence network.

He realized that the collapse of continental opposition to Napoleon had left Britain in a uniquely vulnerable position. Just how vulnerable became clear to the Foreign Secretary within days when his intelligence network informed him of secret protocols to the Franco-Russian Treaty of Tilsit.

The Tsar had agreed to join Napoleon's 'continental blockade', closing his ports to British trade and thus helping to erect a barrier to British commerce from the Adriatic to the Baltic. Worse still, from Britain's perspective, the Tsar would now use his weight to tilt the balance still further against Britain.

Russia would privately put pressure on the neutral countries of Scandinavia to join the blockade of Britain. And, most threatening of all,

Alexander agreed that France should be allowed to take over the fleet of neutral Denmark, which was the second-largest in the world, behind Britain's. Bonaparte demanded that control of the Danish fleet pass directly to him. If the Danes declined, France would seize it, with Russia's willing support. Canning realized that if the French were to take possession of the Danish navy, then the British mastery of the seas, so dearly bought at Trafalgar, would be grievously threatened.

Faced with a direct threat to his nation's security and commercial interests, possessed of intelligence that showed a hostile tyrant was planning to acquire weapons that could tilt the strategic balance, and conscious that in the battle against tyranny only action could signal resolution, Canning ordered a pre-emptive attack.

On August 27, a British fleet of more than forty ships landed 27,000 men on the coast of Denmark. While the army advanced on Copenhagen, the naval force blockaded the city's harbor. The British forces demanded a surrender of the Danish fleet into their hands. When the Danes refused, the British attacked. After hard fighting the Danes eventually allowed their ships of the line to fall under British control.

Canning had, by his swift action, averted a mortal threat to Britain. And he had demonstrated that Napoleon faced an implacable enemy in Britain, one that would do everything required to maintain the struggle against Bonapartism.

Canning was criticized by the parliamentary opposition of his time for acting dishonorably. Critics argued that he had lowered himself to Bonaparte's level. Alongside the charge of moral equivalency, doubts were raised about his use of intelligence. But Canning won the day. His protégé, Viscount Palmerston, swayed the Commons by arguing that it was 'to the law of self-preservation that England appeals as justification for her proceedings'.

By preserving Britain's strategic position, Canning was able not just to save his country, but also to advance the cause of freedom. With Britain's naval supremacy intact, Canning was quickly able to launch another intervention, in Iberia, to thwart Napoleon's expansionist plans on the peninsula.

The swift dispatch of British troops to Portugal was made possible by the success of the Danish mission. And it was through British intervention in the Iberian peninsula that Napoleon began to be worn down and the war was eventually taken to his soil. Canning's swiftness in intervening in Portugal was acclaimed, even by his parliamentary opponents, as a 'bold stroke for the rescue of the world'.

Britain's strike on Copenhagen was not to be the last occasion on which a democracy launched a pre-emptive assault in a war against a tyranny, as a means both of eliminating a threat and of signalling resolve.

In July 1940, Britain stood alone again. The collapse of French resistance to Hitler left Winston Churchill the only democratic leader standing against fascism. And his position was perilous.

France's defeat had been accompanied by Italy's entry into the war on the Nazi side. Control of the seas, on which Britain's strategic position depended, was gravely threatened. The Mediterranean was a particularly vulnerable theatre. Britain's line of communication to Egypt, and through the Suez Canal to India and the Dominions, was vital to its war effort.

The combination of German and Italian naval forces was itself threatening enough to British interests. But the collapse of France had tilted the balance yet further against Britain. France's leaders were now keener on reaching good terms with the Axis than honoring any commitment to Britain. There was every chance that they could surrender their Mediterranean naval forces to Hitler, or acquiesce in the Axis seizure of their ships.

Churchill at first tried diplomacy to avert disaster. He sought to persuade the French to sail their ships into British waters for safe-keeping. But the new French government in Vichy soon displayed its pro-Axis tilt. The French navy, the bulk of which lay at anchor in North Africa, was ordered back to metropolitan France, and into Axis clutches.

Churchill determined to act before the threat became too great. A British naval force sailed for Mers el-Kebir, in Algeria, where the greatest concentration of French ships lay.

Again, in a spirit of diplomacy, the British commander sought a parley with the French admiral in charge and attempted to persuade him to surrender, transfer, or destroy his fleet. Talks proceeded but it soon became clear that the French were only playing for time. While negotiations were going on, the Admiralty intercepted French signals ordering additional forces to make for Algeria to engage the British.

Churchill's determination that the French ships should never fall into Axis hands was clear and so were the actions that the Royal Navy had to take at Mers el-Kebir. A devastating bombardment began. After an exemplary display of British gunnery, the bulk of the French fleet was disabled in short order. The French pleaded for a halt to the action, and the British relented in the hope of securing a surrender and minimizing bloodshed. But the French plea for a ceasefire was a feint, and those French ships that were still seaworthy attempted to make a break for it. British forces were compelled to renew their attack and finish off much of what remained of the French strength.

Churchill was roundly condemned for his actions by the French, whom he had been fighting to save just weeks beforehand. Although the Vichy government ordered its remaining warships to engage the British wherever they could, it was a blow Britain could bear, not least because 84 per cent of France's naval strength was now eliminated and could not be used by the fascists or their allies to menace Britain's interests. A grave threat had been averted. However, that was not all.

In the summer of 1940 there was an expectation among many, and a fear particularly in the United States, that Britain would shortly succumb to Nazi aggression. The willingness of the British government to endure and carry on the fight against tyranny was widely questioned. The action at Mers el-Kebir not only neutralized the threat from the French fleet, it also eliminated any doubts that Churchill would fight on. He had proved that he would prosecute the war 'at all costs and despite the odds'.

The American President, Franklin Roosevelt, praised Churchill's bold stroke and applauded it as a contribution to America's own defense. Americans who had thought Britain was vulnerable to invasion, or likely to surrender, changed their minds and it became easier for the U.S. to offer moral, material and, eventually, military support to Britain in the fight against fascism.

A pre-emptive strike, which would have many international lawyers today united in condemnation, helped ensure we live in a world where international law could still be practiced.

The U.S.-led coalition's pre-emptive strike against Iraq in 2003 has been characterized as a break with the past, a revolutionary act incarnating a new approach, the Bush Doctrine, conceived by a radical group, the neoconservatives, who sought to overturn years of inherited foreign-policy wisdom. The case for the Iraq War may well have been influenced by neoconservative principles. But, as we can see, there is nothing revolutionary about the reasoning behind the war. It follows a traditional pattern set by British statesmen of the past. Insofar as neoconservatism is a philosophy for foreign policy, it is one with deep roots in British state thinking and practice.

Of course, as many of the other essays in this volume make clear, neoconservatism is about far more than statecraft. The thinking of those writers and politicians who have become known as neoconservatives touches on almost every area of political practice with which modern leaders must deal. But in judging how appropriate neoconservative principles are for states other than the U.S. it is worth appreciating how robustly rooted many of the insights favoured by neoconservatives are.

It is my belief that neoconservatism offers British – and European – conservatism valuable pointers on how to deal with the challenges of the modern world without succumbing either to impotent reaction or compromised social democracy. Neoconservatism is a disposition attuned to a political environment in which mass democracy and ethnic diversity are accomplished facts, electorates demand strong government and economic growth, and left-wing responses to modernity are proving inadequate. It also provides conservatives with a historically rooted and philosophically robust set of responses to building a strong society in the face of external threat and internal dissension. As such it speaks directly to the needs of twenty-first-century British, and European, conservatism.

But it would be naive not to recognize that there are barriers to the adoption of neoconservative thinking by British and European conservatives. And some of the resistance to what is perceived as a purely American philosophy go beyond current difficulties.

It is in the essence of conservatism to grasp that political responses that have developed in one specific environment may not easily be transplanted. [See George Will's essay, Ed.] While it has been one of the delusions of socialism to believe that societies can, and should, be molded to fit a universal theory of economic and social organization, conservatives instinctively understand that one size does not fit all. The root of Tory distrust toward further European integration is skepticism toward the belief that the same solutions can apply across a diverse continent. Ideas that flourish in the olive groves of Attica are not likely to take root as easily in the forests of Latvia or the cities of south Yorkshire.

In the same way, it would be naive, and un-Tory, to assume that varieties of conservatism which have blossomed in American soil can be transplanted direct to Britain. Because most of those who have become identified as neoconservatives are Americans, there is an understandable resistance among some British Tories to believing there is much to be learned from neoconservative thinking. And the inevitable difficulties that the allied coalition have faced in the war on terror has heightened hostility among some to American thinking in general, and those identified as neoconservatives in particular.

What such hostility ignores, however, is the direct linkage between contemporary neoconservative thinking and Britain's own political traditions. If Canning, Palmerston, or Churchill were alive today they would recognize their policies, being carried on by Paul Wolfowitz, Donald Rumsfeld, and George Bush. Perhaps more importantly, they would see that the principles by which they had guided Britain were now being enacted by the U.S.

The liberal journalist Jonathan Freedland has argued powerfully in his book *Bring Home the Revolution* that the British should understand that the political structures, and underlying democratic temper, of America were 'made in the UK'. The distinctive features of American public life, he maintained, were the fruits of John Locke and Tom Paine's thinking. It is about time, he has asserted, that the British reclaim their legacy and recapture something of the democratic dynamism that English philosophers have bequeathed America. In learning from America, Freedland has pointed out, Britons are only learning from their own past. And so it is with neoconservatism.

When it comes to foreign policy the contemporary neoconservative response to a turbulent world echoes – not just in actions but in fundamental principles – the enlightened conservative approach of past British statesmen.

Contemporary neoconservatives frame their foreign-policy thinking in a manner distinct from both the principle-free realpolitik of other conservatives and the utopian liberalism of the left. They accept, along with most on the right, the requirement to use force when faced with threats, the folly of treating anti-democratic forces with the same courtesy that would be extended to democratic actors, and the indispensability of the nation-state as a political unit that makes power both accountable and effective.

In all those respects they differ from the utopian left, which views negotiation as a good in itself rather than a means to an end, force as illegitimate unless it has universal international sanction, the nation-state as a reactionary construct that stands in the way of progressive transnational governance, and the West as a morally compromised entity that has no right to consider its values superior to its antagonists'.

But where neoconservatives part company with traditional Conservative realists is in their attachment to the maintenance of liberal Enlightenment principles in the conduct of foreign affairs. Neoconservatives believe that a key part of defending the national interest is upholding Western nations' democratic values.

Neoconservatives are therefore more inclined than Conservative realists to countenance interventions to support democratic forces and liberal trends or to prevent tyrannical abuses. While realists argue that such an attachment is a recipe for overstretch and subversion of state sovereignty, neoconservatives maintain that the West will face fewer threats if it acts as handmaiden to democracy abroad rather than allowing enemies to gather, friends to be picked off, and opponents to scent weakness. Moreover, neoconservatives believe that a nation's survival and strength depend upon moral foundations. To purge morality from foreign policy is not just to betray the West's best instincts, it is to undermine the foundations of its continued vigor.

These intuitions, and instincts, are apparent in the actions of British statesmen such as Canning, Palmerston, and Churchill. All three were, as we have seen, unafraid to authorize an audacious use of force in battles against tyranny.

Canning ensured that in the years after Napoleon's demise, Britain retained its military superiority, not least through an aggressive program of naval shipbuilding. The Royal Navy's strength was deployed in liberty's cause in the New World, where British ships helped the nations of Latin America throw off arbitrary Spanish rule. The Monroe Doctrine, by which the United States declared the Americas off-limits to European colonialism, was only made real by British naval power.

That power was also used to support liberalism on the European continent, and a British fleet was sent to Lisbon in 1823 to support Portugal's constitutional monarch in a struggle with his absolutist younger son, who was backed by French reactionaries.

Canning's protégé, Viscount Palmerston, picked up where his master had left off. Throughout his long career in British politics, which took him from the Tories to the Whigs and on to the premiership, he was as muscular a statesman as one could conceive. But his willingness to deploy a gunboat to strengthen his diplomacy was matched by a liberal vision that saw British power as a force for good.

Palmerston was happy to intervene in Spain and Portugal to support liberal monarchs against absolutists, to rattle sabers over the Low Countries to help the infant constitutional monarchy of Belgium become established in the shadow of its more powerful neighbors, and to act decisively in the Middle East against the French-backed troublemaker, Mehemet Ali. In each case Palmerston combined a hard-headed assessment of British national interest with an inbuilt bias against oppression.

That disposition brought him into conflict with the U.S. at one point, when Palmerston's use of naval power to interdict slave trading rubbed against American interests. But Palmerston's most consistent adversary was the master of realpolitik, Prince Clemens Metternich, the brilliant Hapsburg minister. Where Palmerston was a consistent champion of small nations, liberal parliamentarianism, and European emancipation, Metternich was a defender of the *ancien régime* status quo, an enemy of liberalism, a friend of absolutism, and a coolly ruthless calculator of Austrian national advantage. It is perhaps no surprise that he was an object of Henry Kissinger's admiration. Or that Dr Kissinger's own cerebral cynicism meant that his foreign policy became an object of neoconservative criticism.

The approach adopted by Palmerston and Canning was, naturally, an outgrowth of Britain's particular strategic position in the nineteenth century. But even after Britain lost its dominant position in the twentieth century, it produced leaders whose statecraft was firmly in the tradition of Canning and Palmerston, and consonant with what we now call neoconservatism.

Winston Churchill stands pre-eminent as a political leader who had the foresight to demand vigilance against threats to freedom when others preferred denial or appeasement. His record in the thirties as a visionary critic of Nazism and his denunciation of the sacrifice of Czechoslovakia at Munich earned him the scorn of the conservative realists of his time. But Churchill recognized, as also do today's neoconservatives, that the West cannot stand aloof when tyranny spreads its wings. A failure to confront aggression only emboldens the aggressor, who detects weakness and plots his advance. Only support for democracy, wherever it is threatened, can provide real security. Even after fighting alongside Stalin's Russia to defeat Nazism, Churchill was among the first to warn of the dangers of aggressive communism with his Iron Curtain speech.

The defeat of communism had to wait, however, for the premiership of another politician whose record recommends her as a neoconservative – Margaret Thatcher. Although Lady Thatcher's foreign policy record is marked by episodes of appeasement, not least the concessions to terrorism inherent in the Anglo-Irish Agreement and the negotiated surrender of Hong Kong to communist China, her fundamental instincts were resolutely neocon. Whenever she was able to overcome, or set aside, the advice of the Foreign Office, she displayed a resolve that helped freedom advance.

The Falklands War, fought despite the efforts of her own Foreign Secretary to leave Argentina the beneficiary of aggression, was a turning-point in the eighties. It signalled the determination of a new generation of leaders in the West to fight for their interests and values. The right of peoples to self-determination was upheld, on a distant South Atlantic archipelago, and a message was sent around the world. Not only did the Falklands War demonstrate a new confidence on the part of Britain, it also triggered the collapse of the Argentine junta and set off a benign domino effect in South America, which saw democracies supplant authoritarian rule.

The Falklands War, important as it was, did not, however, count as the defining struggle of the time. It was in the fight against communism where Margaret Thatcher played a supremely significant role. While other British political figures were inclined to deprecate the anti-communist 'evil empire' rhetoric of Ronald Reagan, Mrs. Thatcher saw clearly the profound threat that communism posed. She authorized symbolic acts of solidarity with democratic forces in Eastern Europe, dispatching a minister to pay his respects at the grave of the dissident Polish priest Father Jerzy Popieuszko after he had been murdered by Poland's security forces. She provided support for President Reagan's deployment of Cruise and Pershing ballistic missiles in Europe, a key event in demonstrating Western resolve and accelerating communism's collapse. She also countered the forces of appeasement, moral equivalence, and fellow-travelling within Britain, all the time against a background of fashionable sneering.

It was a tragedy, in more ways than one, that the Conservative administration that superseded her was to abandon her principled position on foreign affairs. The history of British Conservative statecraft in the nineties is an unhappy chronicle. A rush to cut defense spending, a failure to counter genocide in either the Balkans or Africa, and maladroitness in the handling of Hong Kong, conveyed an unmistakable message of exhaustion, weakness, and retreat. It was a message that only encouraged the growth of the global threats we face now.

If an abandonment of identifiably neocon principles only led Britain into foreign policy difficulties, and Britain's finest hours in foreign policy were enjoyed under neocon colors, it might be expected that the ascendancy of neoconservatism in America would be matched by a renaissance of similar thinking in Britain. But there are remarkably few British politicians, or writers, on the right who are happy to pin the badge of neoconservative to their coat. Instead, those most likely to talk of neoconservatism in contemporary Britain are on the left, where the term is used as a catch-all denunciation of any reasonably robust conservative.

It may be too much to expect political players to be precise and scrupulous in the heat of ideological battle but the promiscuity with which many on the British left fling around the term neoconservative means that they have drained it of practically all meaning. Any American who is more than a lukewarm supporter of President Bush is characterized as a neocon.

Traditional conservative figures who have little appetite, indeed a positive antipathy, toward the neocon attachment to extending democracy, such as the State Department hawk John Bolton, are termed neocons simply because they are not to the left of President Clinton. The use of neoconservative as a synonym for ultraconservative has become a hallmark of current left-wing rhetoric.

Robin Cook, for example, blamed 'fundamentalist neocons' for disaster in the Middle East in an article for the *Independent* on May 21, 2004. Mr. Cook sought, for rhetorical effect, to unite two bogey words in one phrase. It clearly did not bother him, though, that it is almost impossible to think of a single neoconservative, American or otherwise, who is also a religious fundamentalist – even though these fundamentalists are an important part of President George W. Bush's political coalition. Those American politicians who are inclined to a literal reading of scripture tend to be traditional conservatives of a different stripe to neoconservatives.

But such nuances are beyond figures like Mr. Cook, who is more interested in the vigor of an attack than its accuracy. It is, however, ironic that a politician who delights in damning the U.S. administration for its inability to appreciate the finer points of diplomacy should himself be so blind to detail, nuance, and subtlety.

Although Mr. Cook, as a demoted former Foreign Secretary and an opponent of the Gulf War, has his own axe to grind, he is very far from alone in his penchant for using neoconservative as a modish term of abuse for any conservative considered beyond the pale.

In April 2004, three Blairite former ministers, Alan Milburn, Stephen Byers, and Peter Mandelson, submitted a joint article to the *Guardian* in defense of the proposed new European Constitution. Even though the burden of their argument was entirely about European integration, and all three ministers were supportive of Tony Blair's role in the Iraq War, they still chose to characterize, and damn, opposition to the new EU treaty as 'neoconservative'. The three clearly felt that the term not only conveyed extremism to their readers, but also attached a whiff of sulfur to their opponents. The charge was, however, misplaced.

The three former ministers sought to argue that 'neocon' opposition to the EU Constitution was driven by isolationism. The neoconservative opponents of further European integration were accused of wanting to 'let the Balkans burn, African wars rage, and the Palestinian Authority go without help'.

There may well be opponents of the EU Constitution who want all of those things. But if they do embrace such an isolationist position they are, by definition, not neoconservatives. What defines neoconservatives is their willingness to intervene where others, on the right or left, would opt to stand aloof. Neoconservatism and isolationism are as much contrary trends as monetarism and collectivism, with the former having developed in opposition to the latter.

The definition of neoconservatism may be fuzzy in many British minds, but what both these examples help illustrate is the toxic nature of the term, certainly so far as political actors on the British left are concerned.

Although there is a slapdash quality to the manner in which neoconservative colors are applied to any right-winger whom the left wishes to demonize, there is also a passion that attaches to left-wing attacks on the neocons, which requires analysis.

In the pages of the *Guardian* and the *Independent*, or in the BBC's broadcasts, neoconservativism is treated as a uniquely worrying phenomenon and neoconservatives as peculiarly dangerous creatures.

One recurring trope has been the attribution of sinister influence over American politics to a neoconservative cabal that possesses several disturbing qualities. [See the essays by Boot, Brooks, and Muravchik, Ed.] The neocons are held to exercise disproportionate, and undeserved, power, to exercise it covertly, to operate as a tightly knit mafia, to have beguiled the media, and to have a hidden agenda to put Israel's interests before those of America, or, indeed, the world.

All these charges were made by the BBC in their *Panorama* special 'The War Party', screened on May 18, 2003. And all, it scarcely needs pointing out, veer dangerously close to reprising anti-Semitic rhetoric of the past.

The belief that Jews exercise an unreasonable amount of unaccountable power, hold sway over the media, 'stick together' to look after their own, and place loyalty to 'their people' in Israel over the country whose passport they carry is characteristically anti-Semitic and it is therefore particularly worrying that this ancient prejudice should revive in the media coverage of neoconservatism.

Another of the principal traits of anti-Semitism is the insistence that Jews live on terms set for them by others. In medieval times this prejudice took the form of ghettoization. Jews lived on sufferance, but under conditions decreed elsewhere. The prejudice survives to this day in the insistence, by some, that Jews continue to inhabit spaces allocated by others.

Specifically, there is a tendency for some on the left to restrict sympathy for Jewish individuals and causes to those that perpetuate the position of Jews as victims, supplicants, or allies of radicalism. When Jews are successful, assertive, self-confident or, worst of all, conservative, then they move, metaphorically, beyond the pale. Some of the passionate opposition that neoconservatism inspires can be seen as the rage of the left when it sees Jewish intellectual figures, whether Norman Podhoretz or Paul Wolfowitz, embracing conservative positions.

But the energetic denunciations that neoconservatism provokes go well beyond leftist anger that those whom they have taken for granted have dared to think for themselves. After all, the ranks of neoconservatives include many, many figures, including this author, who are followers of faiths other than Judaism. The underlying reason that neoconservatism inspires such furious opposition is the scale of the difficulty it poses for the left. It is, quite simply, the most powerful ideological opponent that the left faces today.

Neoconservatism provides a particularly potent challenge to the left because it combines both an appeal to moral principles and an understanding of human nature. The old right understood human nature, but often descended into cynicism when framing policy. The new left has offered policies that seek to inspire, but which have become either rigid or oppressive because they fail to take account of individual character and social reality.

In foreign affairs, as has been noted, neoconservatism transcends the limitations of cynical realism and multilateral idealism. In the past the left have been able to deny political legitimacy to conservative foreign-policy choices by arguing that statesmen of the right have been studiedly amoral. In hard terms, it has been easy for the left to damn past Conservative governments, like those of Nixon and Heath, for cozying up to 'friendly' tyrannies such as Chile and China. Conservative foreign-policy practitioners such as Kissinger have become soft targets in public discourse, easily caricatured for putting oil, arms deals, wealthy clients, and 'stability' before human rights and higher principles.

Because neoconservatism places human rights, democracy, and liberal principles at the heart of its foreign-policy vision, the left have become angered that they no longer have a monopoly on the rhetoric of values.

What makes this loss worse for the left is that neoconservatism provides a framework for defending and extending these values, which their own idealistic multilateralism has not, and cannot. From the collapse of the Soviet Union, to the slow toppling of authoritarianism in Latin America, it has been leaders of the right, displaying resolve and acting in alliances of independent nation-states, who have won concrete gains for freedom. The left cannot abide the twin reverses of losing sole possession of the moral high ground and being proved wrong in the realm of action. Because neoconservatism has achieved both, it is attacked with particular venom and smeared with unique energy. The left cannot allow it to prevail.

The neoconservative emphasis on placing enlightened values at the heart of foreign policy is a reflection of another, deeper aspect of the neocon vision, which poses a profound difficulty for the left. Conservatism has, almost axiomatically, traditionally had a problem with modernity.

Politicians and thinkers of the right have tended to prefer nostalgia to optimism. There has been a deep-rooted suspicion toward democracy among some on the European right, who have sought to place constitutional restraints on expressions of the popular will. Others on the right have been ambivalent about economic growth, and in particular the effect on social stability of capitalism's creative destruction. Yet others on the right have expressed their disquiet at the growth of diversity in modern democratic societies, not least through the development of multi-ethnic polities. All these tendencies have allowed the left to paint the right into a backward-looking corner and depict conservatives as poorly equipped to manage the challenges of the future. Neoconservatives, however, are unhampered by many of the disabilities faced by others on the right.

Neoconservatism, as both philosophy and political practice, has developed as a response to democracy and modernity. It celebrates both, as fruits of human creativity, rather than regarding them with rueful concern.

Neoconservatives, as we shall see, draw on the wisdom of the past in making sense of new challenges. But in the very temper and disposition of the neocon there is an ease with democracy that marks out him or her from some others on the right. It is that quality of understanding of the modern world that makes neoconservatism not just an appropriate set of principles for contemporary statecraft but also a useful guide for those in Europe looking to modernize the right.

Most European parties of the right have their roots in throne or altar. Or both in the case of Britain's Tories. For all their subsequent modernizations, most of the conservative parties of the Old World have a pre-democratic component in their DNA. Whether it is the retention of Catholic social doctrine by Italian and German Christian Democrats or the residual monarchism of British and Spanish conservatives, there is a pre-modern element in the make-up of the European right.

Complicating the picture are the strains imposed on the continental European right by the events of the thirties and forties. The role of conservative authoritarians in facilitating the rise of fascism, or collaborating with Nazism, in Germany, Italy, Spain, France, and the Low Countries, raises difficult questions. In France the split attitudes of the right toward Vichy still influence the politics of today, as we can see in the nature of the division between Gaullists and Le Penistes. That split only compounds fractures on the French right over the question of legitimacy that go back to revolutionary times. There has long been an anti-Enlightenment strain of thinking on the French right, which has had a profound, and malign, influence on swaths of continental conservatism. The American right, by contrast, and the neoconservatives in particular, are not hobbled in the same way. While there are elements on the American right – specifically the self-styled paleoconservatives – who position themselves in opposition to the neocons, and who are suspicious of every social development since the Renaissance and every political change since the fall of the Confederacy – the whole temper of American conservative thinking is built on faith in democratic, republican virtues. American conservatives have had, and continue to have, lively differences about the balance of power within the federal system but there is an instinctive confidence in popular sovereignty, which runs deeper than in many parts of the European right. In America the reigning conservative disposition is optimism about human potential. In Europe it is fatalism about the human condition.

And that is increasingly to the disadvantage of the European right. Deference toward many of the institutions that have conferred legitimacy on the right has rapidly diminished in the last twenty years. The Church, family, and traditional social elites no longer exercise the authority they enjoyed just a generation ago. The collapse of communism has also weakened the cohesiveness of the European right, depriving it of a threat that united traditionalists and more liberal elements under one umbrella.

Many on the British right have rushed to fill the space where old certainties used to exist with new fears and reheated animosities. It is striking that British Conservatism has been in eclipse since 1990 and during that time its tone has generally been one of lamentation or rancor.

The British right desperately needs to modernize its theory and practice, and, in particular, to develop a response to a more diverse and demanding society. Neoconservatism can be invaluable in this process. Its optimism, and the ease with which neoconservatives celebrate a society of modern consumers, can help equip British conservatives to change.

One of the right's successes in Britain in the last twenty years has been the economic emancipation of millions of workers who now have the wealth, and the untroubled self-confidence, to act as American consumers have done for years now. Taste has been democratized and, as we can see in the growth of satellite television, car ownership, and home improvement expenditure, democratic taste is often decidedly Atlanticist in form.

It is a source of regret to many traditional British and European conservatives that increasing personal wealth among workers has led to greater expenditure on goods and services that they consider the vulgar artefacts of American culture. But a far-sighted right would celebrate the assertion of popular taste, in food, dress, and entertainment, as a rebuke to the joyless puritanism of the left.

The optimism of neoconservatism and its development in line with America's own democratization of taste equip it to help Britons and Europeans frame a sensible politics for today.

Because many neoconservatives started on the hopeful left and migrated right, they have an instinctive understanding of the need for promise and vision in modern politics. Neoconservatives understand, as many conservatives still fail to, why a JFK or Clement Attlee remain popular heroes. They know that a key element of modern politics is the ability to give the nation a sense of common purpose infused with nobility of thought and generosity of spirit. Where neoconservatives part company with the left is in an understanding of the dangers of utopianism and a determination not to allow human nature to be remolded to fit overgrandiose visions. But neoconservatives know that if the right fails to offer a sense of high national purpose to politics, and either appeals solely to economic self-interest or to a bundle of sectarian concerns, it will lose, and deserves to.

The requirement to appeal to the better instincts of mankind is apparent, naturally, in the realm of neoconservative foreign policy. Neocons know that in a modern state, foreign policy is no longer a matter of elites calculating interests but democracies committing themselves to causes. Support for foreign policy needs to be won, and retained, through the articulation of vision as well as the skillful execution of statecraft.

While neoconservatives recognize that leaders must appeal to a nation's heart as well as its mind when it comes to foreign policy, the insight doesn't end there. Neoconservatives also accept that in modern democratic societies faith in collective provision is more than a matter of calculation of advantage on the part of client groups. There is nobility in a society seeking to spread advantage as widely as possible. That is why neoconservatives instinctively believe in the merits of strong government as much as they accept the importance of limited government. The two are, of course, linked because government authority depends on avoiding governmental overreach. But another factor weighs in neocon thinking.

Neoconservatives such as [New York Democrat Senator] Daniel Patrick Moynihan were the leading voices, pointing out how welfare can erode those characteristics on which a healthy society depends. The foundation of *The Public Interest* by Irving Kristol and Daniel Bell in the 1960s led to a fundamental review of the welfare state and limits being placed on its growth. Neoconservatives recognized that the surest route out of poverty for any citizen depended on the cultivation of virtues such as prudence, hard work, fidelity in marriage, and honesty in social dealings. The capacity of a traditional welfare state to undermine those virtues – by subsidizing sloth, insulating citizens from their own fecklessness, and providing perverse incentives that undermined family stability – worried early neoconservatives. The reform of welfare policy in the 1990s, in both America and Britain, reflects the grain of neoconservative thinking. Allied to those reforms, neocons have been in the van of developing policies on crime and antisocial behaviour that seek to tackle these problems at root. The work of Charles Murray and James Q. Wilson has influenced policy-makers as far afield as Rudi Giuliani, Michael Howard, and Frank Field, contributing to a turn in the tide after years of liberal excuse-mongering for criminal behavior.

The neoconservative emphasis on a political culture that emphasizes virtue reflects the essential dynamic at the heart of neocon thinking. On the one hand neoconservatives are attuned to the requirements of modernity and are at home with mass democratic culture. But they also know that a successful modern society depends on citizens acquiring and retaining the virtues that history's most thoughtful political thinkers have delineated. For neoconservatives the new world in which we all now live is still best understood, and governed, by close attention to the thought of writers within a recognizably conservative tradition. The writings of Aristotle on what makes a good citizen and a stable polity, the thoughts of Thucydides on power politics and statecraft, and the insights of those Renaissance thinkers who considered the 'republican virtues' of ancient Rome worth reprising – all inform neocon thinking. As do the lessons on civility inherent in Irving Kristol's beloved Jane Austen and the observations on democracy itself first made by Alexis de Tocqueville.

The ability to balance history's lessons with today's demands, to distill lessons from the past about unchanging human nature and then apply them with skill to modern popular democracies, is inherent to neoconservatism. An understanding of just how historically singular, and valuable, our current liberal democracies are, imbues neoconservatives with a determination to defend them. That resolution is not always apparent in other political thinkers and actors. Neocons had a sharper appreciation of the dangers of communism than most conservatives in the sixties, seventies, and eighties, and they have a more acute sense of the dangers inherent in Islamic fundamentalist terrorism now. Societies such as ours in Britain could do with a great deal more of the rigor of the neocons in waking up to the threats we currently face.

There is another aspect to neoconservatism, which a modern European right should wish to emulate – its inclusiveness. It is striking that most leading neocon thinkers do not come from those groups that traditionally sustained the U.S. Republicans. The right in America traditionally drew on white Anglo-Saxon Protestants for its leadership. But neoconservative thought-leaders tend not to be WASPs; they are often Jewish like Kristol and Podhoretz, or Roman Catholic, like George Weigel, Daniel Patrick Moynihan, Richard John Neuhaus, and Michael Novak. Coming from groups that traditionally supported the Democrats, the neocons have reinvigorated Republicanism and refitted it for an ever more diverse America. The European right, which has recently had difficulty in adjusting to social diversity, could learn from the American right's experience of transcending traditional political constituencies by appealing to common values.

There is one other area in which Europeans can learn from neocons – the importance of economic growth. From the writings of Irwin Stelzer to the policies of Ronald Reagan, an orientation toward economic growth is a key factor of neocon political thinking. Neoconservatism, as a political philosophy in tune with our democratic times, instinctively recognizes the importance that a modern citizenry places on the delivery of growth and responds warmly to the aspirations of most voters to enrich their lives. [See the essay by Karlyn Bowman, Ed.] Where many European conservatives might prize either economic protection or simple price stability, neocons have an economic vision that goes beyond such business-oriented calculations and speaks to the wishes of the mass of citizens. Given the sorry position of many continental economies trapped in the euro, a device that entrenches protection and fetishizes price stability, the virtues of a pro-growth policy should hardly need emphasizing to the European right.

Indeed, European and British conservatives have a great deal to learn from a conservative movement that is modern, whereas they are seen as of the past;

from a movement that is intellectually self-confident, whereas they are seen as aridly managerial; from a movement that articulates optimism and vision, whereas they are seen as voices of fear and cynicism; and, above all, from a movement that is alive to the great challenges of our time when many in Europe prefer timid and self-defeating insularity.

For Britain in particular, neoconservatism means a reclamation of all that is best, most optimistic, most engaged, and most open in our own conservative tradition. The vigor with which the contemporary left in Britain denounce neoconservatism should make every British Conservative ask why political opponents wish to steer Tories away from this philosophy. Might it be the case that their anathemas reflect their acute concern at the possibility that British conservatism might become as healthy, lively, popular, and powerful as American? And shouldn't that be something to which the best in British Conservatism should aspire?

THE PROSPECT FOR NEOCONSERVATISM IN GERMANY

Jeffrey Gedmin

*It would probably be hard to imagine a less hospitable place
[for neoconservatism] than Germany… Germany today, perhaps
more so than even France, has become hyper-allergic to the
use of American power.*

THE PROSPECT FOR NEOCONSERVATISM IN GERMANY

JEFFREY GEDMIN

Irving Kristol contends that 'there is nothing like neoconservatism in Europe'. Kristol is right. There is a small network of pro-American writers and policy intellectuals who are attracted to some neoconservative ideas. But the environment for neoconservativism as such is an inhospitable one. It would probably be hard to imagine a less hospitable place than Germany. How has Germany responded to George W. Bush's neoconservative foreign policies of the last four years? Is there a constituency in Germany, however modest, for ideas of the neoconservative 'persuasion'?

The debate of the last couple of years about neoconservatism in Germany, like elsewhere in Europe, has been obscured above all by an obsession with who the neoconservatives are, rather than what they think.

'Ich sage nur Wolfowitz' – I'll only say Wolfowitz. That is how one seething citizen put it to two columnists of the center-right daily *Die Welt* during a chat aboard a train last year. The woman apparently felt that those four words were sufficient to express her anger with today's America. A senior German businessman once calmly asked me, after I had delivered a speech in Frankfurt on Iraq, whether it was the Jews who were responsible for American foreign policy that was aimed at removing Saddam Hussein from power. One German commentator speaks of 'unbridled chauvinism', 'right-wing zionism', 'crass materialism', and 'permanent chaos' in the Middle East. Writes the *Financial Times Deutschland*: 'Wolfowitz still has appetite… despite the military misery in Iraq.'

Observe the German debate on neoconservatism and you might get the feeling that Lyndon LaRouche's conspiracy theories have credence and that Aljazeera rantings sound reasonable. Habsburg heir Otto von Habsurg, who has represented the Bavarian CSU in the European Parliament, told an interviewer that the Pentagon has become 'a Jewish institution'.

German views toward neoconservativism are a strange brew. They are a mixture of Republican realism (Brent Scowcroft), anti-Bushism (Paul Krugman), anti-globalization and anti-capitalism (Michael Moore), anti-Semitism (Pat Buchanan), and anti-Americanism (Susan Sontag). These tendencies, all present before the war in Iraq, surely help account for the collapse of favorable opinion across Europe toward the United States. Germany is no exception. A State Department poll from May 2004 found that, just as in France, two out of three Germans hold a negative opinion of the U.S. Only one out of five said they had confidence in the U.S. to deal responsibly with world affairs.

Books berating the United States and belittling American culture have soared in popularity in recent years. One such title, *Schwarzbuch USA* – Black Book USA – by Austrian journalist Eric Frey, is a 497-page chronicle of American crimes throughout history. The author makes no attempt to conceal his contempt for America's neoconservatives and their influence on the Bush presidency. 'Under George W. Bush [the U.S.] has become a threat to world peace,' says Frey. A recent European Commission poll found that a majority of EU citizens share this view. How did we get here?

It has in part to do with differences in opinion over policy choices made by the Bush administration over the past several years. The United States and Europe have differed over the Kyoto Treaty, the International Criminal Court, Iraq, and other important issues. In part it has also to do with the deterioration of U.S. public diplomacy. America has abdicated in the war of ideas. In fact, America's closest friends now routinely complain that we no longer show up for the fight.

In part, this growing divide between the United States and Europe has to do with differing threat assessments and attitudes toward the use of force. These differences are, of course, nothing new. Nor is it a surprise that for some neoconservative is simply another word for hawk, in itself a pejorative in leading political circles on the continent. The culture of appeasement runs strong in Europe.

The Federal Republic has come a long way since the fall of the Berlin Wall fifteen years ago in adjusting to the realities of power and responsibility. German troops are in Bosnia and Kosovo. They fight alongside Americans in Afghanistan. Still, Germany's political culture remains dominated by strong pacifist tendencies. Most Germans see the war on terror as a law enforcement issue, rather than a foreign policy problem requiring military solutions.

It is perhaps difficult to grasp how difficult the Bush administration's strategically ambitious foreign policies must appear to an ally like Germany.

Today's Germany is a medium-size country, a non-nuclear power without a permanent seat on the United Nations Security Council. The country faces significant economic challenges, structural in nature, and a looming demographic crisis. Its defense spending ranks today, in terms of percentage of GDP, in a league with that of Luxembourg. Add to this the legacy of two world wars and the Holocaust, and it is not hard to fathom why Germans would be put off by the idea of global military interventions, grand strategic designs, and the prospect of remaking the Greater Middle East. Germany is just beginning to come out of its Cold War cocoon.

In fact, Germany's foreign policy priorities today are mainly regional: integrating an enlarged European Union, adopting a European constitution, developing a European defense and security policy, cooperating with Russia, and tending to residual problems in the Balkans. Berlin's foreign policy tools are chiefly civilian and economic; its methods are mostly multilateral. It is probably only natural that a confident, assertive America, pursuing a global agenda and threatening the status quo, is anathema to this kind of political culture. Today's arguments are reminiscent of the fissures that the Atlantic Alliance experienced during Ronald Reagan's presidency. Reagan's 'Evil Empire' speech was ridiculed in much the same way President Bush's 'Axis of Evil' speech has been denounced. Reagan, too, was accused of being a dangerous and naive ideologue. Critics charged Reagan, as they do the U.S. today, with dividing the world into friends and enemies, militarizing American foreign policy, and steering the world toward Armageddon.

There is one thing in Europe that Ronald Reagan did not have to contend with, though. Germany today, perhaps more so than even France, has become hyper-allergic to the use of American power. Perhaps this should come as no surprise after Germany's unification. Unlike France, Germany had been divided for four decades and was also unable to pursue an independent foreign policy during the Cold War. Americans probably underestimated the resentment that such dependency would breed. Now many Germans have a palpable yearning for emancipation.

A campaign poster used for recent European parliamentary elections by the PDS [Party of Democratic Socialism], the successor party to the old East German communists, proclaimed: 'Side by Side with the UN and Not in the Shadow of the U.S.!' The idea has traction. It is part of the mainstream. A prominent Christian Democrat says Germany no longer wants to be treated as 'a passive appendage' of the United States. Neoconservative assertiveness about American power and America's unique place in the world highlights the imbalance in power between America and Europe. It increases frustration about German weakness and anxieties about Germany being dominated by the U.S. One reaction? If Americans are more powerful, Germans are at least more moral and sophisticated.

For the popular weekly magazine *Stern*, America's neoconservatives are nothing but 'imperialists'. For the *Financial Times Deutschland*, America's neoconservative foreign policy is 'unilateralism and high-tech Blitz attacks'. Ulrich Wickert, a popular anchor on network television, was warning of Bush's extremist tendencies shortly after September 11. Wickert argued that Bush and Bin Laden share similar 'patterns of thought'. A leading Social Democrat labels Bush 'a neoconservative zealot', responsible for provoking a 'worldwide intifada'.

Rhetoric among prominent conservatives has not been so different. It is true that Angela Merkel, chairman of the CDU [Christian Democratic Union], has tried to dampen anti-Americanism. Others have attempted to blunt the sharp, hysterical attacks on American neoconservatism. Still, the mainstream moves in a different direction. Conservative commentator Peter Boenisch, once a spokesman for the government of CDU Chancellor Helmut Kohl and former editor of the mass circulation daily *Bildzeitung*, wrote before the Iraq War that the America of Bush and the neoconservatives was no longer an America that Boenisch could trust. 'Bush's America is not mine,' he concluded, blaming a clash of cultures.

If Germany finds it difficult to accept American neoconservative foreign policies, it may have to do with the fact that these policies accent precisely those aspects of American thinking that differ sharply from the tenets and tastes of modern German political culture. After all, according to [Irving] Kristol, neoconservatism may be a variant of conservatism, but it is also in the 'American grain'. What is this grain? It includes, says Kristol, optimism, a desire to cut taxes and promote economic growth, a deep love of country, a suspicion of world government, and a commitment to muscular defense. In other words, neoconservatism is at its heart very American. And the very antithesis of today's Germany.

Optimism is surely not in sync with the Zeitgeist. In fact, according to opinion polls, optimism has not been fashionable in Germany for at least a decade. A Gallup poll this past year found that, by a margin of two to one, Germans are more pessimistic than Americans about the future. The U.S. is known among Germans as the rough-and-tumble, 'hire and fire' society; Germans are more worried than Americans about job security (32 per cent vs.

19 per cent). The enlargement of the European Union, a project of historic dimension, causes more anxiety than hope. Germany's new president, Horst Köhler, says he is 'astonished by the optimism of Poland, the Czech Republic, and Slovakia' when compared to the mood of his fellow citizens.

It goes on. A recent Eurobarometer poll found that three out of four Germans say they are unhappy with their lives. One senior bank executive says he has 'never experienced such deep pessimism'. Former chancellor Helmut Schmidt has complained that Germans have become 'Weltmeister' in complaining. None of this is new. For years, Germans have said of themselves that they are champion complainers, but complain 'at a very high standard' – a reference to the fact that a majority of Germans live well, with a short working week, long vacations, and generous welfare benefits.

This malaise may be a phase from which Germans will eventually liberate themselves. But the optimism that seems to be of a piece with that 'American grain', the hopefulness that is accented and celebrated by neoconservatism, looks unlikely to find a home in Germany in the foreseeable future. The same applies to German attitudes toward tax cuts and economic growth, patriotism, and world government.

A British writer once recounted his first trip to the United States. He was sitting in a seaside café when a beautiful sailboat passed by. While he mused: 'That bastard, why should he deserve such a beautiful thing?' the young American waiter had returned to the table with his coffee, barely able to conceal his enthusiasm. 'One day I'll have one of those,' he exclaimed. Americans tend to be interested in seeing the economic pie grow. Europeans tend to be more interested in the rules and regulations that equitably divide the pie. I received an invitation recently to a Düsseldorf conference, which posed the question, 'Is the Anglo-Saxon economy right for Germany?' Some never tire of asking the question.

Envy plays a bigger role in Germany than it does in the U.S. Big government is far more acceptable. The State is guardian of social values and protector of its citizens. Americans call it 'Uncle Sam'. Germans say, 'Vater Staat'. Germany's pro-market Free Democratic Party (FDP), which rarely polls more than 10 per cent, has pushed for years for deregulation, lower taxes, and pro-growth economic policies. Mostly in vain.

The FDP shared power as junior partner in Helmut Kohl's CDU from 1983 to 1998. Economic liberals, real reformers like the FDP's former economics minister Otto Lambsdorff, have struggled. Six years ago Lambsdorff quipped that Germany was a country with nearly 4 million unemployed, but where you still cannot buy a liter of milk on Sundays. Today the figure for unemployed has increased to 4.5 million. The labor market remains heavily regulated, shop hours are still restricted. Berlin has 18 per cent unemployment and you still cannot buy milk on Sundays.

There is a debate on economic reform. There are advocates of modernization in all the major parties. Even the boldest of reformers, however, feel obligated to repeat like a mantra that they are not advocating 'American conditions' nor the development of an 'elbow society'. The socialist idea dies slowly in Germany. There is no Margaret Thatcher in sight.

A vote for tax cuts is a vote against 'social justice'. There is universal allegiance to the 'social market economy'. Suspicion of markets runs deep. When Michael Novak's book, *The Spirit of Democratic Capitalism*, was first translated into German, publishers fretted about an adverse reaction to the word 'capitalism'.

Neoconservatism espouses patriotism. At least the subject of patriotism is no longer a taboo in Germany. While still in office Helmut Kohl had begun to call for a more open discussion of the issue. Gerhard Schröeder now says Germans are developing a healthy, mature sense of patriotism and not the 'flag-waving, hurrah' variety, whatever that means. There are, indeed, signs that the younger generation is beginning to think differently about national identity and love of country.

For years, there was D-Mark nationalism. This was the German pride in the 'Wirtschaftswunder', the competitiveness of German goods in the world market and the strength of the German currency. Others spoke of 'constitutional patriotism', the pride in the Federal Republic's liberal, democratic order established after the war. World War II and the Holocaust had traumatized ordinary Germans and turned love of country into guilt. Patriotism was equated with the malign and lethal nationalism of the past. In October 2000 a leading CDU politician, observing the understandable pride that the French feel for their country, said he himself 'felt proud to be a German'. This simple statement caused a controversy (the sentiment had become the monopoly of skinheads and Neo-Nazis).

This is changing. But change comes slowly. When Germany's new president, Horst Köhler, says, 'I love my country,' it still makes news. The author of a recent best-seller, *The Land of My Father* (to say 'my Fatherland' is still too strong!), argues 'that it must be allowed' for Germans to love their country. It is an odd, contorted debate. Is it any wonder many Germans feel resentment, envy, and discomfort over the unfettered ('flag-waving, hurrah') patriotism of Americans?

Buried in shame, Germans learned after the war that the only acceptable way to pursue their national interest was through the cover of multilateralism. Germany sought reconciliation with France and submerged itself in the European Community. Bismarck once said he often found 'Europe' in the mouths of those politicians who wanted something, but dared not ask for it in their own name.

German historian Heinrich August Winkler says today that the EU's member states, 'even if they do not fully realize it, are no longer traditional nation-states'. Winkler argues that they are post-classical, supranational states that have begun to exercise sovereignty jointly. 'Their commitment to multilateralism,' says Winkler, 'reflects their historical experience and their current political interests.' This is true to some extent. It certainly reflects a German way of looking at things.

Of course, Americans also prefer to act with allies. We are not inherently hostile to working with international organizations. But then we reach limits. Germans continue to cede extraordinary amounts of sovereignty to supranational institutions. 'Building Europe' enhances German influence and Germany's room for maneuver. Germans also tend to have considerable faith in the United Nations to manage the world's affairs. The Security Council is the body that can help rein in the Americans. That's Germany, starting to sound like France. It is not very American at any rate. And it is hardly neoconservative.

NEOCONSERVATISM
IN EUROPE

João Carlos Espada

Neoconservatism does not have to be invented in Europe.
It is already there. Not as doctrine, to be sure, but as a tacit
disposition among the 'little platoons' that mind their own
business and get in return a strong hostility from the
adversarial culture.

NEOCONSERVATISM IN EUROPE
A View from Portugal

JOÃO CARLOS ESPADA

Irving Kristol, often described as 'the godfather of neoconservatism', famously said that a neoconservative is a liberal who has been mugged by reality. This seems to describe with great precision my own intellectual voyage of discovery of neoconservatism. This essay is mainly a recollection of and a reflection on this voyage. Some readers may find it too boringly personal. I would like to think it may be helpful to those Europeans who, like myself, share a sense of admiration for the Anglo-American political culture and worry about the growing anti-Americanism in Europe.

I

OXFORD JOURNEY

This voyage may be said to have started during my Oxford years, 1990–94. I was doing my DPhil under the supervision of Ralf Dahrendorf and was visiting Karl Popper, at his home in Kenley, south of London, on a regular basis. I could hardly summarize here my personal and intellectual debts to these two great men. Suffice it to say, however, that Lord Dahrendorf (Sir Ralf, when we first met) and Sir Karl gently guided my intellectual evolution from a sort of mild left liberalism to a middle-of-the-road liberalism (in the European and not the American sense), which is aware of liberalism's own difficulties. It is not too simplistic to say that two of those difficulties were particularly important to me.

The first one can be described as the problem of John Stuart Mill and an immense literature has of course been written on the subject. To put it in a nutshell, I was wondering whether Mill's 'one very simple principle' could actually suffice to keep a free society alive and robust. To my mind, the question was not so much about the limits of state interference in individuals' lives. I had learned, albeit slowly, that governments tend to do badly whatever can be done fairly well by civil society and free enterprise. My question was thus mainly moral: should we really believe that everything an individual does within his private sphere is beyond moral judgment by others?

This, in my opinion, is a serious moral question regardless of whether or not it corresponds to Mill's interpretation of his own principle. It clearly became the mainstream interpretation of Mill's principle, one that is now held as a sort of sacred dogma by our public culture, especially among academic and media circles. This *reality*, as Irving Kristol would put it, poses serious problems. And these problems become more serious and *real* for young parents who want to raise their children properly against an atmosphere of relativism propagated by television and schoolteachers. This was the condition of my wife, Graca, and me while we were living in Oxford with our two daughters, Isabel and Diana. And our liberalism was mugged by this *reality*: should parents be prepared to teach their children that every type of personal behavior is equivalent to any other, provided these are either self-regarding actions or actions based on mutual consent?

It can certainly be replied that Mill's principle does not compel us to accept all conduct as morally sound. It only compels us to tolerate different conducts as long as they do not harm others. The main moral point, however, remains: can liberalism or liberty rest on a doctrine that is basically silent about the virtues or the character of a free society and of free and responsible persons? I rather doubt it, and my doubts were reinforced while I was writing my DPhil dissertation on Friedrich A. Hayek's liberalism and Raymond Plant's socialism, which was later published as *Social Citizenship Rights: A Critique of F. A. Hayek and Raymond Plant* (London: Macmillan (St Antony's Series); New York: St Martin's Press, 1995), with a foreword by Lord Dahrendorf. These doubts were reinforced by my perception of Hayek's difficulty in presenting a moral argument against relativism and subjectivism. As I have tried to show in the book just quoted, Hayek gives great importance to general rules of just conduct for the maintenance of a free society. But, again, most of these rules are only 'other-regarding' (as contrasted with 'self-regarding') and their justification tends to be merely based on evolutionary self-selection. With all due respect for Hayek's powerful thought, from which I have learned immensely, I do not think it has provided a satisfactory answer for what I have called here my first difficulty within liberalism: *can liberty rest on a doctrine that is mainly silent about the virtues or the character of a free society?*

My second difficulty was related to the first but was of a more specific nature. I had decided to go to Britain and leave my relatively comfortable position in Portugal – where I was political advisor to the President of the Republic, Mario Soares – because I had an intense admiration for the Anglo-American political tradition. I wanted to know more about it and its distinctive ingredients – distinctive, that is, from the continental European tradition, which I knew only too well. It would be impossible to recall here all I have learned about the Anglo-American tradition and way of life during my stay in Britain and, later on, in the U.S. But, again, there was a sort of mismatch between my liberal theory and my experience of reality. This mismatch puzzled me.

From the simple experience of living in Britain, I could get a strong impression of a distinctive British feature, which is and has been absent in most continental cultures, at least southern European ones. I would call it a sense of duty and self-control, which is gently combined with a sense of humor about oneself – as Karl Popper liked to say, an attitude of *not taking oneself too seriously but a preparedness to take one's duties seriously*. Now, curiously enough, most academic literature on liberty and liberalism that I came across hardly mentioned this distinctive moral sense of the British. It was as if the idea of the gentleman had always been a myth invented either by foreigners or for foreigners, and yet I could describe thousands of personal experiences of my life in Britain that showed an underlying gentlemanly spirit. Why could I hardly find a book on contemporary political theory about gentlemanliness and the moral sense? Furthermore, I was getting the impression that this silence about gentlemanliness in the media and in schools was somehow responsible for the evident erosion of youth behavior in Britain. Again, my theoretical liberalism was being mugged by reality.

There is another dimension of this second difficulty, which may be worth referring to now and to which I shall return later. This could be called Lord Quinton's question. In the chapter dedicated to political philosophy of the *Oxford History of Western Philosophy*, Anthony Quinton asks himself the following question: why have the ideas of Locke produced a conservative revolution in seventeenth-century England and a moderate revolution in eighteenth-century America, whereas they have produced *the effect of alcohol in an empty stomach* once they have crossed the English Channel into eighteenth-century France? It is hardly possible to exaggerate the importance of this simple and unassuming question. For the time being, I would simply like to say that this question was always in my mind while living in Britain. And, gradually, I came to conjecture that part of the answer had to be sought outside political theory, strictly speaking. There seemed to be an ethos, a strange combination of habits and dispositions, as it were, distinctive of the English-speaking peoples, to use the famous expression of Winston Churchill. This ethos could hardly be encapsulated by my theoretical liberalism, or perhaps by any other ism. But what on earth could it be?

I I

NEOCONSERVATISM: FIRST CONTACTS

As I was struggling with all these questions, I suddenly came across a book by a certain Gertrude Himmelfarb. Its title is *Victorian Minds* (New York: Knopf, 1968; Chicago: Ivan R. Dee, 1995) and I still vividly remember the tremendous impact it produced on me. I don't know exactly how and why I found it. I think I was looking for Himmelfarb's intellectual biography of Lord Acton in the small and charming library of St Antony's, my Oxford college. The book on Acton was not there, but *Victorian Minds* fell into my path. I started reading it and could not stop until the very end.

There it was, a book speaking of the *moral sense* of the British peoples and British elites in the nineteenth century. There it was, a book saying that a *common ethos* underpinned Victorian Britain and was subscribed to even by progressive intellectuals such as John Stuart Mill. And there it was, a book saying that this *ethos* was that of a gentleman. 'I now believe in nothing, but I do not the less believe in morality... I mean to live and die like a gentleman if possible.' These were the words of [English scholar and critic] Leslie Stephen 'after abandoning the effort to derive an ethic from Darwinism', Gertrude Himmelfarb recalled, among so many other examples (p. 290).

I was immediately conquered by this book. It finally explained to me what I had been experiencing in Britain. But all new insights bring new problems. And *Victorian Minds* brought me a new problem: *religion*. Not that I was against religion. Having studied Karl Popper's critical rationalism, I had learned that dogmatic rationalism is self-defeating and is actually responsible for generating closed societies – curiously enough, not *irrationally* closed societies, but *rationally closed* societies. I also had read my Tocqueville – via Raymond Aron, incidentally – and knew how anti-religious Jacobins had led France to disaster. Gertrude Himmelfarb's argument, however, was not only about toleration for religion on the part of rationalism but about the crucial role that religion had played in the emergence and consolidation of a liberal society in Britain. Himmelfarb, recalling the work of Elie Halévy, was somehow implying that one of the most stable liberal regimes had not been basically, or even mainly, a product of a rationalist philosophy but of a combination of and a tension between religion and philosophy. This itself was not a philosophical argument but a historical one, based on experience. I must say that, to my mind, this made it more plausible – although still quite problematic.

My next encounter with neoconservatism would be no less dramatic. This took place in the summer of 1995 in Chicago, where I had gone with the purpose of attending the American Political Science Association annual meeting. Almost upon arrival I went to visit the usual book fair and immediately came across a book just published: *Neoconservatism: The Autobiography of an Idea* (New York: The Free Press, 1995), by a certain Irving Kristol. I had no idea that Irving Kristol and Gertrude Himmelfarb were husband and wife. I vaguely knew that Kristol was the editor of a quarterly journal, *The Public Interest*, which both Dahrendorf and Popper had praised but which I had rarely read. These references were good enough, though, and I bought the book.

This book was a real discovery. I read its 486 pages almost at a single sitting and missed most of the sessions of the APSA meeting. I was almost immediately converted to neoconservatism and was absolutely sure that I had to meet Irving Kristol and Gertrude Himmelfarb (of whose marriage, by the way, I had just learned from the autobiographical essays in Kristol's book). It is difficult, however, to explain today what in this book most impressed me that summer (incidentally, it was published in Portuguese in 2003).

There was, of course, an affinity of intellectual trajectories, so to speak, even though there were about thirty-five years between ours; from radicalism in his youth, Kristol had later moved to the center-left and then had the feeling not so much of leaving the left and moving toward the right but of the left leaving him and his friends – by embracing more and more lunatic and leftist cultural issues. There could hardly be a better description of my own trajectory. But there was much more in this book than a kinship of intellectual biographies.

There was, first, the combination of a clearly liberal view (in the European sense) on fundamentals – the critique of utopianism, the defense of the Anglo-American tradition versus the French, the critique of egalitarianism – with a strong opposition to the counter-culture, which is so rare among European liberals. Section II of *Neoconservatism*, entitled 'Race, Sex and Family', comprises six devastating chapters on the craziness of present-day schools and television in Britain, Portugal and America – precisely the sort of problems that were worrying my wife and me while in Oxford.

Second, there were several surprising references to the inadequacy of Hayek's and [Milton] Friedman's views in the battle of ideas against the counter-culture (Chapter 9, entitled 'Capitalism, Socialism and Nihilism', is a *must* in this respect, but there are several others). This leads Kristol to present a defense of capitalism that is different from Hayek's and Friedman's in the sense that it is not silent about the moral life. For Kristol, capitalism has always been underpinned by culture and morality – which he sometimes calls 'the bourgeois ethic', or 'the Protestant ethic', or even 'the Judeo–Christian tradition'. At a time when these moral ideas were mainly consensual, it was of course possible, and intellectually tempting, to describe the capitalist society in merely mechanical terms: as a society based on 'the fear of violent death' (Hobbes) or based on 'private vices, public benefits' (Mandeville). It is only when the moral references become controversial and start to be eroded that we notice their importance. Raymond Aron, incidentally, used to say that we best notice the value of economic growth – as well as of liberty – when we start not to have them. The same might be said of the bourgeois ethic.

Now, the question is almost inescapable: where does this 'bourgeois ethic' come from? I do not think Kristol has been entirely clear on this point. But he has been pretty clear, to my mind, on one point: the moral capital on which capitalism, or liberalism, or simply liberty depend is not 'invented' by liberalism. Somehow that moral capital was there and capitalism emerged from it, gradually and not confrontationally. Actually, the societies where liberal regimes were most successful – the English-speaking ones – were precisely those where *liberty and the moral capital were not confronting each other*. In other words, a liberal order will be the more successful the less it aims at total supremacy – the less it will aim at destroying all pre-liberal assumptions just because they have not been deduced from liberal premises. (A similar view, incidentally, can be found in Edmund Burke's *A Vindication of Natural Society* and Karl Popper's 'Towards a Rational Theory of Tradition' in his *Conjectures and Refutations*).

III

RETURNING TO EUROPE

If this is so, it suddenly throws new light on what I have earlier called Lord Quinton's question: why have Locke's ideas produced the effect of alcohol in an empty stomach once they have crossed the English Channel into France? Because on the continent Locke's ideas were reinterpreted as a radical project for the entire redesign of society – politically, socially, and morally.

In Britain and America, on the contrary, Locke's ideas were simply combined with the old English traditions of limited government. Rather than a project for a new society and a new morality, the English Revolution of 1688 and the American Revolution of 1776 were basically, though not only, a reassertion of the rights of free Englishmen to live their lives as they used to live them before – under the common protection of the laws of the land. In other words, what we now call liberal democracy has emerged in Anglo-American lands as a natural outgrowth of existing, law-abiding and moral-abiding ways of life. For this reason, liberal democracy among the English-speaking peoples has been naturally associated with an ethos of virtue and duty. For this reason, too, it has been tremendously stable. And the English-speaking peoples have always been the first to rise in defense of their cherished liberties – their way of life.

In continental Europe, on the other hand, the liberal project has tended to be understood as an adversarial project: adversarial to all existing ways of life simply because, in a sense, they were already there; because they had not been designed by 'Reason'. This has generated a lasting instability in European politics and European 'liberalism'. This, combined with a widespread disregard for limited or constitutional government, has led European politics to be cynically dominated by two illiberal poles: revolutionary 'liberals' and counter-revolutionary 'conservatives'. They both have aimed at using government without limits to push their own particular agendas. And their illiberal clash – the clash between the liberal project, so to speak, and traditional ways of life – has been at the root of the historical weakness of European liberal democracy (when compared with liberal democracy among the English-speaking peoples).

This misleading opposition helps explain two further important features of European politics: why progressives tend to be relativists, on the one hand, and why traditional or popular ways of life do not necessarily seem to spring naturally from liberal democracy. That European 'progressives' have to lean toward relativism is the consequence of their adversarial understanding of liberty. Traditional ways of life in Europe, on the other hand, do not necessarily appear to derive from liberal democracy because liberty has often been artificially associated with an adversarial culture that threatens those ways of life.

Now, this may sound too abstract and too historical. Be that as it may, the fact is that it throws some light on the present circumstances of European politics. To put it in a nutshell, present-day European politics seems to have overcome the above-mentioned difficulties – but I would submit that they are still fairly visible under the current circumstances.

One of the most astonishing features of today's European politics is, to put it bluntly, the virtual monopoly that the counter-culture has managed to gain upon the elites. As an American friend of mine put it, when the expression 'culture wars' is almost unknown in Europe, this is the surest sign that one of the sides is winning those wars: the counter-culture.

It is not easy to explain this state of affairs. It certainly has a strong generational ingredient; the former radicals of the 1960s are now running most of the elite institutions, at least on the left. But this does not explain the absence of a critique of the counter-culture in non-leftist circles. Several reasons, which cannot be developed here, seem to concur with this absence.

First, one might recall, obviously enough, the absence of neoconservatism in Europe. As I have mentioned, and as is otherwise known, Hayekian liberals (or conservatives) do not feel at ease fighting culture wars. But most European conservatives are not even Hayekians. They are mainly 'statist' conservatives who share with the left an unlimited faith in the other monopoly of European elites: the project of a federal Europe, which can leave behind the so-called 'obsolete nation-state'.

This is not the place to discuss the European project, and I would like to say that I am and have been in favor of a reunited Europe of nation-states. But I must add that the federal idea – that somehow Europe can get rid of its centuries-long national histories – is folly. It is just another version of that artificial concept of liberty or liberalism that has led Europe into a sterile conflict between revolution and the past – to paraphrase Tocqueville.

The fact remains, however, that 'federal Europe' has a tremendous appeal to European elites, both on the right and the left. This somehow fosters a common culture that is strongly dominated by the counter-culture – which, in its turn, has a sort of natural tendency to grow among bureaucratic circles.

This is then significantly reinforced by the strong 'statist' tradition of continental Europe and its relatively weak civil society.

Sadly, all this does not amount to good news for Europe. The federal project and the counter-culture hegemony create tensions within European societies that are not eased, to say the least, by the fact that they have almost a monopoly upon the elites. Populist illiberal reactions, sometimes ugly neo-fascist movements, rise to the surface from time to time and sometimes gain popular support – to the astonished surprise of federal elites. And these tensions can only get worse if the federal project is too promptly promoted among the new member states from Central and Eastern Europe – which have more traditional cultures and are very jealous of their national identities. Furthermore, we now have this growing anti-Americanism, already intertwined with anti-Semitism, which most European elites have been irresponsibly allowing to grow – if not actively promoting. Last but not least, we have the serious tensions associated with a growing Muslim population among which radical Islam recruits its terrorists.

I V

NEOCONSERVATISM IN EUROPE

Edmund Burke once said that, for evil to prevail, it was only necessary for good men to do nothing. This is very true. On the other hand, good men do not have to invent what to do. They can just follow their common sense.

This is basically the situation in Europe. Neoconservatism does not have to be invented in Europe. It is already there. Not as doctrine, to be sure, but as a tacit disposition among the 'little platoons' that mind their own business and get in return a strong hostility from the adversarial culture. It is there among families who worry about the poor education their children are receiving in state schools; it is there among scholars who are shocked by the erosion of liberal education in state universities; it is there among religious people who cannot understand why religion – to be more precise, Christianity and Judaism – has suddenly come under suspicion in Europe; it is there among all the common people who now cannot watch television with their own children. It is there, in brief, among all those who cannot accept the destruction of the gentlemanly character that has always underpinned civilized liberty.

What all these little platoons need, what we all need is the clear sense that we are not being attacked by liberty – but by a Jacobin interpretation of liberty, the same one that in the past has made liberal democracy so fragile in Europe. And we need the energy to assert our own views – not to embark upon a utopian journey toward a perfect and impossible society, but only 'to restore the equipoise of the vessel in which we sail', to paraphrase Edmund Burke's lovely expression.

What we need, to put it in a nutshell, is basically a reassertion of Burke and Tocqueville in our times. It is the reassertion of liberal democracy as a framework to protect, and to be protected by, a moral ethos. In other words, we need to understand that the supporters of liberal democracy in Europe do not have to be silent about the moral life that underpins liberty. And that we must defend the moral life of our societies as a crucial element of our defense of liberal democracy. This, I dare say, is the simple program of neoconservatives in Europe – that is, of European liberals who have been mugged by reality.

LIST OF CONTRIBUTORS

Robert L. Bartley
Directed the editorial pages of *The Wall Street Journal* from 1972 until shortly before his death in 2003, and was awarded a Pulitzer Prize for editorial writing. Awarded the Presidential Medal of Freedom, America's highest civilian honor, by President Bush in 2003.

Tony Blair
Prime Minister of Great Britain.

John R. Bolton
Under Secretary of State for Arms Control and International Security. Formerly Senior Vice President of the American Enterprise Institute; Assistant Secretary of State for International Organization Affairs.

Max Boot
Olin Senior Fellow at National Security Studies, Council on Foreign Relations; contributing editor to *The Weekly Standard*. Formerly, editorial features editor on *The Wall Street Journal;* writer and editor of *The Christian Science Monitor*.

Karlyn Bowman
Resident Fellow at the American Enterprise Institute, and a columnist for *Roll Call* magazine. Formerly, a fellow at the Institute of Politics, John F. Kennedy School of Government, Harvard University.

David Brooks
A senior editor at *The Weekly Standard*, a contributing editor at *Newsweek* and *Atlantic Monthly*, and a columnist at *The New York Times*.

João Carlos Espada
Director of the Institute for Political Studies at the Catholic University of Portugal; editor of the quarterly journal, *Nova Cidadania*; president of the Portuguese Political Science Association and the Portuguese chapter of the International Churchill Society. Formerly visiting professor at several U.S. universities, and political advisor to Mario Soares, President of the Portuguese Republic.

Jeffrey Gedmin

Director of the Aspen Institute, Berlin, and frequent contributor to media in the U.S. and Germany. Previously Resident Scholar at the American Enterprise Institute and director of the New Atlantic Initiative.

Michael Gove

Saturday editor and columnist for *The Times* (London); chairman of the Policy Exchange (a think tank); awarded the Charles Douglas-Home Prize for his study of the Northern Island peace process.

Robert Kagan

Senior Associate at the Carnegie Endowment for International Peace; contributing editor at *The Weekly Standard*; columnist for *The Washington Post*. Co-founder with William Kristol of the Project for the New American Century (PNAC). Formerly Deputy for Policy in the State Department's Bureau of Inter-American Affairs and member of its Policy Planning Staff.

George L. Kelling

Professor, School of Criminal Justice, Rutgers University; Research Fellow, Program in Criminal Justice Policy and Management, John F. Kennedy School of Government, Harvard University; Adjunct Fellow, Manhattan Institute.

Jeane Kirkpatrick

Senior Fellow of the American Enterprise Institute, Washington, D.C.; Counselor to the President for Foreign Policy Studies; Thomas and Dorothy Leavey University Professor, Georgetown University. Formerly, Permanent Representative of the United States to the United Nations, and member of President Ronald Reagan's cabinet and the National Security Council.

Irving Kristol

Senior Fellow at the American Enterprise Institute. Awarded Presidential Medal of Freedom by President George W. Bush. Formerly, founder and publisher of *The National Interest* and *The Public Interest*. The author of *Neoconservatism: The Autobiography of an Idea*.

William Kristol

Editor at *The Weekly Standard*; co-founder and chairman of the Project for the New American Century (PNAC). Formerly, chief of staff to Vice President Dan Quayle, and to Secretary of Education William Bennett; Assistant Professor of Public Policy, John F. Kennedy School of Government, Harvard University.

Joshua Muravchik
Resident Scholar at the American Enterprise Institute; Adjunct Professor at
the Institute of World Politics.

Condoleezza Rice
Assistant to the President for National Security Affairs (commonly referred
to as the National Security Advisor). Formerly, Provost and Professor of
Political Science, Stanford University.

Irwin Stelzer
Director of Economic Policy Studies, the Hudson Institute; columnist for
The Sunday Times; contributing editor at *The Weekly Standard*; member of the
editorial review board of *The Public Interest*.

Margaret Thatcher
Prime Minister of Great Britain (1979–90).

Kenneth R. Weinstein
Vice President and chief operating officer, Hudson Institute. Formerly,
managing director, the Shalem Center.

George F. Will
Pulitzer Prize-winning syndicated columnist for *The Washington Post* and 450
other newspapers; columnist for *Newsweek*; political commentator for ABC
Television network.

James Q. Wilson
Professor Emeritus in Government at Harvard University and UCLA, and
chairman of the Council of Academic Advisers, American Enterprise
Institute. Formerly, President of the American Political Science Association;
chairman of the White House Task Force on Crime; and chairman of the
National Advisory Commission on Drug Abuse Prevention.

Adam Wolfson
Editor of *The Public Interest*. Formerly consultant to President George W.
Bush's Council on Bioethics; lecturer in political science at DePaul
University, the University of Chicago, and Johns Hopkins University.

SCHOLARS AND OTHERS MENTIONED

Elliott Abrams
Special Assistant to the President and Senior Director for Near East and North African Affairs. Formerly, member of the National Security Council under the first President Bush; Assistant Secretary of State under President Ronald Reagan.

Kenneth L. Adelman
Trainer and speaker. Adjunct Professor of National Security Studies at Georgetown University's School of Foreign Service. Formerly, Director of U.S. Arms Control and Disarmament Agency; Deputy U.S. Representative to the United Nations; and Assistant to the Secretary of Defense.

Gerard Baker
Correspondent for *The Times* and contributing editor to *The Weekly Standard*.

Steve Bradshaw
BBC journalist. Formerly editor of *Granta* and a rock music disc jockey.

John Campbell
Political biographer of Lloyd George, F. E. Smith, Nye Bevan, Edward Heath, and Margaret Thatcher.

Daniel Casse
Senior director of the White House Writers Group, a public-policy communications firm. Formerly, special assistant to President George Bush in the Office of Cabinet Affairs, and managing editor of *The Public Interest*.

Eliot Cohen
Director of the Center for Strategic Studies, and Professor at Johns Hopkins School of Advanced International Studies; founding member of the Project for the New American Century; Member of the Council of Academic Advisers, American Enterprise Institute. Formerly, served on Policy Planning Staff, Office of the Secretary of Defense, and professor at Harvard University.

Robert Cooper
Director General for Exetrnal and Politico-Military Affairs at the General Secretariat of the Council of the European Union.

Elizabeth Drew
Journalist and author. Formerly, Washington correspondent for *The Atlantic* and *The New Yorker*.

Niall Ferguson
Herzog Professor of Financial History, Stern Business School, New York University; Senior Research Fellow, Jesus College, Oxford; Senior Fellow, the Hoover Institution, Stanford University.

Robert Fisk
Correspondent for the *Independent*, and seven-time winner of the British International Journalist of the Year Award, with a specialty in the Middle East, where he has spent the last twenty-three years. Most recently contributed a chapter to Anthony Arnove (ed.) *Iraq Under Siege: The Deadly Impact of Sanctions and War*.

Douglas J. Feith
Under Secretary of Defense for Policy.

John Lewis Gaddis
Robert A. Lovett Professor of Military and Naval History at Yale University, and Senior Fellow of the Hoover Institution, Stanford University.

Max Hastings
Historian and journalist. Formerly editor-in-chief of the *Daily Telegraph*; editor of the *Evening Standard*. Journalist of the Year (1982); Editor of the Year (1988); knighted (2002).

Gertrude Himmelfarb
Professor Emeritus, Graduate School of the City University of New York; member of the British Academy, the Royal Historical Society, the American Academy of Arts and Sciences, and the Council of Academic Advisers of the American Enterprise Institute.

Charles Krauthammer

Pulitzer Prize-winning syndicated columnist, appearing in *The Washington Post* and 100 other newspapers; television commentator; contributing editor to *The Weekly Standard*. Formerly Chief Resident in Psychiatry at Massachusetts General Hospital; speech-writer to Democratic Vice President Walter Mondale; writer and editor of *The New Republic*.

Michael Lind

Whitehead Senior Fellow at the New America Foundation; director of the American Strategy Project.

Myron Magnet

Editor of the Manhattan Institute's *City Journal*. Formerly, member of the board of editors, *Fortune* magazine.

Joshua Micah Marshall

Contributing writer for the *Washington Monthly* and a columnist for *The Hill*. Contributes to major newspapers and magazines.

Charles Murray

W. H. Brady Scholar, American Enterprise Institute. Formerly, Fellow of the Manhattan Institute; Chief Scientist, American Institutes for Research; Peace Corps.

Michael Novak

George Frederick Jewett Scholar in Religion, Philosophy, and Public Policy, American Enterprise Institute; member of the Board of the National Endowment for Democracy; U.S. Ambassador to the UN Human Rights Commission; member of several university faculties.

Joseph Nye

John K. Price Professor of Public Policy at the John F. Kennedy School of Government at Harvard University. Formerly, Dean; Assistant Secretary of Defense for International Security Affairs in the Clinton administration.

Matthew Parris

Columnist for *The Times* (London) and other publications, as well as television commentator. Formerly, Conservative Member of Parliament for West Derbyshire.

Richard Perle
Resident Fellow of the American Enterprise Institute. Formerly, Assistant Secretary of Defense for International Security Policy; chairman and member of the Defense Policy Board, U.S. Department of Defense; staff member for Senator Henry 'Scoop' Jackson.

Raymond Plant
Professor Lord Plant is professor of Legal and Political Philosophy at Kings College London. Formerly President of the Academy of Learned Societies for the Social Sciences.

John Podhoretz
Columnist for the *New York Post* and contributing editor to *The Weekly Standard*.

Norman Podhoretz
Senior Fellow at the Hudson Institute and former editor of *Commentary* magazine.

Thomas Powers
Pulitzer Prize-winning journalist; member of the Council on Foreign Relations; founding editor of Steerforth Press.

Corey Robin
Assistant Professor, Department of Political Science, Brooklyn College.

Robert Skidelsky
Professor of Political Economy, Warwick University; founder and chairman of the Centre for Global Studies; cross-bench member of the House of Lords. Formerly, chairman of the Social Market Foundation.

Leo Strauss
Political philosopher and teacher at the University of Chicago after escaping Nazi persecution.

George Tenet
Formerly, director of the Central Intelligence Agency.

Martin Wolf
Associate editor and chief economics commentator at the *Financial Times*. Visiting Fellow of Nuffield College, Oxford University, and a Special Professor at the University of Nottingham.

SOURCES

'The Neoconservative Persuasion' by Irving Kristol was first published on August 25, 2003, in *The Weekly Standard*.

'The Neocon Cabal and Other Fantasies' by David Brooks was first published on January 7, 2004, in the *International Herald Tribune*.

'Myths about Neoconservatism' by Max Boot was first published in *Foreign Policy Magazine*, January/February 2004, where it appeared under the title 'Neocons'.

'National Interest and Global Responsibility' by William Kristol and Robert Kagan is reprinted from the Introduction to *Present Dangers: Crisis and Opportunity in American Foreign and Defense Policy* (San Francisco: Encounter Books, 2000).

'The President's National Security Strategy' by Condoleezza Rice is taken from the Walter Wriston Lecture for the Manhattan Institute, and was delivered at the Waldorf Astoria Hotel, New York City, on October 1, 2002.

'New Threats for Old' by Margaret Thatcher is taken from the John Findley Green Foundation Lecture at Westminster College, Fulton, Missouri, and was delivered on March 9, 1996.

'Doctrine of the International Community' by Tony Blair is taken from a speech delivered at the Economic Club in Chicago on April 24, 1999.

'Beyond the Axis of Evil: Additional Threats from Weapons of Mass Destruction' by John R. Bolton is taken from a lecture delivered at the Heritage Foundation on May 6, 2002.

'The Slow Undoing: The Assault on, and Underestimation of, Nationality' by George F. Will is taken from the Walter Wriston Lecture for the Manhattan Institute, delivered in New York City on November 19, 2003.

'A Conservative Welfare State' by Irving Kristol was first published on June 14, 1993, in *The Wall Street Journal*.

'Broken Windows: The Police and Neighborhood Safety' by James Q. Wilson and George L. Kelling is reprinted from *Atlantic Monthly*, March 1982.

'Pornography, Obscenity, and the Case for Censorship' by Irving Kristol is reprinted from *The New York Times Magazine*, March 28, 1971.

'The Dread Deficit' by Robert L. Bartley is reprinted from *The Seven Fat Years and How to Do it Again* (New York: The Free Press, 1992).

'Conservatives and Neoconservatives' by Adam Wolfson is an expanded and modified version of an essay that first appeared in *The Public Interest*, Winter 2004.

'The Neoconservative Cabal' by Joshua Muravchik is taken from *Commentary*, September 2003.

INDEX